Lecture Notes in Computer Science 13829

Founding Editors

Gerhard Goos
Juris Hartmanis

The series Lecture Notes in Computer Science (LNCS), including its subseries Lecture Notes in Artificial Intelligence (LNAI) and Lecture Notes in Bioinformatics (LNBI), has established itself as a medium for the publication of new developments in computer science and information technology research, teaching, and education.

LNCS enjoys close cooperation with the computer science R & D community, the series counts many renowned academics among its volume editors and paper authors, and collaborates with prestigious societies. Its mission is to serve this international community by providing an invaluable service, mainly focused on the publication of conference and workshop proceedings and postproceedings. LNCS commenced publication in 1973.

Charith Mendis · Lawrence Rauchwerger
Editors

Languages and Compilers for Parallel Computing

35th International Workshop, LCPC 2022
Chicago, IL, USA, October 12–14, 2022
Revised Selected Papers

Editors
Charith Mendis
University of Illinois Urbana-Champaign
Urbana, IL, USA

Lawrence Rauchwerger
University of Illinois Urbana-Champaign
Urbana, IL, USA

ISSN 0302-9743   ISSN 1611-3349 (electronic)
Lecture Notes in Computer Science
ISBN 978-3-031-31444-5   ISBN 978-3-031-31445-2 (eBook)
https://doi.org/10.1007/978-3-031-31445-2

This Springer imprint is published by the registered company Springer Nature Switzerland AG
The registered company address is: Gewerbestrasse 11, 6330 Cham, Switzerland

Preface

The 35th Workshop on Languages and Compilers for Parallel Computing (LCPC) was held October 12–14, 2022 in Chicago, Illinois. It was organized by the Department of Computer Science at University of Illinois at Urbana-Champaign. The workshop gathered together more than 25 researchers from academia, corporate and government research institutions spanning three continents.

This year we celebrated the 35th anniversary of the workshop. We included in the program both new contributions as well as invited presentations of compiler and language research for parallel computing. The program included 9 regular papers, 2 invited papers, 3 keynote talks and 3 invited presentations. We received 12 regular paper submissions, which were double-blind reviewed by two or three PC members each. The program committee discussed online and accepted 9 full-length papers. All 9 accepted papers were presented during the workshop.

David Padua (UIUC) gave the opening keynote talk titled, "The Evolution of Parallel Computing since LCPC'88" on October 12th to kick off the workshop. His talk emphasized the key role LCPC played in bringing researchers scattered across the world to come to a single forum to discuss cutting-edge parallel programming and compiler-related research topics. The first day culminated with a dinner that celebrated David Padua's service to the community with his former students, colleagues and other workshop participants. The second day had intriguing keynotes from Saman Amarasinghe (MIT) and Ponnuswamy Sadayappan (Utah). Contributed and invited talks made up the rest of the workshop.

December 2022   Charith Mendis
                                                    Lawrence Rauchwerger

Organization

General and Program Chairs

Charith Mendis	University of Illinois at Urbana-Champaign, USA
Lawrence Rauchwerger	University of Illinois at Urbana-Champaign, USA

Workshop Organization

Lawrence Rauchwerger	University of Illinois at Urbana-Champaign, USA
Charith Mendis	University of Illinois at Urbana-Champaign, USA
Francisco Coral	Texas A&M University, USA

Steering Committee

David Padua	University of Illinois at Urbana-Champaign, USA
Alexandru Nicolau	University of California Irvine, USA
Rudolf Eigenmann	University of Delaware, USA
Lawrence Rauchwerger	University of Illinois at Urbana-Champaign, USA
Vivek Sarkar	Georgia Institute of Technology, USA

Program Committee

Michelle Strout	University of Arizona, USA
Xiaoming Li	University of Delaware, USA
Calin Cascaval	Google Research, USA
Andreas Kloeckner	University of Illinois at Urbana-Champaign, USA
Sunita Chandrasekaran	University of Delaware, USA
Jose Moreira	IBM Research, USA
Rudolf Eigenmann	University of Delaware, USA
Saday Sadayappan	University of Utah, USA
Changwan Hong	Massachusetts Institute of Technology, USA

Sponsors

Parasol Lab and Department of Computer Science
University of Illinois at Urbana-Champaign, USA

Keynote Talks

David Padua delivering the opening keynote

The Evolution of Parallel Computing Since LCPC'88

David Padua

University of Illinois at Urbana-Champaign, USA

Abstract. An overview of the evolution of hardware, programming notations, and compilers for parallel computing during the last 35 years and the impact of the 1988 state of the art on parallel computing today.

Compiler 2.0

Saman Amarasinghe

Massachusetts Institute of Technology, USA

Abstract. When I was a graduate student a long time ago, I used to have intense conversations and learned a lot from my peers in other areas of computer science as the program structure, systems, and algorithms used in my compiler were very similar to and inspired by much of the work done by my peers. For example, a Natural Language Recognition System that was developed by my peers, with a single sequential program with multiple passes connected through IRs that systematically transformed an audio stream into text, was structurally similar to the SUIF compiler I was developing. In the intervening 30 years, the information revolution brought us unprecedented advances in algorithms (e.g., machine learning and solvers), systems (e.g., multicores and cloud computing), and program structure (e.g., serverless and low-code frameworks). Thus, a modern NLP system such as Apple's Siri or Amazon's Alexa, a thin client on an edge device interfacing to a massively parallel, cloud-based, centrally trained Deep Neural Network, has little resemblance to its predecessors. However, the SUIF compiler is still eerily similar to a state-of-the-art modern compiler such as LLVM or MLIR. What happened with compiler construction technology? At worst, as a community, we have been Luddites to the information revolution even though our technology has been critical to it. At best, we have been unable to transfer our research innovations (e.g., polyhedral method or program synthesis) into production compilers. In this talk I hope to inspire the compiler community to radically rethink how to build next-generation compilers by giving a few possible examples of using 21st-century program structures, algorithms and systems in constructing a compiler.

Towards Compiler-Driven Algorithm-Architecture Co-design for Energy-Efficient ML Accelerators

Ponnuswamy Sadayappan

University of Utah, USA

Abstract. The improvement of the energy efficiency of ML accelerators is of fundamental importance. The energy expended in accessing data from DRAM/SRAM/Registers is orders of magnitude higher than that expended in actually performing arithmetic operations on data. The total energy expended in executing an ML operator depends both on the choice of accelerator design parameters (such as the capacities of register banks and scratchpad buffers) as well as the "dataflow" – the schedule of data movement and operation execution. The design space of architectural parameters and dataflow is extremely large. This talk will discuss how analytical modeling can be used to co-design accelerator parameters and dataflow to optimize energy.

Invited Speakers

GPU Collectives with MSCCL: Man vs. Dragons

Saeed Maleki

Microsoft Research, USA

Abstract. Collective communication primitives on GPUs are the primary bottleneck on large neural network models. Although there have been decades of research on optimizing computation kernels, there has been very little done for collective communication kernels on GPUs. There are many challenges in this area including unique GPU interconnection topologies, high P2P transfer latency, the wide range of use cases for neural networks, and software complexities. In this talk, I will present program synthesis as a primary solution for communication algorithms for these topologies and show how a bespoke algorithm can significantly improve the overall performance of a model. Lastly, I will present a high-level DSL along with a compiler for mapping from an abstract synthesized algorithm to a low-level CUDA code for collective communications.

Retire Linear Algebra Libraries

Albert Cohen

Google Research, USA

Abstract. Despite decades of investment in software infrastructure, scientific computing, signal processing and machine learning and systems remain stuck in a rut. Some numerical computations are more equal than others: BLAS and the core operations for neural networks achieve near-peak performance, while marginally different variants do not get this chance. As a result, performance is only achieved at the expense of a dramatic loss of programmability. Compilers are obviously the cure. But what compilers? How should these be built, deployed, retargeted, auto-tuned? Sure, the BLAS API is not the ultimate interface to compose and reuse high-performance operations, but then, what would be a better one? And why did we not build and agree on one yet? We'll review these questions and some of the proposed solutions in this talk. In particular, we will advocate for a new tile-level programming interface sitting in-between the top-level computational operations and generators of target- and problem-specific code. We will also advocate for a structured approach to the construction of domain-specific code generators for tensor compilers, with the stated goal of improving the productivity of both compiler engineers and end-users.

Portable Compilation of Sparse Computation

Fredrik Kjolstad

Stanford University, USA

Abstract. Hardware is becoming ever more complicated and the architects are developing a fleet of new types of accelerators. I will talk about compiling collection-oriented programs to heterogeneous hardware. I will discuss properties that make certain programming abstractions amenable to portable compilation, give some examples, and describe a programming system design. I will then describe how to compile one such programming model, operations on sparse and dense arrays/tensors, to the major types of hardware: CPUs, fixed-function accelerators, GPUs, distributed machines, and streaming dataflow accelerators. Finally, I will briefly discuss how verification may make it easier to program heterogeneous machines.

Contents

Contributed Papers

Invited Papers

Contributed Papers

Compiler Optimization for Irregular Memory Access Patterns in PGAS Programs

Thomas B. Rolinger[1,2(✉)], Christopher D. Krieger[2], and Alan Sussman[1]

[1] University of Maryland, College Park MD, USA
{tbrolin,als}@cs.umd.edu
[2] Laboratory for Physical Sciences, College Park MD, USA
krieger@lps.umd.edu

Abstract. Irregular memory access patterns pose performance and user productivity challenges on distributed-memory systems. They can lead to fine-grained remote communication and the data access patterns are often not known until runtime. The Partitioned Global Address Space (PGAS) programming model addresses these challenges by providing users with a view of a distributed-memory system that resembles a single shared address space. However, this view often leads programmers to write code that causes fine-grained remote communication, which can result in poor performance. Prior work has shown that the performance of irregular applications written in Chapel, a high-level PGAS language, can be improved by manually applying optimizations. However, applying such optimizations by hand reduces the productivity advantages provided by Chapel and the PGAS model. We present an inspector-executor based compiler optimization for Chapel programs that automatically performs remote data replication. While there have been similar compiler optimizations implemented for other PGAS languages, high-level features in Chapel such as implicit processor affinity lead to new challenges for compiler optimization. We evaluate the performance of our optimization across two irregular applications. Our results show that the total runtime can be improved by as much as 52x on a Cray XC system with a low-latency interconnect and 364x on a standard Linux cluster with an Infiniband interconnect, demonstrating that significant performance gains can be achieved without sacrificing user productivity.

Keywords: PGAS · Chapel · irregular applications · compiler optimizations

1 Introduction

Implementing parallel software that can effectively utilize distributed-memory systems poses many challenges for programmers. Specifically, modifying an existing serial or shared-memory parallelized application to run in a distributed setting often requires significant programmer effort to orchestrate data distribution and communication. The Partitioned Global Address Space (PGAS) model

The Author(s), under exclusive license to Springer Nature Switzerland AG 2023
Mendis and L. Rauchwerger (Eds.): LCPC 2022, LNCS 13829, pp. 3–21, 2023.
https://doi.org/10.1007/978-3-031-31445-2_1

attempts to address these challenges by providing programmers with a view of a distributed-memory system that resembles a single shared address space. The PGAS model has been implemented in various languages and libraries, such as UPC [11], GlobalArrays [14] and Chapel [6]. Within PGAS languages, details regarding data distribution and communication are often abstracted from the programmer. For example, in Chapel simply specifying an array as "distributed" automatically maps the data across the system and remote communication is performed implicitly. The PGAS model therefore encourages programmers to write code in a shared-memory manner but aims to provide good performance on distributed-memory systems without requiring the program to be rewritten.

Irregular memory access patterns are commonly found in applications that perform graph analytics [13], sparse linear algebra [20] and scientific computing operations [10]. Such access patterns pose significant challenges for user productivity on distributed-memory systems because the access patterns are not known until runtime, making it difficult to orchestrate communication amongst remote processes. However, with the PGAS model coding irregular communication patterns becomes more straightforward, as they can be implemented via one-sided communication. Unfortunately, the performance of such codes will be significantly hindered due to the fine-grained remote communication that arises from the irregular memory accesses. While the abstractions provided by the PGAS model can be manually bypassed to achieve better performance, such an effort would significantly degrade user productivity.

In this paper, we present the design and implementation of a compiler optimization that automatically applies the *inspector-executor* technique [16] to parallel loops in PGAS programs written in the Chapel language. The inspector performs memory access analysis at runtime to determine remote communication to an array of interest within a loop. The executor replicates the remote data and runs the original loop, but redirects remote accesses to replicated local copies to avoid repeated remote communication. Our compiler optimization automatically identifies candidate loops and array accesses, and then performs code transformations to construct the inspector and executor routines. As a result, the user is not required to change their original code in order to achieve significant performance gains. The contributions of our work are as follows:

- Design and implementation of an inspector-executor based compiler optimization for Chapel programs that specifically targets irregular memory accesses to distributed arrays. To the best of our knowledge, this work presents the first such optimization within the Chapel compiler.
- Discussion on the unique features of Chapel, such as implicit processor affinity, as they relate to the compiler optimization. While the inspector-executor technique has been employed for a long time [15–17], and applied to other PGAS languages [1,18], our design within Chapel requires a different approach due to Chapel's high-level features.
- Performance evaluation of our optimization across two irregular applications and two different distributed-memory systems. Our results show that the optimization can improve performance by as much as 52x on a Cray XC

system with a low-latency interconnect and 364x on a standard Linux cluster with an Infiniband interconnect.

The rest of the paper is organized as follows. Section 2 presents an overview of Chapel. We present our compiler optimization and discuss its details in Sect. 3. Section 4 presents a performance evaluation of the optimization across two irregular applications, and the Appendix contains additional performance results. Prior work as it relates to our paper is described in Sect. 5. Finally, Sect. 6 provides concluding remarks and discusses future work.

2 Overview of the Chapel Language

Chapel is a high-level language that implements the PGAS model and is designed for productive parallel computing at scale, providing constructs for distributed arrays, remote communication and both data and task parallelism. In this section we provide a brief overview of Chapel, focusing on the features most relevant to our work. For a more in-depth description of Chapel, we refer readers to the work by Chamberlain et al. [6].

2.1 Terminology: Tasks, Threads and Locales

Chapel enables parallelism through executing multiple *tasks* in parallel, where a task is a set of computations that can conceptually be executed in parallel, but may or may not do so. Tasks are implemented by a tasking layer, which provides threads on which Chapel tasks are scheduled. For distributed-memory programming, Chapel introduces the concept of a *locale*, which is defined as a unit of machine resources on which tasks can execute. In practice, a locale is mapped to an entire compute node in a cluster and the number of locales on which a program runs is specified when launching the program. Chapel programs initially start with a single task executing on locale 0. Parallel loops and other constructs then create tasks that can execute across the locales, but ultimately join back to a single task on locale 0 when they are done. This differs from other PGAS languages, such as UPC [11], which use a single program multiple data (SPMD) model that defines the amount of parallelism at program startup.

2.2 Domains and Arrays

Chapel splits an array into two first-class objects in the language: a *domain* and the array itself. A domain is a representation of an index set and can be used to define the indices in an array or the indices iterated over by a loop. Once defined, a domain can then be used to declare an array. Modifications to a domain (e.g., adding/removing indices) propagate to all arrays defined over the domain. Lines 1–2 in Listing 1 present a simple example of defining a domain D that has indices 1 through 5 and then declaring an array of integers, data, over that domain. Of particular relevance to our work is an *associative* domain, which is similar to a dictionary. Lines 4–7 in Listing 1 declare an associative domain C that stores strings and adds the key "foo" via the += operator. The associative array dict is declared over C and provides a mapping of strings to reals. Associative domains also provide parallel-safe modifications by default.

```
1 var D = {0..5}; // rectangular domain
2 var data : [D] int;
3
4 var C : domain(string); // associative domain
5 C += "foo";
6 var dict : [C] real;
7 dict["foo"] = 2.0;
```

Listing 1. Chapel domains and arrays

```
1 var D = newBlockDom({0..15});
2 var arr : [D] int;
3
4 for i in 0..15 {
5   arr[i] = here.id;
6 }
```

Listing 2. Block distributed domain/array in Chapel

The code in Listing 1 only declares domains and arrays that are located on a single locale. Our work focuses on *distributed arrays*, whose data is spread across multiple locales according to some distribution policy. Chapel provides several built-in distribution policies, such as block, cyclic and block-cyclic. Listing 2 shows a simple example of declaring a block-distributed domain and then the corresponding distributed array. The block distribution will partition the array into contiguous chunks and assign one chunk to each locale. The underlying distribution implementation automatically handles the index remapping, allowing users to write arr[i] to access the ith element of the array, rather than having to specify which block the index is in. Furthermore, Chapel performs implicit remote communication, which means that users can access the remote elements of a distributed array in the same way that they would access the local elements. This can be seen on lines 4–6 in Listing 2, which sets the value of arr[i] to be equal to the ID of the locale where the task is executing (here.id). The loop will execute all iterations on locale 0, so any access to an element of arr that is not on locale 0 will result in communication.

2.3 Forall Loops

Chapel provides data parallelism via a forall loop, which allows the loop iterations to be parallelized and distributed across the system. How the iterations are mapped to cores/locales depends on what the forall loop is iterating over, which is referred to as the *iterand*. Non-distributed arrays and domains have default *iterators* defined, which partition the iterations into contiguous chunks and assign each chunk to a task. The tasks then execute concurrently on a single locale. For distributed arrays and domains, the default iterator provides both shared- and distributed-memory parallelism by executing a given iteration of the loop on the locale where that iteration's data element is mapped. Consider the example in Listing 3, which iterates over the domain of a distributed array `arr`. This loop is similar to the non-parallel loop on lines 4–6 in Listing 2, but it will execute the ith iteration on the locale on which `arr[i]` is stored. Therefore, `here.id` will return the locale ID of where `arr[i]` is located. This avoids the remote communication that would occur for the code in Listing 2. Therefore the iterand of a `forall` loop implicitly controls where the computation is performed. We refer to this as controlling the `forall`'s *locale affinity* and note that it is a feature of Chapel that differs from the more explicit affinity-controlling constructs of languages like UPC. Furthermore, users can define their own custom iterators to alter the way in which a `forall` loop is parallelized.

```
1 var D = newBlockDom({0..15});
2 var arr : [D] int;
3 forall i in arr.domain {
4     arr[i] = here.id;
5 }
```

Listing 3. `forall` loop in Chapel

3 Compiler Optimization

In this section we describe the design and implementation of the inspector-executor compiler optimization for irregular memory accesses. We focus specifically on read-only accesses with the form $A[B[i]]$ found inside `forall` loops, where A and B are arrays and A is a distributed array. However, we do support more complex non-affine expressions if certain conditions are met (see Sect. 3.3). The overall goal of the optimization is to selectively replicate remotely accessed elements of A so that they can be accessed locally during execution of the loop. Full replication of A can be prohibitively expensive in terms of both memory consumption and communication overhead, but knowing which elements are accessed remotely requires knowledge only revealed when the loop is executed. This motivates the design of our compiler optimization that creates an inspector o determine at runtime which accesses are remote.

The optimization targets `forall` loops that execute multiple times, which llows for the cost of the inspector phase to be amortized over multiple executions f the optimized loop (i.e., the executor). Such patterns are commonly found in parse iterative solvers [10], molecular dynamics simulations [17] and some graph nalytics applications [5]. Figure 1 presents a high-level overview of Chapel's ompiler passes, where the shaded passes in the dotted box correspond to the asses where the optimization performs static analysis and code transformations. here are roughly 40 passes in Chapel's compiler to date, but most are omitted Fig. 1 to simplify the diagram.

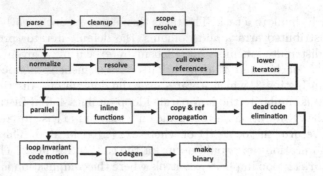

Fig. 1. High-level overview of the Chapel compiler. The shaded passes within the dotted box represent those where our optimization performs code transformations and static analysis.

3.1   High-level Overview

Our optimization operates solely on Chapel's intermediate representation of the program, which we refer to as the abstract syntax tree (AST). The optimization process begins during the normalize pass, at which point the AST has not been heavily modified, thus making the code transformation tasks easier to perform. The optimization considers each `forall` loop that is present in the program and looks for accesses of the form $\mathbf{A}[\mathbf{B}[\mathbf{i}]]$. However, array accesses do not have their own syntax in the AST, meaning that $\mathbf{A}[\mathbf{B}[\mathbf{i}]]$ is represented as a call expression that is indistinguishable from a function call. To address this issue, an irregular access candidate expression is replaced with a compiler primitive that will be acted on during the resolve pass, at which point the optimization can determine whether $\mathbf{A}$ and $\mathbf{B}$ are arrays. If a `forall` loop has a candidate access, the optimization clones the `forall` into the inspector and executor loops.

During the resolve pass of compilation, function calls and types are resolved, which allows the optimization to carry out much of the necessary static analysis to ensure the validity of the code transformations performed during the normalize pass. If anything is found to invalidate the optimization then the code transformations are removed and replaced with the original `forall` loop. Otherwise, the primitive that represents $\mathbf{A}[\mathbf{B}[\mathbf{i}]]$ is replaced with a library call to either "inspect" or "execute" the access, depending on whether the primitive is in the inspector or executor loop. Determining which accesses are remote is performed at runtime via the inspector. The static analysis performed by the optimization only determines that the access is of the form $\mathbf{A}[\mathbf{B}[\mathbf{i}]]$ and that $\mathbf{A}$ is a distributed array.

Finally, at the end of the cull-over references pass, the optimization performs the remaining analysis necessary to ensure the transformations are valid, which focuses on locating modifications (writes) to the relevant arrays and domains for the irregular accesses in the loop. Such writes can change the $\mathbf{A}[\mathbf{B}[\mathbf{i}]]$ access pattern, which would require the inspector runtime analysis to be rerun to ensure that the executor has the correct elements replicated. The cull-over references pass resolves the *intents* of function arguments, where an argument's intent refers to whether it is passed by value or reference. This pass statically sets the intent of the argument to different values depending on whether the procedure reads or writes to the argument. Writes to arrays are performed via Chapel procedure calls where the array is passed in as an argument, which allows the optimization to check the intent of the array to determine whether it is written to.

3.2   Code Transformations

Listing 5 presents code that is functionally equivalent to the output from our optimization's AST-level transformations when applied to the program in Listing 4. We next describe the details of the code transformations and how they support selective data replication.

```
1  forall i in B.domain {
2    C[i] = A[B[i]];
3  }
```

Listing 4. Example `forall` loop with an irregular memory access pattern

```
1  if doInspector(A, B) {
2    inspectorPreamble(A);
3    forall i in inspectorIterator(B.domain) {
4      inspectAccess(A, B[i]);
5    }
6    inspectorOff(A,B);
7  }
8  executorPreamble(A);
9  forall i in B.domain {
10   C[i] = executeAccess(A, B[i]);
11 }
```

Listing 5. Output of code transformations performed by the optimization for the code in Listing 4

Internal Chapel Data Structures: For a distributed array **A** in a `forall` loop that is being optimized, we add a Chapel record (i.e., C struct) for each locale that contains the remote communication information about **A[B[i]]** on that locale. We refer to the complete set of these records as a *communication schedule*. A communication schedule is essentially a set of associative arrays that map **B[i]** to **A[B[i]]** when **A[B[i]]** is a remote access issued from a given locale. If **A** is associated with multiple `forall` loops that are being optimized, the optimization will create different communication schedules for **A** that are linked to each `forall` loop.

Inspector Loop: The compiler optimization starts by cloning the original `forall` loop into two copies, one that will be transformed into the inspector and one that will be transformed into the executor. For the inspector loop (lines 1-5), the optimization replaces the original `forall` loop's iterator with a custom one (`inspectorIterator`). This custom iterator creates one task on each locale to execute that locale's portion of the original `forall` loop serially. While this does reduce the total amount of parallelism that the default iterator provides, it enables turning off parallel-safety for the underlying associative arrays in the communication schedule, which generally provides performance improvements. Once the loop structure is generated, the optimization replaces the original expression `C[i] = A[B[i]]` with a call to `inspectAccess`, which is a procedure we create to perform the memory access analysis. Note that any code in the original loop that does not pertain to the **A**[**B**[i]] access is removed to keep the inspector as lightweight as possible. Furthermore, the call to `inspectAccess` does not perform the actual access to **A**, but instead queries whether **B**[i] would be a remote access to **A**, since remote accesses are expensive. Finally, the optimization inserts a call to `inspectorPreamble` (line 2) before the inspector loop, which initializes some of the communication schedule internal structures.

Turning the Inspector On/off: One of the key steps of the optimization is determining when the inspector should execute. After the inspector runs for the first time, it does not need to be run again unless the memory access pattern changes. The static analysis phase (in Sect. 3.3) determines when such changes occur and the optimization inserts calls to a procedure that sets flags associated with **A** and **B** to indicate that the inspector should be executed. The `doInspector` call on line 2 checks these flags and the `inspectorOff` call on line 6 turns off the flags.

Executor Loop: For the executor loop, the optimization replaces the original **A**[**B**[i]] access with a call to `executeAccess` (line 10), which redirects remote accesses to the replicated copies. The optimization also inserts a call to `executorPreamble` (line 8) just before the executor loop, which initializes the replicated elements with the current values in **A**, ensuring that up-to-date values will be used in the executor. While this does perform remote communication, the optimization only communicates a remote element once, regardless of how many times it is accessed in the loop. As a result, the cost of the remote access is amortized over multiple local accesses.

3.3 Static Analysis

There are two main goals of the static analysis: (1) to detect scenarios where the code transformations could lead to different program results compared to the original program and (2) to only apply the optimization when performance gains are likely. Each goal imposes different requirements that must be resolved at compile-time, where violating any requirement will cause the optimization to revert to the original code. We briefly describe the analysis that is performed to achieve these two goals. We then discuss additional analyses that were developed to increase the generality of the optimization.

Program Results: Since the optimization is applied automatically by the compiler, it must detect scenarios where the code transformations could produce program results that differ from the original code. The primary scenario that could lead to different program results is not running the inspector when necessary, resulting in communication schedules that are out of date. To determine when the inspector needs to execute, the optimization must be able to statically reason about the locale affinity of the `forall` loop and the source/destination locales of the remote accesses for **A**[**B**[**i**]]. The following criteria summarize the static checks performed for these purposes:

1. The `forall` loop must iterate over a distributed array or distributed domain.
2. The `forall` loop cannot be nested inside of another `forall` or any other statement that could create multiple parallel tasks.
3. The index **i** in **A**[**B**[**i**]] must be the loop index variable for the loop that contains **A**[**B**[**i**]], and the loop must iterate over a domain or array.
4. Neither **A** nor **B**, nor their domains, can be modified within the `forall` loop.

Check (1) ensures that the optimization can reason about the `forall` loop's locale affinity (i.e., which locales the iterations will execute on). Check (2) ensures that multiple tasks will not execute the entire `forall` loop at the same time, which would result in potential concurrent updates to the communication schedules. Check (3) ensures that the optimization can statically reason about the index **i** into **B**, specifically when the values of **i** would change. Such changes would happen if the array/domain over which the loop iterates is modified. Check (4) ensures that the values in **B** that are analyzed by the inspector will be the same as the values used within the executor (and the original loop). When applied to **A**, this check avoids the complexities of writing to replicated elements of **A** and having to propagate those values back to the original elements. If these checks are met, then the optimization will determine all modifications to **A**, **B**, their domains and the various other arrays/domains involved in the loop. If these objects are modified, it indicates that **A**[**B**[**i**]] could exhibit an access pattern that differs from when the inspector was last performed, whether it be different indices used to access **A** or the accesses themselves being issued from different locales. When modifications are found, the optimization will set the corresponding flags to rerun the inspector to update the communication schedule.

Program Performance: The goal of the optimization is to improve the runtime performance of an input program. Therefore the static analysis attempts to determine whether the optimization is likely to provide performance gains. This analysis can be summarized as determining that the `forall` loop will execute multiple times without requiring the inspector to be executed each time, which would incur significant overhead. The following criteria summarize the static checks performed for these purposes:

a) The `forall` loop must be nested in an outer serial loop (i.e., `for`, `while`, etc.).
b) Neither **B** nor its domain can be modified within the outer loop that the `forall` is nested in.
c) **A**'s domain cannot be modified within the outer loop that the `forall` is nested in.

Check (a) ensures that the `forall` loop is likely to be executed multiple times, though it is not guaranteed to do so. Checks (b) and (c) ensure that the inspector will not be executed each time the `forall` loop runs. Recall that part of the code transformation phase is to "turn on" the inspector after modifications to **B**, its domain or **A**'s domain. Such modifications have the potential to alter the memory access pattern of **A**[**B**[i]], and therefore require the inspector to be executed again. The array **A** is allowed to be modified within the outer loop, as any changes to its values will be propagated to the replicated copies via the `executorPreamble`. However, modifying **A**'s domain could alter the access pattern **A**[**B**[i]] by adding/removing elements in **A**.

Non-affine Expression Analysis: Thus far we have focused our discussion on accesses of the form **A**[**B**[i]]. However, the optimization can support more complex non-affine expressions, such as **A**[**B**[i*j]%k+1], if certain conditions are met. Specifically, the expressions must be binary operations between immediates or variables yielded by loops that iterate over arrays/domains. This requirement is needed so that the optimization can statically reason about when/how the accesses to **A** and **B** could change. This is accomplished by locating modifications to the arrays/domains that yield the variables used in the expressions. Note that outside of our optimization, Chapel's current compiler does not perform affine/non-affine expression analysis.

Interprocedural and Alias Analyses: The optimization performs interprocedural and alias analyses to support the static checks described previously. The interprocedural analysis computes the call graph starting from the function that contains the `forall` and checks for any invalid call paths. We deem a call path invalid if there is a lack of an outer serial loop or if there is an enclosing statement that creates multiple parallel tasks. When an invalid call path is detected the compiler inserts flags that are set at runtime to "turn off" the optimization temporarily along the invalid path. Also, the interprocedural analysis detects modifications to the arrays/domains of interest across arbitrarily nested function calls. Alias analysis is necessary because Chapel allows users to create references to arrays/domains, which operate similarly to pointers in C. To address this issue, we developed static checks to detect such references and determine the original array/domain. This analysis works for arbitrarily long alias chains (e.g., `var arr = ...; ref a1 = arr; ref a2 = a1`), where the optimization will detect modifications to any of the references along the chain.

4   Performance Evaluation

To demonstrate the performance benefits of the compiler optimization described in Sect. 3, we performed an evaluation of two irregular applications running on two different distributed-memory systems. The applications we evaluate are implemented in a high-level manner, consistent with Chapel's design philosophy, which is to separate data distribution/communication details from the algorithm design. As a result, our exemplar applications closely match standard shared-memory implementations and are representative of direct use of the

PGAS model. Our goal is to show that the performance of these Chapel programs suffer from implicit fine-grained remote communication, but can be significantly improved via automatic optimization without requiring the user to modify the program. Therefore, users can take advantage of the productivity benefits that Chapel provides while also achieving good performance.

4.1 Experimental Setup

For our evaluation, we run experiments on a Cray XC cluster and an Infiniband-based cluster. For the Cray XC, we utilize up to 64 nodes connected over an Aries interconnect, where each node has two 22-core Intel Xeon Broadwell CPUs and 128 GB of DDR4 memory. For the Infiniband cluster, we utilize up to 32 nodes connected over an FDR Infiniband interconnect, where each node has two 10 core Intel Xeon Haswell CPUs and 512 GB of DDR4 memory. On the Cray XC, Chapel is built using the ugni communication layer and the `aries` communication substrate. On the Infiniband system, Chapel is built using the GASNet communication layer and the `ibv` communication substrate. All applications on both systems are compiled using the `---fast` flag. For each experiment, we execute the given application multiple times and measure the total runtime, including the inspector overhead. The results represent the average of these trials. We observed that the runtime variation between trials did not exceed 4%.

4.2 Application: NAS-CG

```
1  forall row in Rows {
2    var accum : real = 0;
3    for k in row.offsets {
4      accum += values[k] * x[col_idx[k]];
5    }
6    b[row.id] = accum;
7  }
```

Listing 6. `forall` loop for NAS-CG

The conjugate gradient (CG) method solves the equation $Ax = b$ for x, where A is a symmetric positive-definite matrix and is typically large and sparse, and x and b are vectors. Unstructured optimization problems and partial differential equations can be solved using iterative CG methods. For the evaluation, we use the NAS-CG benchmark specification and datasets [3]. Table 1 describes the problem sizes evaluated, where each problem size corresponds to the size of the A matrix. Each iteration of NAS-CG performs a total of 26 sparse matrix-vector multiplies (SpMVs), which is the kernel of interest for the optimization and is shown in Listing 6. The implementation uses a standard Compressed Sparse Row (CSR) format to represent A, where Rows is a block distributed array of records that contains the offsets into the distributed array(s) containing the non-zero data values. This approach closely resembles the Fortan+OpenMP implementation of NAS-CG [3]. The irregular access of interest is on line 4, x[col_idx[k]]. For the optimization, the inspector only needs to be executed once since the memory access pattern remains the same across all SpMV operations. In regards to memory storage overhead due to replication, we observed an average increase in memory usage of 6%.

Table 1. Datasets for NAS-CG

Name	Rows	Non-zeros	Density (%)	# of SpMVs
C	150k	39M	0.17	1950
D	150k	73M	0.32	2600
E	9M	6.6B	0.008	2600
F	54M	55B	0.002	2600

Table 2. Runtime speed-ups achieved by the optimization on the NAS-CG problem sizes from Table 1 relative to the unoptimized code in Listing 6. Missing values indicate that the problem size required too much memory to execute and "NA" values indicate that the system did not support the specified number of nodes/locales.

Locales (Nodes)	Cray XC				Infiniband			
	C	D	E	F	C	D	E	F
2	3.2	2.8	—	—	8.9	6	357	—
4	3.6	3.4	17.5	—	15.8	10.4	345	—
8	5.7	6.2	36.7	—	115	127	364	—
16	8.6	11	22.5	—	238	330	258	270
32	6.4	8.4	34	52.3	160	240	195	165
64	4.1	4.9	16.7	25.4	NA	NA	NA	NA
geomean	5	5.5	24.1	36.4	57.3	57.5	296	211

Table 2 presents the NAS-CG runtime speed-ups achieved by the optimization on each system relative to the unoptimized code shown in Listing 6. We observe large speed-ups on both systems, but most notably on the Infiniband system because fine-grained remote communication exhibits higher latency compared to the Aries interconnect on the Cray XC. On both systems, such speed-ups are obtained because of a large amount of remote data reuse in the SpMV kernel, which is due to the sparsity pattern of the matrices generated by the benchmark. The optimization incurs the cost of reading the remote element once, but can then access the element locally throughout the rest of the forall loop. Without the optimization, each access to the remote element likely pays the full latency cost of a remote access since the access pattern is sparse and irregular. Additionally, the SpMV kernel is executed many times during the NAS-CG benchmark, which allows for the inspector overhead to be amortized. We observe that the percentage of runtime devoted to the inspector is 3% on average across all locale counts for the Cray XC and 2% for the Infiniband system.

Beyond relative speed-ups, the optimization significantly improves the overall runtime, as can be see in Tables 5 and 6 in the Appendix. We observe very poor runtime performance and scalability for the unoptimized code, which is due to the implicit fine-grained remote communication required in the straightforward implementation shown in Listing 6. On the other hand, the optimized version of the code generally gets faster with more locales, since the optimization can take advantage of remote data reuse. Overall, these results demonstrate the usefulness of our optimization in automatically providing faster runtimes without sacrificing user productivity.

4.3   Application: PageRank

```
1 forall v in Graph {
2   var val = 0.0;
3   for i in v.offsets {
4     ref t = Graph[neighbors[i]];
5     val += t.pr_read / t.out_degree;
6   }
7   v.pr_write = (val * d) + ((1.0-d)/num_vertices) + sink_val;
8 }
```

Listing 7. forall loop for PageRank

PageRank [5] is an iterative graph algorithm that provides an importance measurement for each vertex in a graph. Listing 7 presents the PageRank kernel and is the target of the optimization, where the irregular memory access of interest is on line 4. Similar to NAS-CG, we use a CSR data structure to represent the graph. The distributed array Graph stores records that correspond to vertices, where each vertex has two importance measurements: pr_write and pr_read. This allows for a straightforward parallel implementation of the kernel by treating one value as read-only during an iteration, and closely matches the GAP Benchmark Suite implementation [4]. Unlike NAS-CG, PageRank adds the complication of storing records in the array of interest rather than base type data (i.e., int, real, etc.). The optimization recognizes this feature and will only replicate the fields that are accessed in the forall loop, namely, pr_read and out_degree.

We evaluate PageRank on two real web graphs obtained from the SuiteSparse Matrix Collection [8], which are described in Table 3. The right-most column denotes the number of iterations that are required to converge with a tolerance value of 1e-7 and a damping factor of 0.85 (d on line 7 in Listing 7). Our choice for these values matches what is used in Neo4j [19], an open source graph database. Each PageRank iteration performs one execution of the entire forall in Listing 7 and the inspector is only executed once since the graph does not change throughout the execution. The memory storage overhead of the optimization for

PageRank is 40–80%, which is much larger than what we observed for NAS-CG. For NAS-CG, the array of interest that is replicated constitutes a small portion of the total memory required. But for PageRank, the array of interest is much larger by comparison, resulting in a larger relative increase in memory storage. However, the memory storage overhead incurred by the optimization is significantly less than what full replication would incur.

Table 3. Datasets for PageRank

Name	Vertices	Edges	Density (%)	Iterations
webbase-2001	118M	992M	7.1e−6	33
sk-2005	51M	1.9B	7.5e−5	40

Table 4. Runtime speed-ups achieved by the optimization on PageRank for the graphs from Table 3 relative to the unoptimized implementation. "NA" values indicate that the system did not support the specified number of nodes/locales.

Locales (Nodes)	Cray XC		Infiniband	
	webbase-2001	sk-2005	webbase-2001	sk-2005
2	0.88	1.2	5.2	2
4	0.98	1.6	8.6	7.1
8	0.97	1.3	12	6
16	0.94	1.7	9.6	5.4
32	1.3	1.4	4.5	4.2
64	1.2	2.1	NA	NA
geomean	1.04	1.5	7.3	4.5

Table 4 presents the runtime speed-ups for the optimization on both graphs from Table 3, and Tables 7 and 8 in the Appendix presents the runtimes without and with the optimization. As we observed for NAS-CG, the speed-ups on the Infiniband system are larger than those on the Cray XC due to the Aries interconnect. However, we observe significantly smaller speed-ups overall when compared to NAS-CG. This is largely because the PageRank kernel is executed fewer times than the NAS-CG kernel, and the graphs exhibit significantly less data reuse when compared to NAS-CG. As a result, there is a larger inspector overhead and smaller performance gains from the executor. For these reasons, speed-ups are not achieved on the webbase-2001 graph on the Cray XC until 32 locales, which is when the remote data reuse reaches its peak. Furthermore, due to the highly irregular nature of the graphs (whose degree distributions follow a power law), the runtime performance fluctuates as the number of locales increase due to the partitioning of the graph across the system. This can change where the elements are located, which may lead to a once heavily accessed remote element now being local. This is more significant for the unoptimized code, as the optimization would have only incurred the cost of the remote access once due to replication. Nevertheless, the scalability of the optimization generally tracks the scalability of the code without the optimization applied.

5   Related Work

Techniques to perform runtime optimizations for irregular memory accesses have been worked on for many years, and of particular relevance to our work is the *inspector-executor* technique [9,16,17]. Das et al. [7] presented an inspector-executor optimization similar to ours, but that work predates the PGAS model, so is not directly applicable due to fundamental differences in programming model design and implementation. For PGAS languages, Su and Yelick [18] developed an inspector-executor optimization that is similar to ours but for the language Titanium. However, Titanium differs from Chapel in its execution model as well as its language constructs for parallel loops, since it is based on Java. This leads to an overall different approach to static analysis. Alvanos et al. [1,2] described an inspector-executor framework for the PGAS language UPC [11], which also differs from Chapel. UPC uses a SPMD model and requires explicit constructs to control the processor affinity of parallel loops. Like Titanium, these differences lead to a significantly different approach to the static analysis used for the optimization. However, we plan to explore some of their techniques in future work. For compiler optimizations related specifically to Chapel, Kayraklioglu et al. [12] presented an optimization to aggregate remote accesses to distributed arrays. However, their optimization does not specifically target irregular memory accesses, which leads to significantly different approaches to static analysis and code transformation. Furthermore, the applications we evaluate in Sect. 4 are not candidates for their aggregation optimization.

6   Conclusions and Future Work

While the PGAS model provides user productivity advantages for writing distributed irregular applications, the resulting code often has poor runtime performance due to fine-grained remote communication. In this work we have presented a compiler optimization for Chapel programs that specifically targets irregular memory access patterns within parallel loops and automatically applies code transformations to replicate remotely accessed data. We demonstrated that the optimization provides runtime speed-ups as large as 52x on a Cray XC system and 364x on an Infiniband system. To this end, we have shown that significant performance gains can be achieved without sacrificing user productivity.

For future work, we plan to improve upon our compiler optimization framework and address some of the limitations, such as optimizing multiple irregular accesses in the same loop. We also plan to design additional compiler optimizations to serve as alternatives to selective data replication when that cannot be applied, as it currently is only applicable for read-only data. Future optimizations will specifically target writes.

Acknowledgements. We would like to thank Brad Chamberlain, Engin Kayraklioglu, Vass Litvinov, Elliot Ronaghan and Michelle Strout from the Chapel team for their guidance on working with the Chapel compiler, as well as providing access to the Cray XC system that was used in our performance evaluation.

Appendix

In this appendix we provide additional performance results for the experiments performed in Sect. 4. Table 5 presents execution runtimes for the unoptimized implementation of NAS-CG and Table 6 presents the runtimes for the automatically optimized implementation of NAS-CG. Due to the amount of time required by the unoptimized code for problem sizes E and F, we project their total runtime based on their average iteration runtime. Each iteration of NAS-CG performs the same computation and communication, and we note that the variation between iterations is no more than 2% on problem sizes C and D. Tables 7 and 8 present similar data for the PageRank application.

Table 5. Execution runtimes (in minutes) for the unoptimized implementation of NAS-CG when executed on the problem sizes from Table 1. Missing values indicate that the problem size required too much memory to execute and "NA" values indicate that the system did not support the specified number of nodes/locales. Runtimes for problem sizes E and F are projected from single iteration runtimes.

Locales (Nodes)	Cray XC				Infiniband			
	C	D	E	F	C	D	E	F
2	1.8	3.9	—	—	9	15	2.3e+5	—
4	1.7	3.4	2882	—	12	17	1.7e+5	—
8	2.2	4.8	3069	—	58	131	1e+5	—
16	2.7	6.1	1005	—	96	242	5.7e+4	4.7e+5
32	1.8	4	845	9927	64	156	3.1e+4	2.4e+5
64	1.2	2.6	285	3501	NA	NA	NA	NA

Table 6. Execution runtimes (in minutes) for the automatically optimized implementation of NAS-CG when executed on the problem sizes from Table 1. Missing values indicate that the problem size required too much memory to execute and "NA" values indicate that the system did not support the specified number of nodes/locales. Runtimes for problem sizes E and F are projected from single iteration runtimes.

Locales (Nodes)	Cray XC				Infiniband			
	C	D	E	F	C	D	E	F
2	0.6	1.4	—	—	1.1	2.6	655	—
4	0.5	1	165	—	0.7	1.7	489	—
8	0.4	0.8	84	—	0.5	1	279	—
16	0.3	0.6	45	—	0.4	0.7	221	1732
32	0.3	0.5	25	190	0.4	0.6	156	1437
64	0.3	0.5	17	138	NA	NA	NA	NA

Table 7. Execution runtimes (in minutes) for the unoptimized implementation of PageRank when executed on the graphs from Table 3. "NA" values indicate that the system did not support the specified number of nodes/locales.

Locales (Nodes)	Cray XC		Infiniband	
	webbase-2001	sk-2005	webbase-2001	sk-2005
2	1.1	4.1	14.6	14
4	0.9	3.8	14.6	28
8	0.7	4.4	14.9	23
16	0.6	7.3	9.7	29
32	0.6	5.7	6.9	26
64	0.7	10	NA	NA

Table 8. Execution runtimes (in minutes) for the automatically optimized implementation of PageRank when executed on the graphs from Table 3. "NA" values indicate that the system did not support the specified number of nodes/locales.

Locales (Nodes)	Cray XC		Infiniband	
	webbase-2001	sk-2005	webbase-2001	sk-2005
2	1.2	3.3	2.8	6.9
4	1	2.4	1.7	3.9
8	0.8	3.4	1.2	3.9
16	0.7	4.2	1.1	5.5
32	0.5	4.2	1.5	6.2
64	0.6	4.7	NA	NA

References

1. Alvanos, M., Farreras, M., Tiotto, E., Amaral, J.N., Martorell, X.: Improving communication in PGAS environments: static and dynamic coalescing in UPC. In: Proceedings of the 27th International ACM Conference on Supercomputing (ICS 2013), pp. 129–138. Association for Computing Machinery (2013). https://doi.org/10.1145/2464996.2465006
2. Alvanos, M., Tiotto, E., Amaral, J.N., Farreras, M., Martorell, X.: Using shared-data localization to reduce the cost of inspector-execution in Unified-Parallel-C programs. Parallel Comput. **54**, 2–14 (2016). https://doi.org/10.1016/j.parco.2016.03.002
3. Bailey, D., Harris, T., Saphir, W., Van Der Wijngaart, R., Woo, A., Yarrow, M.: The NAS parallel benchmarks 2.0. Technical report, Technical Report NAS-95-020, NASA Ames Research Center (1995)
4. Beamer, S., Asanović, K., Patterson, D.: The GAP benchmark suite (2015). https://doi.org/10.48550/ARXIV.1508.03619
5. Bianchini, M., Gori, M., Scarselli, F.: Inside PageRank. ACM Trans. Internet Technol. **5**(1), 92–128 (2005)
6. Chamberlain, B.L., Callahan, D., Zima, H.P.: Parallel programmability and the Chapel language. Int. J. High Perform. Comput. Appl. **21**(3), 291–312 (2007)
7. Das, R., Uysal, M., Saltz, J., Hwang, Y.S.: Communication optimizations for irregular scientific computations on distributed memory architectures. J. Parallel Distrib. Comput. **22**(3), 462–478 (1994)
8. Davis, T.A., Hu, Y.: The university of Florida sparse matrix collection. ACM Trans. Math. Softw. **38**(1), 1:1-1:25 (2011). https://doi.org/10.1145/2049662.2049663
9. Ding, C., Kennedy, K.: Improving cache performance in dynamic applications through data and computation reorganization at run time. In: Proceedings of the ACM SIGPLAN 1999 Conference on Programming Language Design and Implementation, pp. 229–241. ACM (1999). https://doi.org/10.1145/301618.301670
10. Dongarra, J., Heroux, M.A., Luszczek, P.: High-performance conjugate-gradient benchmark: a new metric for ranking high-performance computing systems. Int. J. High Perform. Comput. Appl. **30**(1), 3–10 (2016)
11. El-Ghazawi, T., Carlson, W., Sterling, T., Yelick, K.: UPC: Distributed Shared Memory Programming, Wiley Series on Parallel and Distributed Computing, vol. 40. John Wiley & Sons (2005)
12. Kayraklioglu, E., Ronaghan, E., Ferguson, M.P., Chamberlain, B.L.: Locality-based optimizations in the chapel compiler. In: Li, X., Chandrasekaran, S. (eds.) LCPC 2021. LNCS, vol. 13181, pp. 3–17. Springer, Cham (2022). https://doi.org/10.1007/978-3-030-99372-6_1
13. Lumsdaine, A., Gregor, D., Hendrickson, B., Berry, J.: Challenges in parallel graph processing. Parallel Process. Lett. **17**(01), 5–20 (2007)
14. Nieplocha, J., Harrison, R.J., Littlefield, R.J.: Global arrays: a nonuniform memory access programming model for high-performance computers. J. Supercomput. **10**(2), 169–189 (1996)
15. Rauchwerger, L., Padua, D.: The LRPD test: speculative run-time parallelization of loops with privatization and reduction parallelization. IEEE Trans. Parallel Distrib. Syst. **10**(2), 160–180 (1999). https://doi.org/10.1109/71.752782
16. Saltz, J.H., Mirchandaney, R., Crowley, K.: Run-time parallelization and scheduling of loops. IEEE Trans. Comput. **40**(5), 603–612 (1991)

17. Strout, M.M., Carter, L., Ferrante, J.: Compile-time composition of run-time data and iteration reorderings. In: Proceedings of the ACM SIGPLAN 2003 Conference on Programming language Design and Implementation, pp. 91–102. ACM (2003)
18. Su, J., Yelick, K.: Automatic support for irregular computations in a high-level language. In: IEEE International Parallel and Distributed Processing Symposium, vol. 2, pp. 53b–53b. IEEE (2005)
19. Webber, J.: A programmatic introduction to Neo4j. In: Proceedings of the 3rd Annual Conference on Systems, Programming, and Applications: Software for Humanity, pp. 217–218. ACM (2012). https://doi.org/10.1145/2384716.2384777
20. Williams, S., Oliker, L., Vuduc, R., Shalf, J., Yelick, K., Demmel, J.: Optimization of sparse matrix-vector multiplication on emerging multicore platforms. In: SC'07: Proceedings of the 2007 ACM/IEEE Conference on Supercomputing, pp. 1–12. IEEE (2007)

Tensor Iterators for Flexible High-Performance Tensor Computation

John Jolly[1]($\boxtimes$), Priya Goyal[1], Vishal Sahoo[1], Hans Johansen[2], and Mary Hall[1]

[1] University of Utah, Salt Lake City, UT, USA
jjolly@cs.utah.edu
[2] Lawrence Berkeley National Laboratory, Berkeley, CA, USA

Abstract. The explosive growth of machine learning applications has consequently created a demand for high-performance implementations of tensor contractions, both for dense and sparse tensors. Compilers, code generators and libraries are often limited in what sparse tensor representations are supported. We observe that tensor contractions can be thought of as iterating over the elements of a sparse tensor to perform an operation and accumulation; co-iteration over multiple tensors can be implemented with iteration and lookup. We recognize that the resulting code can be restructured by specifying a computation, its data layout, and how to iterate over that. We illustrate the need for this generality with two different implementations of block-based data layouts implementing sparse matrix-vector multiplication (SpMV). We show how to generate these implementations with a tensor iterator abstraction designed to be integrated into the MLIR compiler, and present measurements of nearby manual implementations to demonstrate the tradeoffs and complexities with these different implementations.

Keywords: Sparse tensors · code generation

1 Introduction

High-performance sparse tensor computations have been an important building block for scientific computing, and recently have become critical to scalable machine learning applications. A sparse tensor reduces the data footprint of a tensor by only storing the nonzeros and sufficient auxiliary information to reconstruct the location of the nonzero in a dense version of the tensor. Accesses to the nonzeros through auxiliary information leads to memory indirection, and consequently, significant data movement. This data movement frequently has poor spatial locality and can cause increased memory access latency. For this reason, there is significant current as well as historical interest in compiler technology to optimize sparse tensor computations [1,3,6,7,9].

In this paper, we make the observation that such systems are limited by the set of tensor data layouts they support. We recognize that the compiler

Supported by the DOE Exascale Computing Project.

C. Mendis and L. Rauchwerger (Eds.): LCPC 2022, LNCS 13829, pp. 22–28, 2023.
https://doi.org/10.1007/978-3-031-31445-2_2

can be restructured by specifying a computation, its data layout, and how to iterate over that. We focus on what we call a *tensor iterator*, a domain-specific compiler building block which provides generality to expand the set of data layouts supported. It is hard to find a unified method for iterating over the indices of these disparate tensor layouts. An iterator that works for Compressed Sparse Row (CSR) will not work well for Block Compressed Sparse Row (BCSR). Therefore, we describe tensor iterators within a uniform disjoint iteration space using common functions that iterate over the values of the tensor; we map their locations to corresponding ones in other tensors to perform operations. This work is part of project to develop high-performance sparse tensor implementations using compiler and code generation technology that we plan to integrate into the MLIR compiler [8].

This paper makes the following contributions: (1) it highlights the role of a tensor iterator with examples of block-structured representations that are designed to reduce data movement; (2) it describes the tensor iterator abstraction and its role in high-performance sparse tensor code generation.

2 Motivation

To motivate our approach, we examine array layouts that are not well-supported by current code generators, and then make observations about how we might generalize the generated code to support these and other representations.

2.1 Example: SpMV on GPUs

As an illustration of the complexity of sparse tensor layouts, we consider two different blocked data layouts that are variations on Block Compressed Sparse Row. These are difficult to represent in the Tensor Algebra Compiler (TACO), which rely on level formats to describe the physical storage of different index dimensions of a tensor, with each level also associated with an index dimension in the tensor computation [6]. Level formats are unable to directly support blocked layouts such as block compressed sparse row (BCSR), which have additional physical dimensions not present in the computation. With the addition of the extra block dimensions, the user must also increase the dimensionality of the dense column and output vectors. In addition, iteration over a bitset is not supported in other compilers.

We discuss GPU implementations of Sparse Matrix Vector Multiply for both of these data layouts. This computation corresponds to, in Einstein notation, $y^i = A^{ij} * x^j$, but with a sparse data layout for array A as shown in Fig. 1(a).

In Fig. 1(b), we illustrate the *zero-padded BCSR*, which is what is typically referred to as BCSR; pseudo-code for the GPU implementation is shown in Fig. 1(d). In zero-padded BCSR, all blocks have the same size, 2×2 in this example, with a fixed starting point for each block. It is sparse because blocks where all values are 0 are excluded from the representation. The GPU parallelization is similar to Version 3 of prior work [5]. To enable global memory coalescing, the blocks are stored in column-major order.

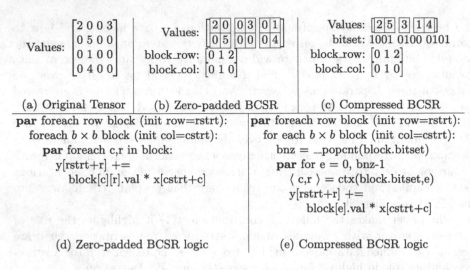

(a) Original Tensor (b) Zero-padded BCSR | (c) Compressed BCSR

par foreach row block (init row=rstrt):	**par** foreach row block (init row=rstrt):
foreach $b \times b$ block (init col=cstrt):	for each $b \times b$ block (init col=cstrt):
par foreach c,r in block:	bnz = _popcnt(block.bitset)
y[rstrt+r] +=	**par** for e = 0, bnz-1
block[c][r].val * x[cstrt+c]	⟨ c,r ⟩ = ctx(block.bitset,e)
	y[rstrt+r] +=
	block[e].val * x[cstrt+c]

(d) Zero-padded BCSR logic | (e) Compressed BCSR logic

Fig. 1. Illustration of iteration indexing variations of BCSR layout for SpMV.

While the code of the zero-padded BCSR implementation is simple and efficient, the zero padding leads to unnecessary computation, which may dominate execution as block sizes get larger. An alternative to zero padding is to compress the blocks such that only the nonzeros are represeented, and a $b \times b$ bitvector is used to identify the locations of the nonzeros in the block [4]. This *compressed BCSR* representation is illustrated in Fig. 1(c), with the pseudo-code in Fig. 1(e). Since there is more overhead to indexing the nonzero elements, we expect this code to perform worse than the other version of the code for small block sizes or mostly-dense matrices.

Performance measurements for these two manual implementations confirm the previously-described tradeoffs on an Nvidia P100 GPU as shown in Fig. 2; that is, as block size gets larger for the same density, performance of the compressed version is much better than zero-padded BCSR.

3 An Abstraction for Tensor Iterators

The goal is to create iterators that can strictly increase without regard to the underlying tensor data layout. This is done with mapping functions that are generated for a specific tensor layout. These functions will perform the necessary computations to convert between the index space and the iterator space. This should allow for iteration code that looks like the code in Listing 1.1.

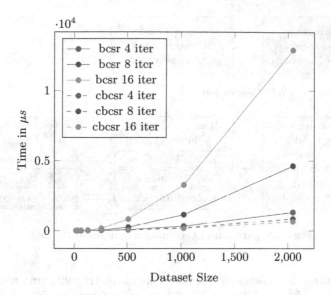

Fig. 2. Performance comparison: zero-padded (BS) vs. Compressed (CBS) BCSR.

```
1  void SpMV(dense_vector y, sparse_matrix A, dense_vector x
      ) {
2     Context ctx;
3     context_init(ctx, y, A, x);
4     int lbound_i, ubound_i = get_bounds(ctx);
5     for(int i = lbound_i; i < ubound_i; i++) {
6        double yv = get_value(ctx, y, i);
7        double Av = get_value(ctx, A, i);
8        double xv = get_value(ctx, x, i);
9        yv += Av * xv;
10       set_value(ctx, y, i, yv);
11    }
12 }
```

Listing 1.1. Matrix-Vector Multiply

Overview. While outside the scope of this paper, the code found in Listing 1.1 an be generated starting from Einstein notation, and integrated into code genration such as in the MLIR SparseTensor dialect [2] or the Tensor Algebra Compiler (TACO) [6]. The code necessary to perform the mapping to the sparse ensor data can be generated using a tensor layout language that identifies the arious components of the tensor layout, as can be seen in Fig. 3.

Iteration Ranges. Central to iteration mapping functions is the definition of 1 iteration range for a combination of tensor layouts. One iteration range will ε used to traverse the data in all tensors of the calculation. An iteration range is rictly increasing and abstracts the actual underlying data layouts. For example,

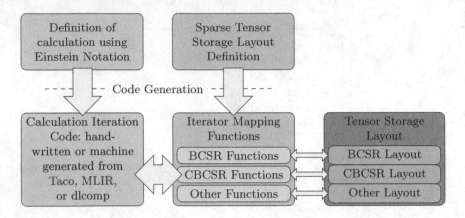

Fig. 3. Separation of Calculation and Tensor Layout

an iteration range for a dense vector and a sparse matrix with nnz non-zeros can be represented as $[0..nnz)$. Internal to the mapping functions the current iterator value will directly access elements of the sparse matrix, but will use information from the sparse matrix to access the corresponding element in the dense vector.

Mapping Functions. The iterator mapping functions have two requirements:

1. Return the iterator range that can be iterated using a single-step incrementer
2. Return and set iterator values that can be mapped back to a specific index point in the index space of the tensor

A key feature of these mapping functions is the potential to be inlined for optimization, and thus should avoid complexities that may hinder the inlining process. The four mapping functions are shown in Table 1.

Table 1. Iterator Range Mapping Functions

Signature	Description
`context_init(ctx, ...)`	Get the iteration context for the associated data structures
`get_bounds(ctx)`	Get the lower and upper bounds of the iteration range as a tuple
`get_value(ctx, tensor, iter)`	Retrieves value in the specified tensor at the specified iterator
`set_value(ctx, tensor, iter, value)`	Sets the value in memory in the specified tensor at the specified iterator

An example of mapping functions for the calculation in Listing 1.1 can be seen in Listing 1.2.

The iterator spans the non-zeros of the sparse matrix $[0..nnz)$ as provided by line 7. For each step of the iterator, the sparse matrix value within the non-zeros can be returned (line 13). For the dense vectors the coordinate array of the sparse matrix is used to index into the value arrays (lines 15 and 17).

This can be further optimized by memoizing the values in the x vector, or memoizing the outer coordinate of the sparse matrix to remove the frequent indexed access into the coordinate array of the sparse matrix.

```
void context_init(Context ctx,
    dense_vector y, sparse_matrix A, dense_vector X) {
  ctx.y = y; ctx.A = A; ctx.x = x;
}

(int, int) get_bounds(Context ctx) {
  return (0, length(ctx.A.values));
}

double get_value(Context ctx, int iter, tensor src) {
  double value = 0.0;
  if(src == ctx.A)
    value = ctx.A.values[iter];
  else if(src == ctx.x)
    value = ctx.x.values[ctx.A.coord[1][iter]];
  else if(src == ctx.y)
    value = ctx.y.values[ctx.A.coord[0][iter]];
  return value;
}

void set_value(Context ctx,
    int iter, tensor dst, double value) {
  if(src == ctx.A)
    ctx.A.values[iter] = value;
  else if(src == ctx.x)
    ctx.x.values[ctx.A.coord[1][iter]] = value;
  else if(src == ctx.y)
    ctx.y.values[ctx.A.coord[0][iter]] = value;
}
```

Listing 1.2. Memoized Mapping Functions

4 Future Work

We plan to develop and evaluate this concept over many challenging tensor layouts such as ELL and DIA. We also plan to implement and measure this concept across various high-performance computing architectures and environments. Performance comparisons will be made against current tensor code generation implementations such as the Tensor Algebra Compiler and the MLIR SparseTensor Dialect.

Acknowledgments. This research was supported in part by the Exascale Computing Project (17-SC-20-SC), a joint project of the U.S. Department of Energy's Office of Science and National Nuclear Security Administration and by the National Science Foundation under project CCF-2107556.

References

1. Bik, A., Koanantakool, P., Shpeisman, T., Vasilache, N., Zheng, B., Kjolstad, F.: Compiler support for sparse tensor computations in mlir. ACM Trans. Archit. Code Optim. **19**(4) (2022). https://doi.org/10.1145/3544559
2. Bik, A., Koanantakool, P., Shpeisman, T., Vasilache, N., Zheng, B., Kjolstad, F.: Compiler support for sparse tensor computations in MLIR. ACM Trans. Arch. Code Optim. **19**(4), 1–25 (2022). https://doi.org/10.1145/3544559
3. Bik, A.J.C.: Compiler Support for Sparse Matrix Computations. Ph.D dissertation, Leiden University (1996)
4. Buluç, A., Williams, S., Oliker, L., Demmel, J.: Reduced-bandwidth multithreaded algorithms for sparse matrix-vector multiplication. In: 2011 IEEE International Parallel & Distributed Processing Symposium, pp. 721–733 (2011). https://doi.org/10.1109/IPDPS.2011.73
5. Evtushenko, G.: December 2019. https://medium.com/gpgpu/block-sparse-matrix-vector-multiplication-with-cuda-4e616b30267
6. Kjolstad, F., Kamil, S., Chou, S., Lugato, D., Amarasinghe, S.: The tensor algebra compiler. Proc. ACM Program. Lang. **1**(OOPSLA) (2017). https://doi.org/10.1145/3133901
7. Kotlyar, V., Pingali, K., Stodghill, P.: A relational approach to the compilation of sparse matrix programs. In: Lengauer, C., Griebl, M., Gorlatch, S. (eds.) Euro-Par 1997. LNCS, vol. 1300, pp. 318–327. Springer, Heidelberg (1997). https://doi.org/10.1007/BFb0002751
8. Lattner, C., et al.: Mlir: scaling compiler infrastructure for domain specific computation. In: 2021 IEEE/ACM International Symposium on Code Generation and Optimization (CGO), pp. 2–14. IEEE (2021)
9. Zhao, T., Popoola, T., Hall, M., Olschanowsky, C., Strout, M.M.: Polyhedral specification and code generation of sparse tensor contraction with co-iteration (2022). https://doi.org/10.48550/ARXIV.2208.11858, accepted for publication, ACM Transactions on Architecture and Code Optimization

Learning from Automatically Versus Manually Parallelized NAS Benchmarks

Parinaz Barakhshan[✉][iD] and Rudolf Eigenmann[iD]

University of Delaware, Newark, DE, USA
{parinazb,eigenman}@udel.edu

Abstract. By comparing automatically versus manually parallelized NAS Benchmarks, we identify code sections that differ, and we discuss opportunities for advancing auto-parallelizers. We find ten patterns that challenge current parallelization technology. We also measure the potential impact of advanced techniques that could perform the needed transformations automatically. While some of our findings are not surprising and difficult to attain – compilers need to get better at identifying parallelism in outermost loops and in loops containing function calls – other opportunities are within reach and can make a difference. They include combining loops into parallel regions, avoiding load imbalance, and improving reduction parallelization.

Advancing compilers through the study of hand-optimized code is a necessary path to move the forefront of compiler research. Very few recent papers have pursued this goal, however. The present work tries to fill this void.

Keywords: source-to-source automatic parallelizer · Cetus · NPB Benchmark · manually-parallelized programs · automatically-parallelized programs

1 Introduction

Since the end of Dennard scaling [21] at the turn of the millennium, nearly all computer systems include parallel architectures that are exposed to their programmers. In the past two decades, we have witnessed a significant increase in computer applications in nearly all domains of science, engineering, business, and our daily lives. As a result, the number of program developers has drastically increased, including many software engineers trained on the intricacies of parallel computer architectures and applications, but also an even larger number of non-experts. Tools that help create and efficiently implement parallel applications on modern architectures are more important than ever. While the relevance of automatic parallelizers is obvious for non-expert programmers, the same tools can also greatly benefit the specialists, assisting them in efficiently performing many of the tedious programming tasks.

After four decades of research in automatic parallelization, a large number of techniques have been developed. Nevertheless, automatic parallelization tools succeed only in about half of today's science and engineering applications.

The Author(s), under exclusive license to Springer Nature Switzerland AG 2023
Mendis and L. Rauchwerger (Eds.): LCPC 2022, LNCS 13829, pp. 29–46, 2023.
ps://doi.org/10.1007/978-3-031-31445-2_3

And there is little success in many of the business and daily-life applications, which represent the major part of today's software. Users of parallelizers are often frustrated by the unpredictable performance of automatic tools, which at times degrade the speed below that of the original program. Manual paralleliza-tion is often a necessity, but its complexity and tediousness make it amenable to only a minority of highly trained experts. Even for these experts, creating parallel applications is an expensive and time-consuming task.

Developing tools that automate these tasks is even more challenging. The Languages and Compilers for Parallel Computing (LCPC) community has been at the forefront of this development. Its importance is paramount. One of the biggest questions for this community is how to bring about advances. The premise of this paper is that we need to study representative applications, inves-tigate how manual programmers have performed their tasks, compare the trans-formations they have applied with those of automatic parallelizers, and learn from these comparisons how to improve our tools. Amazingly, there are very few papers that pursue this direction. We will discuss these papers in the section on related work.

The present paper tries to fill this void. We identify programming patterns that differ between manually parallelized and auto-parallelized codes, find the limitations of auto-parallelizers, and suggest improvements for such tools so that they generate programs that are closer to hand-parallelized code.

We do this by studying the NAS Parallel Benchmark (NPB) applications [14]. The NPB applications are a representation of real-world applications. While their first release was in 1991, they are continually being modernized and include pro-grams with irregular code and data patterns. The OpenMP versions of NPB are used as our hand-parallelized applications, which we compare to the serial versions parallelized automatically by the Cetus translator [20]. Cetus is an advanced parallelizer and compiler infrastructure for C programs. We use it to represent modern parallelization technology.

The remainder of the paper is organized as follows. Section 2 outlines our experimental design. Section 3 identifies and measures the code sections that dif-fer between manual and automatic parallelization. Section 4 presents the main findings, including a description of the code patterns that differ between auto-matically and manually parallelized applications, an assessment of the perfor-mance impact of each pattern, and a discussion of opportunities for compilers. We describe related work in Sect. 5, followed by conclusions in Sect. 6.

2   Experimental Design

Application Benchmarks: We use the NAS Parallel Benchmarks NPB 3.3, which provide serial, OpenMP, and MPI codes for ten applications. The original codes are written in Fortran, but we use the variants written in C [18]. We evaluate the codes EP, IS, BT, SP, MG, and CG, which present opportunities for automatic parallelization. For our experiments, we measured the performance of the applications for input Class A, which is a small data set, but representative of larger sets. We have verified the validity of our findings on a larger data set, described in a technical report [2]. We measure the average performance of three program runs.

Automatic Parallelization: We use the Cetus open-source automatic parallelizer, which is a source-to-source translator for C programs. Cetus represents some of the most advanced parallelization technology [4,13,16], including symbolic program analysis. It generates OpenMP-annotated C code on output, invoking GCC as a backend code generator (GCC v4.8.5 with option -O3).

We ran Cetus with its default option to parallelize the codes. Among the major passes applied [5] are range analysis, points-to and alias analysis, data dependence analysis, data privatization, induction variable substitution, and reduction parallelization. This experiment uses Cetus as a representative of current auto-parallelizers, as it represents some of the most advanced parallelization technology. Additionally, it has been actively maintained, with recent enhancements and bug fixes [4].

Platform: The measurements are performed on a 4-core system. All CPUs are located on one NUMA node. Each CPU has a 512 KiB L1d cache and a 512 KiB L1i cache, as well as a 4 MiB L2 cache. Our extended technical report [2] also validates our results against a larger system.

3 Code Sections that Differ Between Manual and Automatic Parallelization

This section presents overall experimental results. We compare the performance of the automatically and manually parallelized applications (Sect. 3.1) and identify program sections that exhibit differences (Sect. 3.2) between auto- and hand-optimized. These measurements were taken on the 4-core system, introduced in Sect. 2, using data class A. Our findings have been validated on a larger data set, as described in Sect. 3.4 and Sect. 3.5 of the technical report [2].

3.1 Performance of Serial, Auto-Parallelized and Hand-Parallelized Applications

The execution times of the serial, auto-parallelized, and hand-parallelized codes, as well as their speedups, are shown in Table 1.

Table 1. Execution times of the serial, auto-parallelized and manually parallelized codes in seconds. Parallel Execution is measured on 4 cores. The Speedup is calculated as the sequential divided by the parallel runtime.

Application Name	Serial Execution Time(s)	Auto-Parallelized Code		Manually-Parallelized Code	
		Execution Time	Speedup	Execution Time	Speedup
SP	416	362	1.2	110	3.8
BT	414	356	1.2	116	3.6
EP	86	63	1.4	22	3.8
MG	35	15	2.3	8	4.0
IS	8	7	1.1	3	2.8
CG	12	5	2.5	3	4.0

With auto-parallelization, the SP, BT, EP, MG, and CG applications have gained speedup. For the IS application, there is almost no speedup reported; the code has not been parallelized substantially due to irregular data patterns.

The hand-parallelized code yields speedup gains for all applications. On average, the hand-parallelized codes perform 2.5 times faster than auto-parallelized ones.

We examine the reasons behind the differences between the auto-parallelized and hand-parallelized execution times in Sect. 4 and discuss the programming patterns responsible for these differences.

3.2 Performance of Individual Code Sections

Table 2 on page 4 shows the differences between Cetus-parallelized and manually parallelized code sections. The execution times for these code sections are reported in both auto-parallelized and manually parallelized variants. In addition, the table identifies all patterns applied to the hand-parallelized code sections that were not present in the auto-parallelized sections.

We number adjacent (nests of) loops in each subroutine from 0. For example, main#1-#3 indicates the second through the fourth *for loop* in function *main*.

Our comparison of auto-parallelized and manually parallelized codes revealed program patterns that differentiate them. The table shows which of these programming patterns have been applied to the manually parallelized code sections. Section 4 explains each of these patterns in more detail and explores the differences these patterns can make in terms of improving code performance. We omit code sections that differ but whose execution times are insignificant.

Table 2. Differences in execution times between hand-parallelized and auto-parallelized codes

App	Loop Name	Auto	Manual	P1	P2	P3	P4	P5	P6	P7	P8	P9
CG	main#1-#3	2.13	0.57	1	0	3	0	0	1	0	0	0
CG	conj_grad#0-#4	0.15	0.15	0	0	5	0	0	0	0	1	1
CG	sparse#6	0.03	0.01	1	0	1	0	0	0	0	0	0
CG	**Program**	5.00	3.00	3	0	8	0	0	1	0	1	1
IS	create_seq#0	3.48	0.88	0	1	1	0	0	1	0	0	1
IS	full_verify#0	0.12	0.05	1	0	1	1	1	1	0	0	1
IS	rank#1-#7	0.38	0.09	1	0	3	1	1	1	0	0	1
IS	**Program**	7.39	2.80	2	1	5	2	2	3	0	0	3
MG	rprj3#0	0.32	0.08	1	0	1	0	0	0	0	0	0
MG	norm2u3#0	0.42	0.12	1	1	1	0	0	0	0	1	1
MG	comm3#0	0.003	0.003	0	0	3	0	0	0	0	1	1
MG	zran3#0	1.77	0.43	1	1	1	0	0	0	0	0	1
MG	zran3#1-#3	0.25	0.03	1	1	3	0	0	0	0	0	1
MG	**Program**	15.4	8.54	4	3	9	0	0	0	0	2	4
EP	main#0	0.002	0.007	0	0	1	0	0	1	0	0	0
EP	main#3	62.5	22.4	1	1	1	0	0	1	1	0	1
EP	**Program**	63.0	22.0	1	1	2	0	0	2	1	0	1
BT	initialize#0-#7	0.44	0.12	8	7	8	0	0	0	0	6	0
BT	exact_rhs#0-#4	0.52	0.14	5	3	5	0	0	1	0	2	0
BT	compute_rhs#0-#10	20.5	20.4	0	0	11	0	0	0	0	7	0
BT	x_solve#0	110	31.3	1	1	1	0	0	1	0	0	0
BT	y_solve#0	110	31.5	1	1	1	0	0	1	0	0	0
BT	z_solve#0	113	32.2	1	1	1	0	0	1	0	0	0
BT	error_norm#1	0.08	0.02	1	1	1	0	0	0	1	1	1
BT	rhs_norm#1	0.004	0.003	0	0	1	0	0	0	1	1	1
BT	**Program**	356	116	17	14	29	0	0	4	2	17	2
SP	error_norm#1	0.04	0.01	1	1	1	0	0	0	1	1	1
SP	rhs_norm#1	0.003	0.002	0	0	1	0	0	0	1	1	1
SP	exact_rhs#0-#4	0.77	0.13	1	3	5	0	0	1	0	2	0
SP	initialize#0-#7	0.14	0.04	1	7	8	0	0	0	0	6	0
SP	lhsinit#0	0.71	0.13	1	0	1	0	0	1	0	0	0
SP	lhsinitj#0	1.10	0.30	0	0	0	0	0	1	0	0	0
SP	compute_rhs#0-#10	23.3	20.1	0	0	11	0	0	0	0	7	0
SP	x_solve#0	87.2	20.4	1	1	1	0	0	1	0	0	0
SP	y_solve#0	123	20.8	1	1	1	0	0	1	0	0	0
SP	z_solve#0	123	21.4	1	1	1	0	0	1	0	0	0
SP	**Program**	362	111	7	14	30	0	0	6	2	17	2

Auto– Execution time of auto-parallelized code (seconds) on 4 cores

Manual– Execution time of manually-parallelized code (seconds) on 4 cores

P1– Number of loops in which the outermost loop is parallelized; more on Sect. 4.1

P2– Number of loops containing function calls inside the region; more on Sect. 4.2

P3– Number of loops inside the parallel region; more on Sect. 4.3

P4– Dynamic schedule (1 means the pattern is applied); more on Sect. 4.4

P5– Irregular patterns like indirect array accesses (1 means the pattern is applied); more on Sect. 4.5

P6– Threadprivate data access (1 means Threadprivate data has been accessed); more on Sect. 4.6

P7– Array reduction (1 means the pattern is applied); more on Sect. 4.7

P8– Number of NOWAIT clauses; more on Sect. 4.8

P9– Code modification (1 means the pattern is applied); more on Sect. 4.10

4   Code Patterns, Performance Impact, Opportunities for Compilers

We now analyze the program sections in each benchmark that differ between the manually and automatically parallelized versions. We have identified ten programming patterns that represent these differences. In rough order of importance, we first explain the pattern, followed by assessing the performance impact of enabling/disabling the pattern. We then discuss the potential for improving compilers to implement the pattern.

4.1   Parallelizing Nested Loops at the Outermost Level Possible

The Pattern. It is well understood that outermost parallelism yields the best performance and that automatic parallelization may fail to do so, finding parallelism in inner loops, only. Running outermost loops in parallel minimizes the number of parallel loop invocations, and the associated fork/join overheads, including implicit barriers at the loop end. Not surprisingly, we found several program sections that differed between manually and automatically parallelized in this way. Among the causes were irregular data accesses, function calls (discussed later), or dependences that could not be disproven.

Performance Impact. Subroutines x_solve(), y_solve(), and z_solve() in programs BT and SP are examples of compute-intensive functions that are not parallelized at the outermost level by the Cetus compiler – due to function calls present in the outermost loop. Table 3 shows the differences between the auto- and hand-parallelized code execution times.

Table 3. Impact of parallelizing the outermost loop in nested loops, comparing the execution time of the Cetus-parallelized code with the manually parallelized code.

Application Name	Loop Name	Technique Not Applied	Technique Applied	Impact
BT	x_solve#0	110	31	255%
BT	y_solve#0	110	31	255%
BT	z_solve#0	113	32	253%
BT	**program**	356	116	206%
SP	x_solve#0	87	20	335%
SP	y_solve#0	123	21	486%
SP	z_solve#0	123	21	486%
SP	**program**	362	111	226%

Opportunities for Compilers. The presence of function calls requires inter-procedural analysis or inline expansion capabilities, which we will discuss in the following subsection. Irregular access patterns have long been a challenge for compilers, with both run-time and recent compile-time approaches pursuing improvements. For disproving data dependences, we have often found that the opportunity is in the propagation of information across the program (such as interprocedural symbolic analysis) rather than in increasing the power of data dependence tests themselves.

4.2 Parallelizing Loops Containing Function Calls

The Pattern. Most auto-parallelizers, including Cetus, do not consider loops with function calls or I/O statements, for parallelization, unless those functions are known to be side-effect free. Our study found many examples in which a function call inside a loop prevented auto-parallelization. The same loops were parallelized in the manually transformed codes. Inline expansion, which replaces a function call with the body of the called subroutine, can help parallelize such patterns. Users of the Cetus compiler have that option available. We measure the effect of doing so.

Performance Impact. We performed an experiment to determine how much parallelization is enabled through inline expansion in Cetus-parallelized codes. Table 4 shows the result.

We found that auto-parallelization indeed could detect additional parallelism in several of the loops in question after applying inlining. As displayed in Table 4, subroutine *initialize()* in both BT and SP shows significant performance gain, due to parallelization of the outermost loops. However, in *exact_rhs()*, the transformation led to performance degradation. While additional loops could be parallelized, these were inner loops where parallelization was not profitable. What's more, the most compute-intensive loops, in subroutines x_solve(), y_solve(), and z_solve() of both applications, remained unaffected by inline expansion, as Cetus is still unable to disprove data dependences.

Opportunities for Compilers. Despite studies on interprocedural analysis IPA) that have been carried out for more than three decades, IPA is not available in most compilers. Among the reasons are the complexity of the technique, the fact that most analyses need specialized IPA algorithms, and the resulting increase in compilation times.

By interacting with the user, it is possible to identify user functions that have no side effects and add them to the default list of side-effect-free functions, which consist primarily of math functions. Other opportunities include selective subroutine inline expansion during the compiler analysis only. The former technique could identify additional parallelism with user input, while the latter could eliminate overheads, such as excessive code growth.

Table 4. Impact of inlining in parallelizing automatically parallelized codes; Comparing the execution time of auto-parallelized codes before and after inlining.

App Name	Loop Name	Number of Inlined Functions	Parallelized after Inlining?	Technique Not Applied	Inlining Technique Applied	Impact
BT	initialize#0-#7	9	Yes[1]	0.44	0.14	214%
BT	exact_rhs#0-#4	3	Yes[2]	0.52	0.63	-17%
BT	x_solve#0	8	No	110	122	-10%
BT	y_solve#0	8	No	110	123	-11%
BT	z_solve#0	8	No	113	124	-9%
BT	error_norm#1	1	Yes[3]	0.08	0.03	167%
BT	**Program**			356	395	-10%
SP	initialize#0-#7	9	Yes[1]	0.14	0.04	250%
SP	exact_rhs#0-#4	3	Yes[2]	0.77	0.7	10%
SP	x_solve#0	1	No	87	87	0%
SP	y_solve#0	1	No	123	124	-1%
SP	z_solve#0	1	No	123	123	0%
SP	error_norm#1	1	Yes[3]	0.04	0.03	33%
SP	**Program**			362	377	-4%

[1] In nested loop structures, the outermost loops are parallelized. In manually parallelized code, however, all parallel loops are included in a parallel region.
[2] In nested loop structures, inner loops are parallelized.
[3] While the outermost loop is parallelized, the array reduction implementation differs from the hand-parallelized code that will be discussed later.

4.3   Parallel Regions Enclosing Multiple Parallel Loops

The Pattern. In OpenMP, multiple adjacent parallel loops can be converted into a *parallel region*. This way, the parallel threads are spawned only once, at the beginning of the region, reducing fork/join overhead. The original parallel loops will become *worksharing constructs*, which simply distribute their iterations onto the available threads. In some cases, the programmers had inserted *NOWAIT* clauses to eliminate barrier synchronizations at the end of the worksharing constructs.

In the hand-parallelized codes, we found this pattern frequently. By contrast, auto-parallelizers, including Cetus, typically examine and parallelize loops individually.

Performance Impact. We have measured the impact of such a technique by converting the hand-parallelized programs to variants without parallel regions. The loops inside the regions were changed to individual parallel loops. Note that doing so also forces a barrier synchronization at the end of each parallel loop. The results are presented in Table 5.

Opportunities for Compilers. Developing transformations that combine adjacent parallel loops into a parallel region seems feasible in some situations but we are not aware of auto-parallelizers that do so. In other cases, creating parallel regions can be challenging because sequential code sections may be present

Table 5. Impact of enclosing multiple parallel loops in a parallel region – comparing the execution times of the code containing individual parallel loops with the hand-optimized code containing a parallel region.

App Name	Loop Name	Number of Loops	Technique Not Applied	Technique Applied	Impact
MG	comm3#0-#2	3	0.003	0.003	0%
MG	zran3#1-#3	3	0.034	0.033	4%
MG	**Program**	6	9	8.5	6%
BT	initialize#0-#7	8	0.124	0.116	7%
BT	exact_rhs#0-#4	5	0.167	0.142	18%
BT	compute_rhs#0-#10	11	0.117	0.108	8%
BT	**Program**	24	129	116	11%

between the parallel loops. There exists work on eliminating barrier synchronization, which can be incorporated into such techniques.

4.4   Avoiding Load Imbalance Through Dynamic Scheduling

The Pattern. Load imbalance can be caused by the uneven distribution of work across worker threads. Loop scheduling defines chunks of loop iterations and their distribution onto the threads. In loops that are prone to uneven workload, due to conditional execution or work that depends on the iteration number, loop scheduling can affect performance noticeably. Two schedule clauses offered by OpenMP for resolving load imbalance are *dynamic* and *guided*. They make scheduling decisions at run-time, assigning chunks of iterations to idle threads.

The developers of the hand-parallelized codes have made use of these clauses. By contrast, the Cetus compiler currently does not change the default loop schedule, which is the static distribution of an equal share of iterations to all worker threads.

Performance Impact. We have found some loops where loop scheduling made a substantial difference. Table 6, shows two such loops in the IS program. The improved code performance of 43% and 17%, respectively, translates to a noticeable overall program speed improvement of 6%. The impact of dynamic scheduling on the whole application is significant, as the rank function is invoked multiple times.

Opportunities for Compilers. Program and loop workloads are affected by both program and execution characteristics. Dynamic factors, such as external programs in shared machines, and conditional executions guided by input data, are difficult to assess. However, the compiler *can* analyze programs for conditional execution patterns that may depend on input data, iteration numbers that tend to load threads unevenly, and inner loops whose workload depends on outer loop iterations (e.g., triangular loops).

Table 6. Impact of adding dynamic scheduling. The execution time of the code when scheduling is disabled is compared to the execution time of the manually parallelized code.

Application Name	Loop Name	Technique Not Applied	Technique Applied	Impact
IS	full_verify#0	0.07	0.05	43%
IS	rank#1-#7	0.10	0.09	17%
IS	**program**	2.14	2.02	6%

4.5 Analyzing Irregular Patterns in Hand-Parallelized Codes

The Pattern. Applications that have irregular data access patterns with complex code structures prevent auto-parallelizers from succeeding.

The IS application exhibits such patterns. The loops full_verify#0, rank#0, rank#2, rank#4, and rank#6 include indirect array accesses, which prevent Cetus from detecting parallelism.

Performance Impact. Table 7 reports execution times of these loops in the IS application when they are not parallelized by the auto-parallelizer due to such patterns, and when they are parallelized in the manually optimized code.

Table 7. Impact of parallelizing irregular patterns. The execution time of the auto-parallelized code, where irregular patterns remain serial, is compared to the execution time of the manually parallelized code, where the same loops are parallelized.

Application Name	Loop Name	Technique Not Applied	Technique Applied	Impact
IS	full_verify#0	0.12	0.05	135%
IS	rank#1-#7	0.38	0.09	318%
IS	**program**	7.39	2.80	163%

Opportunities for Compilers. Loops containing subscripted subscripts are among the most complex patterns for compilers to analyze. A number of run-time techniques have been developed, such as run-time data-dependence tests and inspector-executor schemes. Recent work has also begun to develop compile-time techniques based on the observation that, in some cases, the information needed to prove the absence of data dependences is present in the application program [4] [6].

4.6   Threadprivate Data

The Pattern. The OpenMP *threadaprivate* directive specifies that variables are replicated, with a copy being kept in each thread. It privatizes static or global variables that are modified by multiple parallel regions. Threadprivate variables persist across regions. The manually parallelized benchmarks make use of this concept in a number of program sections.

Auto-parallelizers, including Cetus, do not create threadprivate data. Data that need to be replicated across threads and persist across parallel regions or loops need to be implemented through data expansion or copying region/loop-private data in and out – sometimes through first/last-private clauses.

Performance Impact. We measured the impact of using threadprivate data by considering those program sections where conversion to loop-private data was possible. We compared the performance of the variants without threadprivate data (loop-private data only) with the hand-parallelized variants, which use threadprivate data.

The result was unexpected. Table 8 shows that using threadprivate data lowers the performance in all of our cases. The compute-intensive loops in BT, subroutine x/y/z_solve, see a 25% performance reduction. The superior performance of regions without the use of threadprivate data is consistent with the findings of others [12], who attribute this effect to inefficient OpenMP implementations.

We did not measure other program sections where additional programming steps would be necessary for the transformation to region/loop-private data. In these cases, the additional steps would likely add overhead, making the threadprivate variant more desirable.

Table 8. Impact of using *threadprivate* directives. We compare the execution time of the code where threadprivate data is replaced by loop-private data, with the execution time of the manually parallelized code.

Application Name	Loop Name	Technique Not Applied	Technique Applied	Impact
EP	main#0	0.003	0.006	-50%
EP	main#3	20.93	22.40	-7%
EP	**Program**	21.0	22.5	-7%
BT	exact_rhs#0-#4	0.055	0.142	-61%
BT	x_solve#0	23.43	31.24	-25%
BT	y_solve#0	23.63	31.51	-25%
BT	z_solve#0	24.45	32.17	-24%
BT	**Program**	93	116	-20%

Opportunities for Compilers. Identifying threadprivate variables would involve analyses similar to current data privatization, combined with liveness analysis across loops. While this appears feasible, careful consideration will need to be given to profitability, so as to avoid situations with negative impacts.

4.7 Array Reductions

The Pattern. Reduction operations are parallelized as follows: Each thread concurrently performs a reduction operation on the assigned loop iterations, creating partial results, followed by a step that combines the partial results. We have found differences in this combination step. For array reductions, the hand-parallelized versions perform the needed mutual exclusion operation on each element individually, using an OpenMP *atomic* construct. By contrast, the Cetus implementation performs the mutual exclusion for the entire array, by means of a *critical section*. This is the major difference, next to a minor variation in how data is allocated. The extended technical report [2] provides an example describing the pattern and the differences between the auto- and hand-parallelized versions.

Performance Impact. We compared the two variants, individual element synchronization (manual) and overall synchronization (automatic), by replacing two of the array reduction patterns in the hand-parallelized codes with the Cetus implementation scheme. We measured the execution time of those code sections and the entire program.

Table 9 shows a significant performance impact on the two loops. The overall effect in the programs is minor, as loop rhs_norm#1 is small and executed once per application in both SP and BT. In general, as reduction operations can show up in compute-intensive sections of programs, the impact may be much larger, however.

Table 9. The table compares the performance of the Cetus-applied array-reduction transformation versus the manually applied technique in the hand-parallelized codes.

Application Name	Loop Name	Technique Not Applied (Cetus)	Technique Applied (Manual)	Impact
BT	rhs_norm#1	0.005	0.003	66%
BT	**program**	117	116	1%
SP	rhs_norm#1	0.006	0.002	200%
SP	**program**	112	111	1%

Opportunities for Compilers. Compilers can easily transform array reductions in either of the described variants. The choice of best implementation depends on several factors, including the efficiency of implementation of the OpenMP atomic directive. If the implementation simply uses a critical section (which we have seen in some OpenMP libraries), the current Cetus transformation likely performs the same or better. This calls for compilers having knowledge of architectural and platform parameters, which we will discuss more in Sect. 4.9 on conditional parallelization.

4.8   NOWAIT – Eliminating Barrier Synchronizations

The Pattern. A barrier is implicitly included at the end of some OpenMP constructs, including *parallel, for, and single constructs*. This barrier is the safe default so that all threads have completed their share of work before proceeding with the execution. This synchronization is not needed if threads do not access data previously operated on by a different thread or on the last worksharing loop inside a parallel region. The OpenMP NOWAIT clause eliminates the barrier.

NOWAIT clauses have been inserted on many parallel loops inside the parallel regions in the hand-parallelized programs, reducing substantial overhead. The auto-parallelized code do not include such techniques.

Performance Impact. In order to test the performance impact of the technique, we have created program variants of hand-parallelized codes with removed NOWAIT clauses. Table 10 on page 14 compares these codes with the hand-parallelized variants. The impact in most of the programs is only about 1%, even though individual loops see a gain of up to 16%. It is likely that the impact would increase with a larger number of threads (recall that we use four) or in programs/loops with imbalanced load.

Opportunities for Compilers. Compile-time techniques for barrier elimination have been explored. Engineering them into available compilers is still an opportunity to be seized. Given the relatively minor impact, other techniques may be prioritized. Note also that this technique is related to enclosing loops in a parallel region.

Table 10. Impact of Eliminating Barrier Synchronization: Execution times of removed versus present NOWAIT clauses in hand-parallelized codes.

Application Name	Loop Name	Number of NOWAIT Clauses	Technique Not Applied	Technique Applied	Impact
CG	Conj_grad#0–4	1	0.173	0.149	16%
CG	**program**	1	3	2.98	**1%**
MG	norm2u3#0	1	0.121	0.119	2%
MG	comm3#0	1	0.003	0.003	0%
MG	**program**	2	8.7	8.5	**2%**
BT	initialize#0-#7	6	0.116	0.116	0%
BT	exact_rhs#0-#4	2	0.142	0.142	0%
BT	compute_rhs#0-#10	7	21.343	20.345	5%
BT	error_norm#1	1	0.019	0.019	0%
BT	rhs_norm#1	1	0.003	0.003	0%
BT	**program**	17	117	116	**1%**
SP	initialize#0-#7	6	0.043	0.043	0%
SP	exact_rhs#0-#4	2	0.133	0.132	1%
SP	compute_rhs#0-#10	7	21.452	20.050	7%
SP	error_norm#1	1	0.012	0.011	9%
SP	rhs_norm#1	1	0.002	0.002	0%
SP	**program**	17	111.5	110.5	**1%**

4.9   Conditional Parallelization

The Pattern. A technique present in auto-parallelized codes, but not in the manual variants, is the conditional parallelization of loops. The Cetus compiler estimates the workload of loops, as the product of the number of statements and iterations. It parallelizes only those with high workloads. If the estimate is an expression that cannot be computed at compile time, it uses OpenMP's conditional parallelization clause with an if condition that the expression exceeds a threshold. The manually parallelized programs do not use such conditional parallelization. One can expect that conditional parallelization benefits programs with small data sets, as some of the loops will not beneficially run in parallel.

Performance Impact. We have found some conditionally parallelized loops that are too small to run in parallel beneficially. But their impact on the overall programs was very small, even when they were executed in parallel, as these loops do not take significant execution time. We have also found some loops that Cetus did not parallelize since they were not profitable. While conditional parallelization adds a small runtime overhead, due to the if clause added to the OpenMP directive that checks for exceeding a threshold, the technique is generally beneficial.

To estimate the overhead conditional parallelization may add to the execution time of the loop, we measured the execution time of the rhs_norm#1 loop of the BT application with and without conditional parallelization in the Cetus parallelized code. The results of this measurement are presented in Table 11.

Opportunities for Compilers. Like many other optimizers, Cetus uses crude profitability model. There is much room for improving these models t

Table 11. Impact of conditional analysis; A comparison is made between the execution time of the code with and without conditional analysis in Cetus-parallelized code.

Application Name	Loop Name	Technique Applied	Technique Disabled	Impact
BT	rhs_norm#1	0.004	0.003	33%

estimate the execution time of loops or program sections under various optimization variants.

4.10   Code Modifications in Hand-Parallelized Codes

The Pattern. Our comparison of hand-parallelized and auto-parallelized versions of the codes revealed additional modifications that were made to the hand-parallelized codes. They include:

- Enclosing a mix of parallel loops and serial sections in a parallel region.
- Changing the scope of variables to enable the creation of parallel regions.
- Explicitly mapping tasks or iterations to threads.
- Resolving some dependences (mostly output dependences) to enable parallelization.
- Improving cache performance.
- Merging loops that perform similar tasks.

Performance Impact. These modifications were often applied to enable later parallelization steps. Their impact was thus difficult to isolate. In general, they contributed significantly to the good performance of the parallel applications.

Opportunities for Compilers. While, at a high level, the mentioned modifications seem automatable, they tend to make use of application-specific knowledge. They are thus non-trivial to implement with general benefit.

5   Related Work

Many studies have been conducted on the NAS Parallel Benchmarks, including analyses, evaluation, parallelization, and tuning, but no comparison has been made between automatically and manually parallelized codes. Some studies do propose improvements to auto-parallelizers, based upon limitations of such tools that they have encountered in their experiments. The following are studies in this regard.

A study by Prema et al. [15] comparing different auto-parallelizers such as Cetus, Par4all [1], Pluto [8], Parallware [11], ROSE [17], and Intel C++ Compiler (ICC) [19] while parallelizing NAS Parallel Benchmarks (NPB) finds that auto-parallelizers have limitations, which programmers should be aware of in order to intervene manually if necessary during parallelization. The development of an interactive environment that highlights the difficulties encountered while parallelizing loops is proposed.

Blume [7] and Eigenmann et al. [10] discuss the successes and limitations of auto-parallelizers, based on a study performed on the Perfect Benchmarks. A modified version of the KAP restructurer and the VAST restructurer were used as representatives of parallelizing compilers for Fortran programs. Based on the limitations of auto-parallelizers at that time, this study proposes new techniques.

Dave et al. [9] have measured the serial performance as well as the performance of the manually parallelized codes on a subset of the NAS Parallel and SPEC OMP2001 benchmarks. In contrast to the present paper, their experiment compared the performance of these programs with that of auto-tuned codes.

A distinguishing feature of the present paper is that it compares auto-parallelized with hand-parallelized codes in order to identify opportunities for compiler improvements. Performance differences attributable to the identified program patterns are also measured, so as to quantify their importance for future compiler developments. Our proposed improvements could help auto-parallelizers reach performance approaching that of hand-parallelized code.

6   Conclusion

We compared how expert programmers parallelize programs with how automatic parallelization does the same. The goal is to learn how to improve auto-parallelizers so as to approach hand-optimized performance. We believe that such studies are essential to push the forefront of research in compilers for parallel computing.

Currently, auto-parallelized codes are not as efficient as hand-parallelized codes. Our analysis of a subset of the NAS Parallel benchmarks found that auto-parallelized codes perform better than serial codes in many programs, but hand-parallelized codes perform significantly better. We have identified code sections, their program patterns, and the performance where differences occur. Additionally, we found examples in which hand-parallelized codes performed better after the use of threadprivate data was undone.

Among the patterns that showed the biggest performance differences were: Parallelizing the outermost loop in nested loops, parallelizing loops that enclose function calls, parallelizing loops with irregular patterns, enclosing loops in parallel regions, applying dynamic scheduling to cases with imbalanced loads, and using NOWAIT clauses to eliminate implicit barriers.

Opportunities for advancing compilers exist in several areas, including in advancing analysis techniques, improving transformation techniques, and efficient OpenMP code generation. These opportunities are explained along with the differentiating patterns that have been identified. The findings of this study will be used to guide future developments of the Cetus parallelizing compiler platform and an interactive Cetus parallelization tool (iCetus) [3].

Acknowledgements. This work was supported by the National Science Foundation (NSF) under Awards Nos. 1931339, 2209639, and 1833846.

References

1. Amini, M., et al.: Par4all: from convex array regions to heterogeneous computing. In: 2nd International Workshop on Polyhedral Compilation Techniques, Impact (Jan 2012) (2012)
2. Barakhshan, P., Eigenmann, R.: A comparison between automatically versus manually parallelized NAS Benchmarks. Technical Report, Department of Electrical and Computer Engineering, University of Delaware, Newark, DE, USA (Aug 2022). https://arxiv.org/abs/2212.00165
3. Barakhshan, P., Eigenmann, R.: iCetus: a semi-automatic parallel programming assistant. In: Li, X., Chandrasekaran, S. (eds.) Lang. Compilers Parallel Comput., pp. 18–32. Springer International Publishing, Cham (2022)
4. Bhosale, A., Barakhshan, P., Rosas, M.R., Eigenmann, R.: Automatic and interactive program parallelization using the Cetus source to source compiler infrastructure v2.0. Electronics 11(5), 809 (2022)
5. Bhosale, A., Barakhshan, P., Rosas, M.R., Eigenmann, R.: The Cetus compiler manual (2022). https://sites.udel.edu/cetus-cid/the-cetus-compiler-manual/
6. Bhosale, A., Eigenmann, R.: On the automatic parallelization of subscripted subscript patterns using array property analysis. In: Proceedings of the ACM International Conference on Supercomputing, pp. 392–403 (2021)
7. Blume, W.J.: Success and limitations in automatic parallelization of the perfect benchmarks programs. Master's thesis, University of Illinois at Urbana-Champaign, Center for Supercomputing Res. & Dev. (July 1992)
8. Bondhugula, U., Hartono, A., Ramanujam, J., Sadayappan, P.: A practical automatic polyhedral parallelizer and locality optimizer. In: Proceedings of the 29th ACM SIGPLAN Conference on Programming Language Design and Implementation, pp. 101–113. PLDI '08, Association for Computing Machinery, New York, NY, USA (2008). https://doi.org/10.1145/1375581.1375595
9. Dave, C., Eigenmann, R.: Automatically tuning parallel and parallelized programs. In: Languages and Compilers for Parallel Computing, pp. 126–139 (2010)
10. Eigenmann, R., Hoeflinger, J., Padua, D.: On the automatic parallelization of the perfect benchmarks(R). IEEE Trans. Parallel Distrib. Syst. 9(1), 5–23 (1998)
11. Gomez-Sousa, H., Arenaz, M., Rubinos-Lopez, O., Martinez-Lorenzo, J.A.: Novel source-to-source compiler approach for the automatic parallelization of codes based on the method of moments. In: 2015 9th European Conference on Antennas and Propagation (EuCAP), pp. 1–6 (2015)
12. Martorell, X., et al.: Techniques supporting threadprivate in openMP. In: Proceedings 20th IEEE International Parallel & Distributed Processing Symposium, p. 7 (2006). https://doi.org/10.1109/IPDPS.2006.1639501
13. Mosseri, I., Alon, L.-O., Harel, R.E., Oren, G.: *ComPar*: optimized multi-compiler for automatic openmp S2S parallelization. In: Milfeld, K., de Supinski, B.R., Koesterke, L., Klinkenberg, J. (eds.) IWOMP 2020. LNCS, vol. 12295, pp. 247–262. Springer, Cham (2020). https://doi.org/10.1007/978-3-030-58144-2_16
14. NASA Advanced Supercomputing (NAS) Division: NAS Parallel Benchmarks (2022). https://www.nas.nasa.gov/software/npb.html

15. Prema, S., Jehadeesan, R., Panigrahi, B.K.: Identifying pitfalls in automatic parallelization of NAS parallel benchmarks. In: 2017 National Conference on Parallel Computing Technologies (PARCOMPTECH), pp. 1–6 (Feb 2017). https://doi.org/10.1109/PARCOMPTECH.2017.8068329
16. Prema, S., Nasre, R., Jehadeesan, R., Panigrahi, B.: A study on popular auto-parallelization frameworks. Concurr. Comput. Pract. Experience **31**(17), e5168 (2019). https://doi.org/10.1002/cpe.5168
17. Quinlan, D., Liao, C.: The ROSE source-to-source compiler infrastructure. In: Cetus users and compiler infrastructure workshop, in conjunction with PACT, vol. 2011, p. 1. Citeseer (2011)
18. SNUNPB(2013): NAS Parallel Benchmarks C version (2019). http://aces.snu.ac.kr/software/snu-npb/
19. Tian, X., Bik, A., Girkar, M., Grey, P., Saito, H., Su, E.: Intel® OpenMP C++/Fortran compiler for hyper-threading technology: implementation and performance. Intel Technol. J. 6(1) (2002)
20. University of Delaware: Cetus, a parallelizing source-to-source compiler for C programs (2022). https://sites.udel.edu/cetus-cid/
21. Wikipedia: Dennard scaling (2022). https://en.wikipedia.org/wiki/Dennard_scaling

Employing Polyhedral Methods to Reduce Data Movement in FPGA Stencil Codes

Florian Mayer[✉], Julian Brandner, and Michael Philippsen

Friedrich-Alexander Universität Erlangen-Nürnberg (FAU) Programming Systems Group, Erlangen, Germany
{florian.andrefranc.mayer,julian.brandner,michael.philippsen}@fau.de

Abstract. Due to the ubiquity of stencil codes in scientific computing there is a strong need to optimize their runtimes. When using a GPU as an accelerator, programmers need to amortize the cost of shipping data to/from the device. When using an FPGA as an accelerator, the situation is worse as programmers also need to build a cache-like data shipment on the device. To avoid this tedious and error-prone task, our source-to-source compiler takes OpenMP **pragma**-annotated stencil codes, derives a polyhedral model from them, finds and merges overlapping contiguous read accesses, and instruments the code with vendor-specific annotations that guide the FPGA synthesis to generate efficient stencil hardware with fast data shipment and fast on-FPGA cache-like structures. Our data movement optimization improves the runtime of a set of stencil codes from three different sources by between $1.3\times$ and $5.8\times$, on average.

1 Introduction

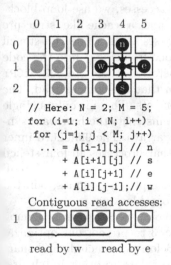

```
// Here: N = 2; M = 5;
for (i=1; i < N; i++)
 for (j=1; j < M; j++)
  ... = A[i-1][j] // n
      + A[i+1][j] // s
      + A[i][j+1] // e
      + A[i][j-1];// w
```

Contiguous read accesses:

read by w   read by e

Fig. 1. Original 5-point stencil.

As stencils are building blocks in scientific computing that are used extensively at the core of simulation codes, their runtime performance matters. Due to their regular computation pattern – Fig. 1 shows a 5-point stencil – there have been attempts to use accelerator hardware for them. Whenever an accelerator accesses external memories and especially when the local memory of the accelerator can only hold fragments of all the problem data, there is the need to reduce, optimize, or at least hide time-consuming shipment of data between external memory and the accelerator and to also improve temporal locality by reusing data that is already on the device.

Known solutions for GPUs do not suffice for FPGAs. Whereas on the GPU there are caches that let the GPU processors efficiently

Mendis and L. Rauchwerger (Eds.): LCPC 2022, LNCS 13829, pp. 47–63, 2023.
ps://doi.org/10.1007/978-3-031-31445-2_4

access the data, on FPGAs there is no such hardware for data movement. Programmers have to either apply some generic hardware block (IP) with cache functionality or build a faster stencil-specific data shipment themselves that reuses data that has already been read. The latter is desirable but also tedious and error-prone.

The main contribution of this paper is to show how a compiler can add such structures automatically to the generated FPGA hardware. The main technical idea is to employ polyhedral techniques to detect overlapping burst-like access patterns and use them to generate the pragmas for the hardware synthesis tools that cause cached stencil hardware that initiates memory bursts to fill its caches and that reuses the data from the overlapping accesses.

```
for (i = 1; i < N; i++) {
 for (j = 1; j < ...; j += 4) {
  float n[4], we[6], s[4];
  #pragma USE_FLIPFLOPS (n,we,s)
  BURST_CPY(n , A+..., sizeof(n));
  BURST_CPY(we, A+..., sizeof(we));
  BURST_CPY(s , A+..., sizeof(s));
  for (k = 0; k < 4; k++) {
   #pragma UNROLL
   ... = n[k]   + s[k]
        + we[k] + we[k+2];
  }}
 // remaining iterations (M%4)
 for (j...;...;j++) { ... }
}
```

Fig. 2. Optimized stencil code for Fig. 1.

When the stencil code of Fig. 1 is fed into an FPGA synthesis tool, it detects that a contiguous stretch of array elements (called a burst) is read as w moves from left to right over the first line of the array, see the bottom of Fig. 1 Similarly there are bursts for e, s, and n. For each of the bursts, the synthesis generates pipelining circuits that hide the transfer times. But as the bursts overlap and have elements in common, the generated FPGA wastes time by re-reading them. This is the optimization potential that we harvest. After identifying the overlapping contiguous read accesses, we use loop blocking and add a cache-like structure that reads all the w and e elements once and reuses them while the stencil processes each block. To do so we transform the code from Fig. 1 into the code in Fig. 2. Before the inner loop with the stencil operation, there are BURST_CPY operations that fill into temporary arrays the data that the stencils read. The combined array we holds both the w and the e elements. There is only a single burst operation for it. The USE_FLIPFLOPS pragma instructs the hardware synthesis to generate register banks for the temporary arrays. The UNROLLed inner loop turns into a SIMD-like hardware component that processes all four stencil iterations in parallel since the register banks permit concurrent accesses to all elements. For simplicity of this example, we used simplified pragmas, omitted offset calculations, and glossed over the details of loop blocking.

The remainder of this paper is organized as follows. Sec. 2 covers common polyhedral terms and notations that we use in Sec. 3 to present our optimization method. Sec. 4 holds our evaluation results. Before we conclude and share our plans for future work, Sec. 5 discusses how we relate to other polyhedra approaches for FPGAs.

2 Notation of Polyhedral Techniques

Let us first cover the common polyhedral terms and notations that we use in Sect. 3. The polyhedral model [12] is well-known to represent, analyze, and optimize highly regular program fragments [2,3,6,8] that are also known as static control parts (SCoP). Informally, SCoPs are code fragments that consist of possibly imperfectly nested loops and branches, where each condition is an affine function of the surrounding parameters or loop indices [1]. Most stencils are SCoPs as they can be defined in terms of a canonical loop nests, load/store statements, and arithmetic/logical operations. Figure 3 holds the polyhedral description for the stencil in Fig. 1. It represents the loop iterations and the load/store access behavior of the stencil.

$$\text{Dom} := \overbrace{[N, M]}^{parameters} \rightarrow$$
$$\{S[i,j] : 1 \le i < N \wedge 1 \le j < M\}$$
$$R_n := [] \rightarrow \{S[i,j] \rightarrow A[i-1,j]\}$$
$$R_s := \{S[i,j] \rightarrow A[i+1,j]\}$$
$$R_e := \{S[i,j] \rightarrow A[i,j+1]\}$$
$$R_w := \{\underbrace{S[i,j]}_{domain} \rightarrow \underbrace{A[i,j-1]}_{range}\}$$

Fig. 3. Polyhedral description for the code in Fig. 1. R_i are read access relations.

The notation uses a description syntax that is based on the Integer Set Library (ISL) [25]. A named tuple $S[i,j]$ represents a point in the iteration space of the stencil. The constraints $1 \le i < N$ and $1 \le j < M$ express the loop bounds and constrain the number of tuples in the Domain set. In this description, an access relation, for example R_n, models that the iteration $S[i,j]$ reads the element $A[i-1,j]$. Below we always omit empty parameter lists "[]". While a full polyhedral description also defines the order of the iterations in the Domain, we can omit this because we do not need it to generate code from it. The ISL comes with operations on sets and relations. As we use them in Sect. 3 let us informally show their semantics.

- *set ∩ set*: Set intersection, e.g., $\{S[1,2]; S[2,3]\} \cap \{S[2,3]\} = \{S[2,3]\}$.
- *relation(set)*: Set application. Conceptually each element of the *set* is used as an argument for the *relation*. This yields a set of results. For the running example, consider the access relation $R_e = \{S[i,j] \rightarrow A[i,j-1]\}$ and the set of two iterations $I = \{S[1,1]; S[1,2]\}$. Then $R_e(I)$ yields the set of two array elements $\{A[1,0]; A[1,1]\}$.
- *set ∪ set*: Set union, e.g., $\{S[1,2]; S[2,3]\} \cup \{S[3,4]\} = \{S[1,2]; S[2,3]; S[3,4]\}$.
- *card(set)*: Number of elements in the set, e.g., $card(\{S[1,2]; S[2,3]\}) = 2$.
- *lexmin(set)*: Find the lexicographic minimum and return a one element set, e.g., $lexmin(\{S[1,2]; S[2,3]; S[0,5]\}) = \{S[0,5]\}$.
- *set → set*: Build a relation from the cross product of both input sets, e.g., $\{S[0,1]; S[2,4]\} \rightarrow \{S[2]\} = \{S[0,1] \rightarrow S[2]; S[2,4] \rightarrow S[2]\}$.
- *deltas(relation)*: Calculate the delta $y - x$ for each tuple $x \rightarrow y$ in *relation*, e.g., $deltas(\{S[1,4] \rightarrow S[4,1]; S[2] \rightarrow S[1]\}) = \{S[3,-3]; S[-1]\}$.

3   Optimization Method

For an n-point stencil code that processes k-dimensional rectangular arrays and is written in C, our optimization can create a cache-like structure whose size is only limited by the number of register banks on the target FPGA. The stencil must consist of a single canonical loop nest that only increments its loop counters by ± 1. To simplify the search for bursts, array accesses may either only have index expressions for each of their multiple dimensions that have the form $i \pm c$ where i is a loop counter and c is a constant integer, or they can use a pointer plus an offset expression, i.e., they are one-dimensional array accesses. While the stencil can contain multiple load operations, we only allow stores without loop-carried data dependencies. Such dependencies would keep the hardware synthesis tool from creating parallel hardware for the FPGA. This restriction is not too severe as many stencil codes let all stencils write to a shadow array in a pass over the data, before the next pass uses that shadow data as input, i.e., before the array and its shadow switch places.

Our optimization procedure has five steps. First, we find the stencil loop in the source code and represent it as an intermediate object. Second, we extract the bursts from this object and generate polyhedral descriptions for them. Third, we check these access relations for overlaps and construct a graph that represents them. Fourth, we fuse the nodes in this overlap graph until there are no edges left. Fused nodes hold crucial information for the code generation. Fifth, we check if it is reasonable to apply the transformation and if so, we generate a transformed loop with added vendor tool pragmas from the intermediate object and the fused overlap graph. We only discuss read accesses below. Write accesses are similar.

Step 1 locates the stencil in the AST of the source code and skips non-perfect loop nests or stencils that do not match the criteria from above. We represent the stencil as an intermediate object that stores all the relevant information about the loop (loop counters, ranges, statements of the loop body). We later use this representation to transform the code and to pretty-print the result as C-code, as hardware synthesis tools only accept C-codes as their inputs.

Step 2 derives the polyhedral representation of the stencil, i.e., its domain and the access relations of its read accesses. While the domain information is explicit in the intermediate object, extracting the read access relations is harder. To do so, we visit each load operation to build the access relation from it. There are two cases. (a) The load reads from a static array, there is an index expression per dimension of the array, and each of them conforms to $i \pm c$. In this case the polyhedral access relation is straightforward. Figure 3 holds the resulting access relations for the code in Fig. 1. They are all bursts as they use the loop counter of the innermost loop in the index expression of their last dimensions. (b) In the harder to analyze case, the load reads from a pointer plus an expression. For the running example assume that in Fig. 1 there would be a pointer B &A[0][0]. Instead of the north read access A[i-1][j] the stencil code could have B[(i-1)*M + j], which addresses the same element, but in a linearized representation of the array data. Here we use a delinearization technique [9,16] to try to map the expression (back) to index expressions for each of the dimensions of the original array. If that succeeds, the result has the form of case (a) and we can turn it into the access relation.

```
proc overlapGraph(D, BAR, SZ)
do
   G := (V = BAR, E = ∅);
   C := combinations(BAR);
   D_span :=
      [K] → {S[i_0, i_1, ..., i_inner] :
         i_0 = lb_0 ∧ i_1 = lb_1...∧
         K ≤ i_inner < K + SZ};
   D_extract := D ∩ D_span;
   foreach (x, y) in C do
      r_x := x(D_extract);
      r_y := y(D_extract);
      if r_x ∩ r_y ≠ ∅ do
         G.addEdge(x, y);
      end
   end
   return G;
end
```

Fig. 4. Overlap detection algorithm. D = loop domain, BAR = set of <u>b</u>urst <u>a</u>ccess relations, SZ = <u>s</u>pan <u>s</u>ize, G = overlap graph.

Step 3 starts with the loop Domain D and the set BAR of all the access relations that are flagged as bursts. For the running example it starts with D $= [N, M] \to \{S[i,j] : 1 \leq i < N \wedge 1 \leq j < M\}$ and BAR $= \{R_n, R_e, R_s, R_w\}$. Let us abbreviate the loop boundaries with *Bnds* below. The overlap detection algorithm in Fig. 4 constructs an undirected overlap graph G that has as its vertices one node per burst access relation. The algorithm adds an edge for any two nodes whose bursts overlap. For the running example, it constructs the graph G shown in the upper left corner of Fig. 5. To do so, the foreach considers all combinations of read access relations and checks whether they overlap, i.e., whether there are iterations in the iteration space that access the same

array element. Overlap detection has been studied in the polyhedral literature before. Some published techniques only detect re-reads in *adjacent* iterations [20], which is too restrictive as we can build an FPGA that accesses SZ elements concurrently. More general techniques can find re-reads *anywhere* in the iteration space [10]. These are too complex, as our cache-like structure on an FPGA can only help for re-reads that are at most SZ iterations away.

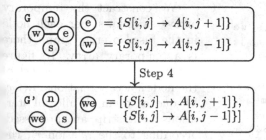

Fig. 5. Overlap graph G and fused overlap graph G'. Empty parameter lists and access relations R_n and R_s are omitted.

In our overlap detection, D_{span} are SZ consecutive iterations of the innermost loop. As the lb_i are the lower bounds of the outer loops, in the running example D_{span} only considers the single row with $i_0 = 1$. $D_{extract}$ removes from D_{span} all iterations that do not exist in the iteration space D of the loop. For the example and a span size SZ $= 4$ this gives $D_{span} = [K] \to$

$\{S[i_0, i_{inner}] : i_0 = 1 \wedge K \leq i_{inner} < K+4\}$ and $\text{D}_{extract} = [K, N, M] \rightarrow \{S[i,j] : i = 1 \wedge K \leq j < K + 4 \wedge Bnds\}$. When the $\texttt{foreach}$ considers a pair $(\texttt{x}, \texttt{y})$, we calculate $\texttt{r}_x = \texttt{x}(\text{D}_{extract})$ and $\texttt{r}_y = \texttt{y}(\text{D}_{extract})$, i.e., the sets of array elements that the stencil loop reads within a span. They overlap if $\texttt{r}_x \cap \texttt{r}_y$ is non-empty. In the running example, the $\texttt{foreach}$ at some point processes $\texttt{x} = R_e = \{S[i,j] \rightarrow A[i, j-1]\}$ and $\texttt{y} = R_w = \{S[i,j] \rightarrow A[i, j+1]\}$. The intersection of $\texttt{r}_x = \texttt{x}(\text{D}_{extract}) = [K, N, M] \rightarrow \{A[i,j] : i = 1 \wedge K - 1 \leq j < 4 + K - 1 \wedge Bnds\}$ and $\texttt{r}_y = \texttt{y}(\text{D}_{extract}) = [K, N, M] \rightarrow \{A[i,j] : i = 1 \wedge K + 1 \leq j < 4 + K + 1 \wedge Bnds\}$ contains $A[1, K+1]$ and $A[1, K+2]$, i.e., exactly the two elements of row $i = 1$ that the bottom of Fig. 1 shows in a darker gray.

Step 4 uses the overlap graph and iteratively fuses its connected nodes until no edges are left. Initially, each node in the graph represents one load operation. A node is attributed with a list that holds its access relation. If two nodes are fused, their lists are concatenated. For the running example, Fig. 5 shows the overlap graph after Step 3 (top) and after node fusion (bottom). The connected nodes w and e correspond to the stencil's west and east load operations. They are fused into the node we with the concatenated list of read access relations.

Step 5 outputs the original code if there is no data reuse (i.e., if there is no fused node) as the transformation would yield slowdowns (see Sect. 4, Table 1). Otherwise this step uses the fused overlap graph and the intermediate object that contains the stencil to generate an optimized loop with added pragmas to guide the hardware synthesis. We first strip-mine the original inner loop. For each strip, we add cache-like structures and burst operations to fill temporary arrays. In the *body* of the payload loop, we finally replace the original load operations with loads from the fast cache-like structures. Figure 6 shows the resulting template. It is straightforward to transform the loop into two nested loops (the inner of which processes a strip of size $\texttt{SZ}$) plus an extra loop that deals with the remaining iterations if the original loop count is not divisible by $\texttt{SZ}$. What needs to be discussed here are the sizes of the temporary arrays that work as cache-like structures, how to burst-load them, and how to redirect array accesses to use the temporary arrays instead of the original arrays.

```
for (j=...;...;j+=SZ) {
  #pragma USE_FLIPFLOPS (n,s,we)
  float n[as_n], s[as_s], we[as_we];
  BURST_CPY(n , A + off_n, as_n);
  BURST_CPY(s , A + off_s, as_s);
  BURST_CPY(we, A + off_we, as_we);
  for (...) {body} // SZ times
}
// remaining iterations (%SZ)
for (j=...;...;j++) { ... }
```

Fig. 6. Strip-mining the innermost loop of the stencil in Fig. 1. $as_i = $ <u>a</u>rray <u>s</u>ize, $off_i = $ fill <u>off</u>set. Tool pragmas are omitted.

We construct the temporary arrays as follows. For each node in the fused overlap graph there is a temporary array. To figure out its size we process the list of the node's access relations. Let r_i be one of them. While all iterations of a strip are processed according to the relation r_i, the set $s_i = r_i(\text{D}_{span})$ of data elements are accessed, and as the strip reads all the data element $s = \bigcup_i s_i$, the size of the temporar array needs to be $as = card(s)$. Since in the running example the node n holds only the read access relation R_n, the size of the temporary array n is $as_n = card(R_n(D_{span})) = 4.$[1] Similarly, each of the two read access relations of node we accesses 4 elements per strip. The union of these sets have the two darker gray elements in Fig. 1 in common. Hence, the resulting array size is $as_{we} = 6$.

```
proc lessOrEq(x, y) begin
  r_xmin  := lexmin(x(D_span));
  r_ymin  := lexmin(y(D_span));
  Q  := (r_xmin → {I_x[]})∪
        (r_ymin → {I_y[]});
  r_min  := lexmin(r_xmin ∪ r_ymin);
  R  := Q(r_min);
  return
      (R = {I_x[]} ∨ R = {I_x[]; I_y[]});
end
```

Fig. 7. Algorithm to compare two access relations. x, y = access relations, Q = comparison query, R = comparison result.

For each node of the fused overlap graph, we also insert a BURST_CPY operation to fill its temporary array. (For write accesses the BURST_CPY operations are at the end of the template. They copy values back into the original array.) The address offset *off* with respect to the base address of the original array is determined by the lexicographically smallest element accessed by the list of read access relations of a node in the fused overlap graph. If the list only has a single access relation r that element is $r_{rmin} = lexmin(r(D_{span}))$, which is simple to derive from the *range* of r.

(see Fig. 3). For longer lists we iteratively use the lessOrEq comparator shown in Fig. 7 to determine the smallest access relation.[2] Note that the comparator does not return the smallest array element that two access relations x and y read but instead returns the access relation that is responsible for accessing the smallest array element. To do so, it constructs a relation Q that maps the smallest array element r_{xmin} accessed by a relation x to an identifier I_x of that relation. Hence, R is the identifier of the access relation that is responsible for accessing the smallest array element. (R may hold both access relations if they both access the same smallest element.)

For the fused node we in Fig. 5, we need to compare $R_w = x = \{S[i,j] \to A[i, j - 1]\}$ and $R_e = y = \{S[i,j] \to A[i, j + 1]\}$. The smallest accessed array elements are $r_{xmin} = [K] \to \{A[1, K - 1]\}$, $r_{ymin} = [K] \to \{A[1, K + 1]\}$. The relation $Q = [K] \to \{A[1, K - 1] \to I_x[]; A[1, K + 1] \to I_y[]\}$ uses the tuples $I_i[]$ to store that r_{xmin} comes from x and r_{ymin} from y. Since the total minimum is $r_{min} = [K] \to \{A[1, K - 1]\}$, applying r_{min} to Q yields the id $\{I_x[]\}$ of x and thus $x = R_w \leq y = R_e$. Hence the range of R_w is used to extract off_{we}. We call the lexicographically smallest array element of the smallest read access relation *off*. In the running example $r_{off} = [K] \to \{A[1, K - 1]\}$.

For SZ $= 4$, the result of the set application $R_n(D_{span}) = \{S[i,j] \to A[i-1][j]\}([K] \to \{S[i_0, i_{inner}] : i_0 = 1 \wedge K \leq i_{inner} < K + SZ\}) = [K] \to \{A[i_0, i_{inner}] : i_0 = 1 \wedge K \leq i_{inner} < K + 4\} = \{A[1, K]; A[1, K + 1]; A[1, K + 2]; A[1, K + 3]\}$ has 4 elements.
Other works [10,20] do not define an order on access relations or they compare other polyhedral representations. The ISL only compares the elements of sets and relations.

Finally we construct the *body* of the payload loop by adjusting the stencil's original load operations to read from the cache-like structures instead. There are two load types: (a) non-burst loads do not have a node in the overlap graph as their read access relation has not been flagged as burst and (b) burst loads whose nodes in the fused overlap graph stand for one or more read access relations.

In case (a), we cannot read from a temporary array but instead access the original array. We copy index expressions like `A[0][0]` that do not use the loop counter j of the strip-mined loop verbatim into the new *body*. In other expressions in the strip loop, we reconstruct the original loop counter j as j+k.

Whenever a burst load in case (b) belongs to a node with a single read access relation, there is a BURST_CPY operation that fills into the temporary array all the data for all SZ iterations of the *body*. Hence, instead of accessing the original array the *body* can access the temporary array and any occurrence of the original loop counter j is replaced by the new loop counter k of the strip loop. Note, that the read access finds its elements in the temporary array from offset 0 onward. For the running example, instead of the north load `A[i-1][j]` there is `n[k]` in the *body*.

```
for (k = 0; k < SZ; k++)    {
  #pragma UNROLL
  ... = n[k]      //  A[i-1][j]
      + s[k]      //  A[i+1][j]
          ↓ o_w
      + we[k+0]   //w A[i][j-1]
      + we[k+2];  //e A[i][j+1]
}               ↑ o_e
```

Fig. 8. Payload loop with *body*.

Whenever a burst load in case (b) belongs to a node with more than one read access relation, the temporary array has more than SZ elements. Each of the fused read accesses r_i finds its SZ elements from an offset o_i onward. For the running example, Fig. 8 shows that the west read uses the offset $o_w = 0$ when reading from `we`, compared to the east read with offset $o_e = 2$. Algorithmically, we determine such an offset by calculating the distance between the read access relation that we are about to encode in *body* and the smallest read access relation r_{off} that we determined above when finding the offset needed for the BURST_CPY. We obtain the distance with the *deltas* operation (see Sect. 2) on the smallest array elements from both relations. In the running example R_w was used for the offset of the BURST_CPY that fills the `we` array. Since for the R_w access the distance between r_{off} and $r_{wmin} = lexmin(D_{span}(R_w)) = [K] \rightarrow \{A[1, K-1]\}$ is $deltas(r_{off} \rightarrow r_{wmin}) = \{A[0, \underline{0}]\}$, the *body* uses $o_w = 0$ in the west read. For the R_e access with $r_{emin} = [K] \rightarrow \{A[1, K+1]\}$ we get $deltas(r_{off} \rightarrow r_{emin}) = \{A[0, \underline{2}]\}$, i.e., the desired offset $o_e = 2$. As you can see, encoding read accesses for burst loads of both un-fused and fused nodes work the same way.

To conclude the transformation, we unroll the strip loop by adding the UNROLL tool pragma to it and specify that the temporary arrays can be accessed concurrently via the USE_FLIPFLOPS pragma. In the hardware synthesis, this yields a larger basic block for the strip loop. In general, larger basic blocks yield more parallelism in the resulting hardware blocks. Since there are no loop-carrie dependencies in the original stencil loop, parallel hardware can be synthesized for all the SZ iterations of the strip loop.

4   Evaluation

The evaluation considers 11 stencil codes from three different benchmark suites. We used all stencils from the Adept benchmark suite [11], 3 of 6 Polybench 4.2.1 stencils [21], and 4 stencils found in 3 of 7 benchmarks from the SPEC ACCEL OpenMP suite [24]. From the Polybench suite, we had to exclude both adi and fdtd-2d as they use imperfectly nested loops and seidel-2d because of its loop-carried dependencies (no shadow array toggling). We had to exclude 4 of the SPEC ACCEL codes because of varying reasons: polbm uses a pointer cast that the vendor tool does not support. Both pcsp and pbt use OpenMP syntax that we do not yet support and pep only has loops that are either pure data initializations without any calculations or are imperfectly nested. From pcg and pomriq we excluded the same types of loops, but we measured those that our technique is applicable to.

For each benchmark, our OpenMP-to-FPGA compiler ORKA-HPC [17] off-loaded the stencil to the FPGA by adding a single OpenMP target pragma. We measured the run times of the stencil hardware that resulted from applying the presented transformation on our test system running Ubuntu 20.04.4 LTS on a Intel Core i7-4770 CPU connected to a Xilinx VCU118 FPGA board via PCI express (width x4, 5GT/s). We used float arrays for the stencil data across all benchmarks and synthesized the hardware with Xilinx Vitis 2021.2 for each of them with span sizes SZ of 2^2 to 2^6. The FPGA synthesis used 50 MHz as FPGA clock frequency since the hardware synthesis often fails for higher frequency settings [5].[3] For each synthesized FPGA and for each problem size, we measured 10 runs and used the averages of their runtimes (excluding data shipment times from the host to the FPGA board memory). Tables 1 and 2 show the speedup factors that the resulting FPGA achieves after applying our transformation over its corresponding base FPGA that the vendor tool produces from the original code (without our transformation being applied) using default synthesis settings. Most notably, this included a default implicit PIPELINE pragma for all loops. As our transformation adds an UNROLL pragma that overrides the implicit one, there is the threat that the measured effects are mainly caused by this pragma change instead of the cache-like structures and the burst accesses. We could have added an UNROLL to the plain stencil codes and use the resulting measurements as the baseline. But we sticked with the unmodified stencil codes, because when we synthesized the benchmarks with the added UNROLL pragma (with explicit unroll factors), they either had identical runtimes (differences of ±0.5%) or performed much worse (up to 8×) than the plain codes.

For Polybench 1D-Jacobi and 3D-Heat, Vitis could not build 50 MHz hardware for SZ 16. To get around this hurdle, we generated pairs of FPGAs (with 44 MHz and 56 MHz) for both benchmarks and interpolated the measured speedups. But as we

Table 1. As for bursts without reuse, our tool does *not* apply the transformation, as it would cause the slowdowns (speedup values < 1) shown here.

	SPEC 1D-Pomriq					SPEC 1D-Pcg (Region 1)					SPEC 1D-Pcg (Region 2)				
size SZ	4	8	16	32	64	4	8	16	32	64	4	8	16	32	64
10 000	0.38	0.38	0.54	0.70	0.83	0.24	0.26	0.42	0.47	0.66	0.26	0.48	0.83	1.16	1.42
20 000	0.37	0.37	0.51	0.66	0.82	0.22	0.24	0.39	0.45	0.64	0.26	0.47	0.82	1.18	1.47
90 000	0.37	0.37	0.52	0.68	0.81	0.22	0.24	0.39	0.45	0.64	0.25	0.47	0.82	1.19	1.47
160 000	0.37	0.36	0.52	0.68	0.81	0.22	0.24	0.39	0.45	0.64	0.25	0.46	0.82	1.19	1.47
250 000	0.37	0.37	0.52	0.68	0.81	0.22	0.24	0.39	0.44	0.64	0.25	0.47	0.82	1.19	1.47
262 143+2	0.37	0.37	0.52	0.68	0.81	0.22	0.24	0.39	0.44	0.64	0.25	0.47	0.82	1.19	1.47
262 144+2	0.36	0.36	0.52	0.68	0.81	0.22	0.24	0.39	0.44	0.64	0.25	0.47	0.82	1.19	1.47

Let us first demonstrate why in Step 5 the optimization does not apply the code transformations if a stencil's overlap graph does not have a fused node, i.e., if there is no reuse. The resulting code would only fill the cache-like structures by means of bursts. The bursts alone without any data element reuse would mostly slow down the runtimes, see Table 1 for the three stencils without reuse, for various problem sizes and span sizes SZ. (The exceptions are SZ = 32 and SZ = 64 for 1D-Pcg (Region 2), probably because the burst accesses that we insert (accidentally) hide the bus latencies somewhat better than the bursts created by the vendor tool.) Overall, it is a strength of our approach that we can algorithmically decide when *not* to apply the transformation. This leaves us with 8 benchmark codes for which we discuss the quantitative effects of our optimizations below.

A per-benchmark comparison of the *rows* in Table 2 reveals that for a fixed span size SZ the speedup often increases with a growing problem size, but the gains diminish quickly. The reason is that strip-mining comes with an extra sequential loop that handles the remaining iterations for problem sizes that are not divisible by SZ. The larger the problem size is with respect to SZ, the easier the fixed cost of the extra loop can be amortized. We show this effect quantitatively, with the problem sizes that cause the maximal and minimal iterations of the extra loop. While 512 or 512^2 (for the 1D benchmark) are divisible by SZ, 511 or $512^2 - 1$ cause the maximal number of remaining iterations. As on the edges of the iteration space, a stencil usually reads from halo elements and as all the benchmarks in our set use 2 halo elements (one on each side) we added 2 to get to the problem sizes in the last two rows of each benchmark in Tables 1 and 2. The rows show that the speedup gains going from the size with the maximal remainder loop to the size that does not need a remainder loop is quite strong for a problem size increment of 1. Only for the 1D benchmarks the measurements are the same in the two rows. Whereas in all other benchmarks both the iteration of the strip-loop and the SZ − 1 iterations of the remainder loop are executed

---

cannot guarantee that the speedups scale exactly linearly w.r.t. the clock frequency. Table 2 shows these interpolated numbers in gray.

511 times ($\frac{511 \cdot (SZ-1)}{511^2}$), in the 1D codes both run only once ($\frac{SZ-1}{512^2-1}$). Therefore, each 1D strip loop better hides the cost of the remainder loop.

A per-benchmark comparison of the *columns* in Table 2 shows that up to a span size of 32 larger span sizes lead to better speedups. Between the smallest span size 2^2 and the span size 2^5 we see an increase by more than 2×. Let us postpone the discussion why the speedups often plunge for span size 64, and first discuss two reasons why the speedups grow with SZ up to span size 32. First, a larger span size fills its larger cache-like structures with longer bursts that better amortize the memory latency. This holds for the BURST_CPY operations inserted for both the unfused and the fused nodes of the overlap graph. Second, fused nodes of two or more array accesses use the same temporary array, i.e., they share the cost of their burst operation. Table 3 characterizes the stencils of the benchmarks and quantifies how much reuse potential our optimization harvests.[4] The difference between the number of nodes in the initial overlap graph before Step 3 (G) and after node fusion (G') indicates how many (burst) loads our technique saves compared to what the hardware synthesis needs under the hood for a plain stencil. We show the percentage of saved bursts in a separate column. The next column describes the types of the nodes in the fused overlap graph, i.e., it shows the number of unfused nodes U and fused nodes F_i that represent overlapping array accesses of i normal nodes. The last column details the exact number of saved read accesses w.r.t. SZ. To calculate this term, we first determine for the unfused graph G how many elements all bursts access. From this number we then subtract the number of elements that the fused graph G' accesses. We count a node F_i i times. For example, without node fusion, the running example in Fig. 1 has 4 burst reads of size SZ, one for each of the 4 nodes in G. After node fusion there are 2 unfused U nodes (n and s) with burst reads of size SZ plus one burst of size SZ + 2 for the fused F_1 node we. Hence, fusion saves $4 \cdot SZ - (2 \cdot SZ + SZ + 2) = SZ - 2$. For SZ = 4 this gives savings of 2, i.e., the two dark gray elements in Fig. 1. Note, that since all benchmarks in our set also have a halo size of 2, all their F nodes also represent SZ + 2 element accesses.

In general, the more overlapping bursts our overlap detection finds and fuses, and the more read accesses this saves, the better are the speedups in Table 2. This holds for all benchmarks. Only when comparing the speedups of 3D-Heat to the other benchmarks, its speedup is a little lower than the percentage of saved bursts and the number of saved read accesses would suggest. Since the synthesized FPGA utilized the same number of DSP blocks (ASIC hardware for floating point operations) across each value of SZ, we assume the reason is that the vendor synthesis tool cannot efficiently pipe the data to the DSP blocks and uses a slower fallback instead, even though (or because?) the fused temporary array is reused six times, which is more reuse than in all other benchmarks.

We only discuss read accesses below as the benchmarks in our set all have one single unfused write burst without any overlapping. So there are no differences or effects to be discussed.

Table 2. Benchmark results. 1D, 2D, and 3D indicate dimensionality of the stencil. Cells give speedups over the unmodified code. Interpolated values in light gray.[3]

size SZ	Adept 2D-5P					Adept 2D-9P				
	4	8	16	32	64	4	8	16	32	64
100^2	1.30	1.34	1.85	2.43	1.63	2.00	2.24	3.15	3.92	1.96
200^2	1.37	1.41	1.92	2.56	2.43	2.20	2.42	3.50	4.46	3.89
300^2	1.39	1.45	1.94	2.63	2.10	2.27	2.59	3.62	4.64	2.98
400^2	1.40	1.46	1.95	2.64	2.45	2.31	2.60	3.70	4.77	3.97
500^2	1.41	1.46	2.02	2.63	2.24	2.33	2.67	4.09	4.78	3.30
$(511+2)^2$	1.41	1.47	1.97	2.56	2.18	2.34	2.64	3.84	4.43	3.14
$(512+2)^2$	1.43	1.49	2.07	2.92	2.68	2.39	2.75	4.28	5.79	4.60

size SZ	Adept 3D-19P					Adept 3D-27P				
	4	8	16	32	64	4	8	16	32	64
100^3	1.83	1.94	2.87	4.15	1.95	2.32	2.57	3.62	4.70	2.09
200^3	1.94	2.00	3.00	4.25	3.83	2.50	2.64	3.85	4.78	4.82
300^3	1.96	2.07	3.03	4.24	2.90	2.57	2.88	3.91	4.80	3.38
400^3	1.99	2.08	3.05	4.28	3.85	2.60	2.81	3.98	4.84	4.88
500^3	2.01	2.13	3.37	4.29	3.23	2.62	2.95	4.44	4.83	3.86
$(511+2)^3$	2.00	2.10	3.16	3.95	3.06	2.60	2.89	4.07	4.39	3.59
$(512+2)^3$	2.04	2.15	3.42	5.03	4.44	2.67	3.02	4.58	5.82	5.89

size SZ	Polybench 1D-Jacobi					Polybench 2D-Jacobi					size
	4	8	16	32	64	4	8	16	32	64	
10 000	1.85	2.62	4.22	4.60	3.01	1.54	1.65	2.43	3.12	1.78	100^2
20 000	1.87	2.65	4.06	4.70	2.98	1.69	1.74	2.64	3.33	3.00	200^2
90 000	1.87	2.64	4.31	4.73	3.03	1.75	1.81	2.72	3.46	2.48	300^2
160 000	1.87	2.63	4.32	4.73	2.99	1.76	1.82	2.76	3.49	3.04	400^2
250 000	1.87	2.64	4.32	4.74	3.03	1.82	1.86	2.98	3.55	2.70	500^2
262 143+2	1.87	2.64	4.33	4.74	3.03	1.81	1.85	2.83	3.33	2.58	$(511+2)^2$
262 144+2	1.87	2.64	4.35	4.74	3.03	1.85	1.90	3.08	4.08	3.41	$(512+2)^2$

size SZ	Polybench 3D-Heat					SPEC 3D-Postencil				
	4	8	16	32	64	4	8	16	32	64
100^3	1.35	1.46	2.17	2.79	1.46	1.35	1.45	2.08	2.91	1.77
200^3	1.41	1.51	2.29	2.99	2.39	1.41	1.50	2.18	3.14	2.96
300^3	1.43	1.56	2.32	3.05	1.99	1.43	1.56	2.19	3.23	2.43
400^3	1.45	1.55	2.36	3.13	2.43	1.44	1.55	2.22	3.28	3.00
500^3	1.45	1.58	2.50	3.15	2.16	1.46	1.58	2.34	3.34	2.65
$(511+2)^3$	1.46	1.57	2.41	3.00	2.09	1.46	1.56	2.26	3.16	2.55
$(512+2)^3$	1.48	1.60	2.55	3.53	2.70	1.48	1.59	2.37	3.79	3.34

Table 3. Stencil characteristics, read accesses only. Overlap graph G before Step 3; G' after node fusion. U = Unfused node. F_i = Fused node for i overlapping array accesses.

	#nodes		percentage of saved bursts	type of nodes in G'	saved read accesses
	G	G'			
Figure 1	4	3	25%	$2U + 1F_2$	$SZ - 2$
2D-5P	4	3	25%	$2U + 1F_2$	$SZ - 2$
2D-9P	8	3	62%	$1F_2 + 2F_3$	$5 \cdot SZ - 6$
3D-19P	18	9	50%	$4U + 1F_2 + 4F_3$	$9 \cdot SZ - 10$
3D-27P	26	9	65%	$1F_2 + 8F_3$	$17 \cdot SZ - 18$
1D-Jacobi	3	1	66%	$1F_3$	$2 \cdot SZ - 2$
2D-Jacobi	5	3	40%	$2U + 1F_3$	$2 \cdot SZ - 2$
3D-Heat	10	5	50%	$4U + 1F_6$	$5 \cdot SZ - 2$
3D-Postencil	7	5	28%	$4U + 1F_3$	$2 \cdot SZ - 2$

For span size 64, the measured speedups of the benchmarks plunge. The reason is that the basic blocks of the unrolled strip-loops become too large for the hardware synthesis tool to generate efficient circuits from. In the HLS tool reports, we see an excessive increase (on average 24×) in the number of DSP blocks compared to a span size of 32 with a basic block of half the size. Since there are performance issues for a large number of DSP blocks [14], and since loop splitting has been suggested as an mitigation strategy [15], this is a well-known effect that is in line with the literature.

In total, for stencil loops with data element reuse, even with small span sizes and with benchmarks where we cannot harvest much data reuse (e.g., 2D-5P, $SZ = 4$) we noticed speedups of around 1.3×. For larger span sizes and for stencils with a high proportion of saved bursts and a lot of reuse, our optimization achieves speedups of up to 5.8× (e.g., 3D-27P, $SZ = 32$).

5 Related Work

While our approach is unique in the way it utilizes polyhedral methods to generate burst array accesses to increase data reuse on FPGA platforms, let us discuss some related publications.

Pouchet et al. [20] propose an extensive hardware generation framework capable of optimizing stencil codes. One of its features is a polyhedral-based data reuse optimization. While this work is conceptually similar to ours in that it also uses strip-mining, it only detects and optimizes reuse between two directly consecutive iterations of the stencil.

There is a fundamentally different approach to construct FPGAs that optimize data reuse for stencil codes. Instead of strip-mining the loop and using a cache-like data structure for the accessed array elements, some works [4,18,19] use FIFO memory to store reusable data between stencil iterations exactly as long as it is needed. They use the polyhedral model to identify where and when to use said FIFOs. While designs that rely on FIFOs tend to require less hardware, our method can be fully and elegantly implemented on source level, granting us the full benefits of the state-of-the-art HLS tools. A comparative performance evaluation is future work.

Wang et al. [27] introduce a more generic polyhedral-based compiler AutoSA that can transform stencil codes to systolic arrays for FPGAs that also employ FIFOs. While our approach constructs one processing element (PE) per SCoP and uses overlap detection to reduce data shipment, AutoSA creates a grid of independent PEs connected by FIFO channels that it optimizes for latency, but does not detect data reuse in them.

In the domain of code optimization for ASIC, Issenin et al. [10] use a polyhedral method to improve data reuse with a scratch-pad RAM. Their method DRDU is not specifically aimed towards stencil codes and relies on significantly more complex formula representations. They lead to extensive runtimes that are infeasible for large codes, unless users constrain the runtime of the algorithm and are willing to accept sub-optimal results.

The PPCG source-to-source compiler [26] generates CUDA code from programmer-annotated SCoPs. It mainly focusses on restructuring the input code to SIMT parallelism which also requires to exploit data reuse between PEs of the GPU. Similarly to DRDU, PPCG's reuse method seems to be a lot more computationally expensive than our approach. We have in common with PPCG that we also use temporary arrays as cache-like structures. But to work with these arrays PPCG generates code that is optimized for GPU architectures while we generate HLS primitives that turn into FPGA circuits. Another difference is that PPCG ships all the data to/from the GPU that potentially may be needed for the computation while our support for OpenMP `target`/`target data` allows a manual and more fine-grained control that can reduce data shipment. It may be a fruitful endeavour to port PPCG's reuse detection to our compiler (or the other way around) for quantitative comparisons of both runtimes and efficiencies.

An other reuse detection by Shin et al. [23] achieves speedups by exploiting data reuse in codes that use SIMD parallelism. While our approach harvests data reuse on codes without loop carried dependencies, their algorithm inspects loop carried dependencies in the kernel to find overlaps. It also focusses on the innermost loop nest, but exploits the data reuse with unroll-and-jam transformations instead of strip-mining.

There are some works [2,13,28] that use polyhedral techniques to optimize code for execution on CPUs. These methods can only be transferred to FPGAs to a limited extend, as their main goal is to improve the temporal locality of data accesses. FPGAs lack multi-layered general purpose caches and thus cannot benefit from this kind of optimization. Instead, our work focusses on exploiting the spacial locality with problem-specific cache-like structures that are filled and flushed in bursts.

6   Conclusion and Future Work

We presented an automatic source-to-source transformation for stencil codes that results in more efficient FPGA hardware for them. We showed how to employ polyhedral methods to find overlapping contiguous array accesses in the stencil and how to analyze them to generate fast, stencil-specific cache-like structures to exploit spatial locality. Our transformation also employs strip-mining and inserts the necessary FPGA-vendor specific annotations to let the hardware synthesis generate efficient FPGA accelerators for the stencils. On benchmarks the presented data movement optimization achieves speedups of up to 5.8 compared to hardware synthesized from the plain un-transformed source code of the stencils.

There are three directions of future work. First, it would be interesting to find the ideal span sizes that result in the best speedups. Second, instead of using the default bus width of 32 bit for the channels to the FPGA board memory, it is tempting to increase the width for a higher memory bandwidth. But this needs research to reduce the cost of the necessary alignments of each burst access. And finally, instead of using the default parameters for the vendor tool pragmas a Design Space Exploration (DSE) may lead to better results [7,22,29].

References

1. Benabderrahmane, M.-W., Pouchet, L.-N., Cohen, A., Bastoul, C.: The polyhedral model is more widely applicable than you think. In: Gupta, R. (ed.) CC 2010. LNCS, vol. 6011, pp. 283–303. Springer, Heidelberg (2010). https://doi.org/10.1007/978-3-642-11970-5_16
2. Bondhugula, U., Hartono, A., Ramanujam, J., Sadayappan, P.: A practical automatic polyhedral parallelizer and locality optimizer. In: Proceedings of the International Conference on Programming Language Design and Implementation (PLDI 2008), Tucson, AZ, pp. 101–113, June 2008
3. Boulet, P., Darte, A., Silber, G.A., Vivien, F.: Loop parallelization algorithms: from parallelism extraction to code generation. Parallel Comput. **24**(3–4), 421–444 (1998)
4. Cong, J., Huang, M., Pan, P., Wang, Y., Zhang, P.: Source-to-Source Optimization for HLS. In: Koch, D., Hannig, F., Ziener, D. (eds.) FPGAs for Software Programmers, pp. 137–163. Springer, Cham (2016). https://doi.org/10.1007/978-3-319-26408-0_8
5. Farahmand, F., Ferozpuri, A., Diehl, W., Gaj, K.: Minerva: automated hardware optimization tool. In: Proceedings of the International Conference on ReConFigurable Computing and FPGAs (ReConFig 2017), Cancun, Mexico, pp. 1–8, December 2017
6. Feautrier, P.: Some efficient solutions to the affine scheduling problem. I. One-dimensional time. Int. J. Parallel Program. **21**(5), 313–347 (1992)
7. Ferretti, L., Ansaloni, G., Pozzi, L.: Lattice-traversing design space exploration for high level synthesis. In: Proceedings of the International Conference on Computer Design (ICCD 2018), Orlando, FL, pp. 210–217, October 2018
8. Franke, B., O'Boyle, M.: Array recovery and high-level transformations for DSP applications. ACM Trans. Embedded Comput. Syst. **2**(2), 132–162 (2003)

9. Grosser, T., Ramanujam, J., Pouchet, L.N., Sadayappan, P., Pop, S.: Optimistic delinearization of parametrically sized arrays. In: Proceedings of the International Conference on Supercomputing (ICS 2015), Newport Beach, CA, pp. 351–360, June 2015
10. Issenin, I., Brockmeyer, E., Miranda, M., Dutt, N.: DRDU: a data reuse analysis technique for efficient scratch-pad memory management. ACM Trans. Design Automation of Electronic Syst. 12(2), Article 15, 1–28 (2007)
11. Johnson, N.: The Adept Benchmark Suite (2015). https://github.com/EPCCed/adept-kernel-openmp. Accessed 2 Sept 2022
12. Karp, R.M., Miller, R.E., Winograd, S.: The organization of computations for uniform recurrence equations. J. ACM 14(3), 563–590 (1967)
13. Kodukula, I., Ahmed, N., Pingali, K.: Data-centric multi-level blocking. In: Proceedings International Conference on Programming Language Design and Implementation (PLDI 1997), Las Vegas, NV, pp. 346–357, June 1997
14. Langhammer, M., Pasca, B.: Design and implementation of an embedded FPGA floating point DSP block. In: Proceedings of the International Symposium on Computer Arithmetic, Lyon, France, pp. 26–33, June 2015
15. Liu, J., Wickerson, J., Constantinides, G.A.: Loop splitting for efficient pipelining in high-level synthesis. In: Proceedings of the International of the Symposium on Field-Programmable Custom Computing Machines (FCCM 2016), Washington, DC, pp. 72–79, May 2016
16. Maslov, V.: Delinearization: an efficient way to break multiloop dependence equations. In: Proceedings International Conference on Programming Language Design and Implementation (PLDI 1992), San Francisco, CA, pp. 152–161, June 1992
17. Mayer, F., Brandner, J., Hellmann, M., Schwarzer, J., Philippsen, M.: The ORKA-HPC compiler–practical OpenMP for FPGAs. In: Proceedings of the International Workshop on Languages and Compilers for Parallel Computing (LCPC 2021), Newark, DE, pp. 83–97, October 2021
18. Meeus, W., Stroobandt, D.: Data reuse buffer synthesis using the polyhedral model. IEEE Trans. Very Large Scale Integr. (VLSI) Syst. 26(7), 1340–1353 (2018)
19. Natale, G., Stramondo, G., Bressana, P., Cattaneo, R., Sciuto, D., Santambrogio, M.D.: A polyhedral model-based framework for dataflow implementation on FPGA devices of Iterative Stencil Loops. In: Proceedings of the International Conference on Computer-Aided Design (ICCAD 2016), Austin, TX, pp. 1–8, November 2016
20. Pouchet, L.N., Zhang, P., Sadayappan, P., Cong, J.: Polyhedral-based data reuse optimization for configurable computing. In: Proceedings of the International Symposium on Field Programmable Gate Arrays (FPGA 2013), Montery, CA, pp. 29–38, February 2013
21. Pouchet, L.N.: PolyBench/C - The Polyhedral Benchmark Suite. http://web.cse.ohio-state.edu/~pouchet.2/software/polybench/. Accessed 2 Sept 2022
22. Schafer, B.C., Wakabayashi, K.: Divide and conquer high-level synthesis design space exploration. ACM Trans. Des. Autom. Electron. Syst. 17(3) (2012)
23. Shin, J., Chame, J., Hall, M.: Compiler-controlled caching in superword register files for multimedia extension architectures. In: Proceedings of the International Conference on Parallel Architectures and Compilation Techniques (PACT 2002) Chicago, IL, pp. 45–55, September 2002
24. SPEC: SPEC ACCEL. https://www.spec.org/accel/. Accessed 2 Sept 2022
25. Verdoolaege, S.: ISL: an integer set library for the polyhedral model. In: Fukuda K., Hoeven, J., Joswig, M., Takayama, N. (eds.) ICMS 2010. LNCS, vol. 6327, pp 299–302. Springer, Heidelberg (2010). https://doi.org/10.1007/978-3-642-15582-6_49

26. Verdoolaege, S., Carlos Juega, J., Cohen, A., Ignacio Gómez, J., Tenllado, C., Catthoor, F.: Polyhedral Parallel Code Generation for CUDA. ACM Trans. Archit. Code Optimiz. **9**(4), Article 54, pp. 1–23 (2013)
27. Wang, J., Guo, L., Cong, J.: AutoSA: a polyhedral compiler for high-performance systolic arrays on FPGA. In: Proceedings of the International Symposium on Field-Programmable Gate Arrays (FPGA 2021), pp. 93–104. Virtual Event, USA, February 2021
28. Wolf, M.E., Lam, M.S.: A data locality optimizing algorithm. In: Proceedings of the International Conference on Programming Language Design and Implementation (PLDI 1991), Toronto, Canada, pp. 30–44, June 1991
29. Zhong, G., Venkataramani, V., Liang, Y., Mitra, T., Niar, S.: Design space exploration of multiple loops on FPGAs using high level synthesis. In: Proceedings of the International Conference on Computer Design (ICCD 2014), Seoul, South Korea, pp. 456–463, October 2014

An HPC Practitioner's Workbench for Formal Refinement Checking

Juan Benavides[1], John Baugh[1]([✉])(iD), and Ganesh Gopalakrishnan[2](iD)

[1] North Carolina State University, Raleigh, NC 27695, USA
{jdbenavi,jwb}@ncsu.edu
[2] University of Utah, Salt Lake City, UT 84112, USA
ganesh@cs.utah.edu

Abstract. HPC practitioners make use of techniques, such as parallelism and sparse data structures, that are difficult to reason about and debug. Here we explore the role of data refinement, a correct-by-construction approach, in verifying HPC applications via bounded model checking. We show how single program, multiple data (SPMD) parallelism can be modeled in Alloy, a declarative specification language, and describe common issues that arise when performing scope-complete refinement checks in this context.

Keywords: Formal methods · scientific computing · parallelism · Alloy

1 Introduction

To explain the points of view expressed in this paper, it helps to take the example of how an HPC expert practices their programming craft. The expert has the intended math in their head but then uses the medium of code not just to express intent but also to get the code running efficiently on the chosen computational medium, be it a CPU or a GPU accelerator. Such details end up being baked into the code, including sparse data structure designs and thread-to-array-slice mappings. Even though the final product is arrived at through a succession of *refinements*, it is seldom that these intermediate forms play a continued role in explaining the elaboration of the design. Doing so may in fact be considered counterproductive, since one would be forced to maintain even more code.

While this practice is standard and seemingly successful in some ways, one has to question whether the required apprenticeship is keeping a generation of (otherwise programming-language-aware) students from entering the area. Even absent this, the real price seems to be already getting paid by the expert when they suddenly realize that porting the code to a new platform requires hard-to-hire talent, with bugs crippling productivity [7]. Performance-portability mechanisms such as Kokkos [4] and RAJA [3] seem like a possible answer, but they are not widespread, and are too much to teach at an introductory level.

© The Author(s), under exclusive license to Springer Nature Switzerland AG 2023
C. Mendis and L. Rauchwerger (Eds.): LCPC 2022, LNCS 13829, pp. 64–72, 2023.
https://doi.org/10.1007/978-3-031-31445-2_5

Harking back to the vision of early computer science pioneers, and taking inspiration from the creators of lightweight model-finding "thought calculators" such as Alloy [9], we present our experience-to-date using Alloy as the medium in which to capture refinements. We argue that doing so might encourage the practice of stating refinements in the tangible (and analyzable) medium of formal logic. The benefits of Alloy-style specifications are already evident in their ability to generate test cases—even for GPU memory models [10]—and perhaps they may one day help formally examine code ports at the design level.[1]

Scope and Organization. In what follows, we describe a lightweight modeling approach for reasoning about the structure and behavior of scientific software. We propose abstraction and refinement principles to manage sources of complexity, such as those introduced to meet performance goals, including sparse structure and parallelization. Elements of the approach include declarative models that are automatically checked with (Boolean satisfiability) SAT solvers, akin to the analysis approaches used in traditional engineering domains, so no theorem proving is required. The approach is bounded and therefore incomplete, but we appeal to the *small scope hypothesis*, which suggests that most real bugs have small counterexamples. For data refinement, we adopt a state-based style, which extends well to concurrency and parallelism—typically better than, say, an algebraic one.

We begin with related work, then introduce our refinement-checking approach and demonstrate it in the context of an HPC application, and follow up briefly with conclusions and future directions.

2   Previous Work

Formal methods is an extensive field that we do not intend to survey. Instead, we present a few examples of related work that are most relevant to the HPC community. These studies set a precedent for the framework we present, highlighting refinement, lightweight model-finding, and rich state in scientific computing.

Dyer et al. [5] explore the use of Alloy to model and reason about the structure and behavior of sparse matrices, which are central to scientific computing. Examples of sparse matrix-vector multiplication, transpose, and translation between ELLPACK and compressed sparse row (CSR) formats illustrate the approach. To model matrix computations in a declarative language like Alloy, a new idiom is presented for bounded iteration with incremental updates. The study considers the subset of refinement proof obligations that can be formalized as safety properties—and are thus easier to check—in Alloy.

Baugh and Altuntas [2] describe a large-scale hurricane storm surge model used in production and verification of an extension using Alloy. To explore implementation choices, abstractions are presented for relevant parts of the model, including the physical representation of land and seafloor surfaces as a finite element mesh, and an algorithm that allows for the propagation of overland flows. Useful conclusions are drawn about implementation choices and guarantees about the extension, in particular that it is equivalence preserving.

---

[1] It is well known that running unit tests is a poor way of unearthing conceptual flaws.

Martin [11] shows how a data refinement approach can be used to formally specify parallel programs using a Coarray Fortran (CAF) implementation of an iterative Jacobi routine. At an abstract level, a mathematical description of a step in the iteration is given, and at the concrete level, the corresponding operation is defined for parallel coarray images; an abstraction function relates the two levels. Since it focuses on specification, the roles of state-space invariants and other refinement proof obligations needed for verification are not addressed.

3   Approach

Data refinement is a correct-by-construction approach for the stepwise development of programs and models from a higher-level abstract specification to lower-level concrete ones [13]. The HPC field lends itself well to a data refinement approach as most programs begin with a mathematical specification—often as a theory report—that serves as a guide, to one extent or another, in the implementation of high performance code.

To ensure that a refinement step preserves correctness in a formal, machine-checkable manner, proof obligations must be met and discharged; their articulation and promotion begins with the work of Hoare [8] and thereafter proceeds along both relational and predicate transformer lines; de Roever [13] summarizes and contrasts a variety of modern approaches. While many of these offer some degree of tool support, Alloy's model-finding strengths for expressing rich state, combined with its push-button automation, make it an attractive alternative to those requiring theorem proving, especially for HPC practitioners.

Below we introduce refinement checking and some of the practical details of formalizing the checks in Alloy. Our goal beyond this short paper is to develop a general framework for carrying out data refinement checks in Alloy that will make the approach clear and appealing to practitioners. That includes characterizing a sufficient set of proof obligations for data refinement, showing how to encode them in Alloy, and demonstrating the approach on practical HPC problems.

4   Refinement Checking

The notion of refinement is relative. It makes use of an upper abstract level and a lower level concrete one:

> *Definition: Semantic Implementation Correctness* [13]. Given two programs, one called concrete and the other called abstract, the concrete program *implements* (or *refines*) the abstract program correctly whenever the use of the concrete program does not lead to an observation which is not also an observation of the abstract program.

Refinement as inclusion, above, is a global criterion. To be made practical, local criterion with a finite number of verification conditions can be obtaine by defining a *simulation* in terms of abstraction relations and commutativit diagrams.

In Fig. 1, the commutativity diagram shows the concrete (C) and abstract (A) states related by an abstraction relation α, together with concrete and abstract operations, op_c and op_a, respectively, that define transitions from the non-primed to primed states.

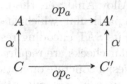

Fig. 1. Data Refinement

There are four different technical notions of simulation that correspond to ways in which commutativity can be defined in terms of the diagram [13]. When α is both total and functional, the four types of simulation coincide and some of the proof obligations simplify, including the condition for *correctness* of the concrete operation op_c:

$$\forall a, a' : A, c, c' : C \mid \alpha(c, a) \wedge op_c(c, c') \wedge \alpha(c', a') \Rightarrow op_a(a, a') \qquad (1)$$

That is, starting from a concrete state in which the corresponding abstract precondition holds, the final concrete state must represent a possible abstract final state. Such a criterion implies inclusion, i.e., that programs using some concrete data type C have (only) observable behaviors of programs using a corresponding abstract data type A. Diagrams satisfying such properties are said to commute *weakly*, whereas strong commutativity would be expressed with material equivalence instead of implication in Eq. 1.

Summarizing the set of proof obligations for data refinement in a state-based formalism [13], we have the following conditions:

1. *Adequacy* – every abstract state must have a concrete counterpart.
2. *Correspondence of initial states* – every concrete initial state must represent an abstract initial state.
3. *Applicability of the concrete operation* – the precondition for the concrete operation should hold for any concrete state whose corresponding abstract state satisfies the abstract precondition.
4. *Correctness of the concrete operation* – as we describe above.

Not every condition applies in every situation, and in some cases a condition may require a special interpretation for the given context. For instance, an adequacy check for a refinement from abstract matrices to coarrays can be satisfied trivially in the one-processor case: a single coarray matrix, equivalent to the abstract one, "refines" it, but one might rather show adequacy for an n-processor case.

To draw sound conclusions from these, the structure of α is clearly important. If the correctness condition of Eq. 1 is to apply, for instance, it must be shown to be both functional (Eq. 2) and total (Eq. 3):

$$\forall a_1, a_2 : A, c : C \mid \alpha(c, a_1) \wedge \alpha(c, a_2) \Rightarrow equal(a_1, a_2) \qquad (2)$$

$$\forall c : C \mid \exists a : A \mid \alpha(c, a) \qquad (3)$$

What would it mean to check these in Alloy? The three equations above are expressions of first order logic, and yet they present different levels of difficulty to the Alloy Analyzer, the model-finding tool supporting the formalism. Equation 3 in particular, which checks whether or not a relation is total, is problematic because its SAT encoding results in an unbounded universal quantifier [9].

Similar checks are required if we have concerns, as we should, about *progress* properties: a concrete operation op_c can "do nothing" and satisfy the correctness check vacuously, e.g., when the term $op_c(c, c')$ is false in Eq. 1, as it might be due to an inadvertently buggy specification. So we add to the set of proof obligations a progress check:

5. *Progress of the concrete operation* – with respect to the operation, every initial state satisfying the concrete precondition must have a corresponding final state.

As with Eq. 3, which requires that α be total, this kind of check introduces an unbounded quantifier in its formulation, and is again problematic for Alloy.

All this points to a limitation of finite instance finding. Various approaches have been devised to try and circumvent it, including the definition of generator axioms [9], though they are sometimes difficult to come by or too computationally expensive to employ, as we later show. Below we describe a new, simpler approach for performing these and other checks in Alloy and do so in the context of HPC.

5   A Parallel HPC Application in Alloy

We illustrate our approach with Alloy models of a parallel program originally specified by Martin [11]. We extend his work by formalizing coarrays in Alloy, adding necessary and sufficient conditions for checking refinement, and defining the state-space invariants required to formally verify them. Our models are available online [1].

Iterative Jacobi Computation. Martin considers an example of the numerical solution to Laplace's equation over a rectangular domain, with fixed values on the boundary, using the technique of Jacobi iteration. The example is implemented in Coarray Fortran (CAF), a single program, multiple data (SPMD) extension to the language. In CAF, designated variables are extended with a parallel dimension, so that each is shared across copies of the same program (images) using the Partitioned Global Address Space (PGAS) model.

At each iteration, the algorithm averages the four-nearest neighbors of all interior elements of a matrix. Because it updates or "displaces" all of the elements at the same time, the Jacobi method is sometimes called the *method of simultaneous displacements,* which contrasts with the Gauss-Seidel method whose elements are successively "updated in place." As a result, extra storage is needed in the Jacobi method to take a step, but, afterward, the previous step' storage can be reused if we swap matrix storage locations at each iteration.

To specify the parallel program, Martin takes a refinement perspective, defining a step in a sequential Jacobi iteration as the abstract level, and a step i a parallel CAF implementation as the concrete level. The abstraction relation maps coarrays at the concrete level (a sequence of image matrices) to a single abstract matrix. Duplicating columns at the image interfaces allows computation and then communication to proceed in separate "stages" in the CAF program.

Figure 2 shows the column mapping between coarray images and the abstract matrix (left) and the role of invariants (right) which we use to tighten the abstraction relation α so that it is total. In the concrete space, the invariant enforces interface conditions between neighboring coarrays, i.e., the duplication of columns necessary for halo or border exchanges, and it ensures that the matrices corresponding to a given coarray variable all have the same dimensions in each image, as dictated by CAF semantics. In the abstract space, another invariant enforces basic matrix index and bounds checking.

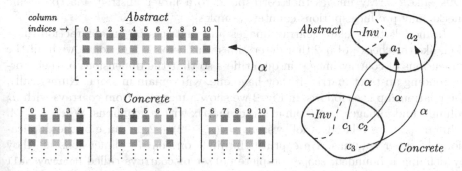

Fig. 2. Mapping coarray images to a matrix (left) and enforcing invariants (right)

Alloy Models and Extensions. We formalize the problem in Alloy using the same matrix structure as Dyer et al. [5], along with new machinery to capture the relevant aspects of Coarray Fortran.

```
sig Matrix {                          sig Value {}
    rows, cols: Int,                  sig Coarray {
    vals: Int → Int → lone Value          mseq: seq Matrix
}                                     }
```

A signature in Alloy introduces both a type and a set of uninterpreted atoms, and may introduce fields that define relations over them. A summary of the language is available online (see alloytools.org/download/alloy-language-reference.pdf).

Here, intuitively, matrices are defined with two-dimensional indexing, and coarrays are defined as a sequence of matrices. Since Alloy provides no means of representing reals or floating point values, matrix elements are modeled as a number of distinct values, depending on scope size. This simple approach suffices for representing the structural properties of matrices, and where more is needed, arithmetic expressions can be built up and checked symbolically [5].

After adding abstract and concrete Jacobi operations, refinement checks can be performed. Below we describe some of the issues that arise when attempting to verify such obligations, along with their resolution, including a new idiom for checking whether or not a relation is total. Further details and other refinement checks appear in models that are available online [1].

Relative Scope Sizes. Alloy has a rich notion of scope that allows users to bound each signature separately. This accommodates, within a model and across the model's signatures, individual scope sizes that are problem dependent and tailored to the domain. With matrices, however, their sizes are naturally determined by row and column dimensions, a numerical quantity that is bound by a single bitwidth specification in Alloy, which sets the scope of all integers [12]. While otherwise not a concern, when a model calls for matrices of relatively different sizes—like coarray images that correspond to a larger abstract matrix—some checks may produce spurious counterexamples.

In models that relate coarray images and matrices by an abstraction function, like the check in Eq. 2 that determines whether α is functional, we limit the dimensions of coarray images in quantifiers so that the dimensions of their corresponding abstract matrix, if they have one, will remain in scope. Numerically, the relationship is as follows: in Fig. 2 we show a mapping from coarrays with n_c columns and i images, say, to an abstract matrix with n_a columns. When $n_a \geq 4$, column sizes are related as follows: $n_a = i(n_c - 2) + 2$, because of the duplication of border columns. We capture the limit on coarray dimensions in Alloy by defining a bounded, scope-complete subset of coarrays called `CoarraySmall` that can be used as a drop-in replacement when expressions are quantified over coarrays and abstract matrices.

Total Relation Check. For checking whether or not α is total, we must contend with the unbounded universal quantifier problem [9]. To do so, we present a novel approach that avoids the need for generator axioms, which are in any case impractical in this context, because they produce a combinatorial number of instances, namely $\mathcal{O}(v^{n \times n})$ for $n \times n$ matrices whose elements each have v possible values. We do so by adding problem structure, i.e., by introducing an additional level of indirection and reformulating the check:

```
sig P {
  con: Coarray,
  abs: lone Matrix
}
check isTotal { all p: P | alpha[p.con, p.abs] ⇒ some p.abs }
```

Here, instances of `P` necessarily hold a single coarray in `con` and *may* hold a matrix in `abs` that is related to it by the abstraction function `alpha`; the `lone` keyword in Alloy (less than or equal to one) allows the `abs` field to be empty. Intuitively, Alloy searches within a given scope for a counterexample in which concrete object exists but there is no abstract counterpart, according to `alpha`. If no counterexample can be found, the check is valid within the specified scope

To show that the approach is equivalent to adding generator axioms, we reformulate the check above as a predicate $isTotal_p$, define another predicate $isTotalNaive_p$ that is equivalent to Eq. 3, and then compare them after including a predicate for the generator axiom:

```
check isTotalₚ ⇔ (isTotalNaiveₚ and generator)
```

The check passes, though with sizes limited to just 2×2 matrices and four values, since `generator` explodes the scope. In cases where generator axioms cannot be circumvented, as `isTotal` manages, parametric reasoning may be considered [6].

Interleaving Specifications. The communication step, as given in CAF by Martin, makes a subtle but important design choice. A coarray image shares the values it computes in interface columns before the next iteration begins, yet no synchronization barrier is needed. Instead of "pulling" values—which may or may not have been computed—from adjacent matrices, an image "pushes" its computed values by writing to its neighbors. Doing so guarantees the absence of race conditions, and eliminates the need for interleaving-style specifications.

Although we can and have used interleaving to detect race conditions in simple CAF models, it is interesting to ask what happens in applications like that of Martin, which are not written in an update-in-place style, and where there is nevertheless interference, such as the inadvertent overwriting of values by processes due to a bug. Can we find it? In such a case, overwriting produces a contradiction in the antecedent of the correctness check, so it appears safe. Therefore, one needs both safety and progress checks, which we include. That is to say, interference of this kind manifests as lack of progress, which is detectable.

6   Conclusions and Future Work

We present an approach for checking data refinement in Alloy to verify correctness properties of HPC programs. Unlike attempts at after-the-fact verification, our emphasis is on "design thinking," an inherently iterative process that, with tool support, may help practitioners gain a deeper understanding of the structure and behavior of the programs they create. Tangible artifacts from the process include representation invariants that must be maintained by concrete implementations—in languages like Fortran, C/C++, and Julia—and abstraction relations that define and document how they should be interpreted.

Although we believe this to be a promising approach for HPC verification, the work presented in this paper also exposes some of the limitations of finite instance finding in dealing with existential quantifiers, integer bounds, and scope explosion. Practitioners will likely encounter these issues themselves, so developing a common approach for tackling them is necessary. Further work is needed to understand the best Alloy formulations for typical refinement checks as well as addressing technical limitations of the Alloy Analyzer in scientific applications.

Acknowledgments. This work was funded by NSF under the Formal Methods in the Field (FMitF) program, awards #2124205 (NCSU) and #2124100 (Utah).

References

1. Alloy models from the paper. https://go.ncsu.edu/alloy/
2. Baugh, J., Altuntas, A.: Formal methods and finite element analysis of hurricane storm surge: a case study in software verification. Sci. Comput. Program. **158**, 100–121 (2018)
3. Beckingsale, D.A., et al.: Raja: portable performance for large-scale scientific applications. In: 2019 IEEE/ACM International Workshop on Performance, Portability and Productivity in HPC (P3HPC), pp. 71–81 (2019)
4. Carter Edwards, H., Trott, C.R., Sunderland, D.: Kokkos: enabling manycore performance portability through polymorphic memory access patterns. J. Parallel Distrib. Comput. **74**(12), 3202–3216 (2014)
5. Dyer, T., Altuntas, A., Baugh, J.: Bounded verification of sparse matrix computations. In: Proceedings of the Third International Workshop on Software Correctness for HPC Applications, Correctness 2019, pp. 36–43. IEEE/ACM (2019)
6. Emerson, E.A., Trefler, R.J., Wahl, T.: Reducing model checking of the few to the one. In: Liu, Z., He, J. (eds.) Formal Methods Softw. Eng., pp. 94–113. Springer, Berlin, Heidelberg (2006)
7. Gopalakrishnan, G., et al.: Report of the HPC Correctness Summit, 25–26 Jan 2017, Washington, DC. CoRR abs/1705.07478 (2017)
8. Hoare, C.A.R.: Proof of correctness of data representations. Acta Informatica **1**(4), 271–281 (1972)
9. Jackson, D.: Software Abstractions: Logic, Language, and Analysis. The MIT Press (2012)
10. Lustig, D., Wright, A., Papakonstantinou, A., Giroux, O.: Automated synthesis of comprehensive memory model litmus test suites. In: Proceedings of the Twenty-Second International Conference on Architectural Support for Programming Languages and Operating Systems, pp. 661–675. ASPLOS 2017, ACM, New York, NY, USA (2017)
11. Martin, J.M.R.: Testing and verifying parallel programs using data refinement. In: Communicating Process Architectures 2017 & 2018, pp. 491–500. IOS Press (2019)
12. Milicevic, A., Jackson, D.: Preventing arithmetic overflows in Alloy. Sci. Comput. Program. **94**, 203–216 (2014)
13. de Roever, W.P., Engelhardt, K., Buth, K.H.: Data refinement: model-oriented proof methods and their comparison. Cambridge University Press (1998)

MPIRace: A Static Data Race Detector for MPI Programs

Wenwen Wang[⊠]

University of Georgia, Athens, Georgia
wenwen@cs.uga.edu

Abstract. Data races in distributed parallel programs, such as those developed with the message passing interface (MPI), can cause critical correctness and reliability issues. Therefore, it is highly necessary to detect and fix them. However, existing MPI programming error detection tools have rather limited support for data race detection. To address this problem, we present MPIRace, which is a *static* data race detector for MPI programs. It creates several novel and effective static program analysis techniques to overcome the technical challenges of conducting static data race detection for MPI programs. We also implement a research prototype of MPIRace based on LLVM, a widely-used compiler infrastructure. After applying MPIRace to MPI-CorrBench, a recent MPI correctness benchmark suite, and a broad range of real-world MPI applications, we successfully find 20 data races. Among them, 12 are found in the real-world MPI applications and it is the first time they are reported by a data race detector. Moreover, the detection speed of MPIRace is extremely fast, i.e., less than one minute for every evaluated application. We believe MPIRace will tremendously help developers in improving the correctness, reliability, and sustainability of MPI programs.

1 Introduction

The message passing interface (MPI) [18] is the industry-standard programming model of distributed parallel programs. However, even with MPI, developing highly-efficient yet *correct* distributed parallel programs is still not an easy task. This is because developers have to carefully coordinate the communications between different computer nodes. A subtle programming mistake can potentially lead to incorrect execution results. *Data races* are a common source of programming errors in MPI programs. Typically, a data race occurs when two *concurrent* memory accesses read/write the *same* memory location without any synchronization preserving their *happens-before* order, and at least one of the two accesses is *write*. As a consequence, the nondeterministic happens-before order of the two accesses can produce unexpected or incorrect execution results. Therefore, it is highly necessary to detect and fix data races in MPI programs.

Unfortunately, existing MPI programming error detection tools have very limited support for data race detection. Some static detection tools simply omit data races due to the inherent complexity of data race detection [3,24]. For example, MPI-Checker [3] is a static correctness checker to verify the usage of

The Author(s), under exclusive license to Springer Nature Switzerland AG 2023
Mendis and L. Rauchwerger (Eds.): LCPC 2022, LNCS 13829, pp. 73–90, 2023.
https://doi.org/10.1007/978-3-031-31445-2_6

MPI library routines. It only detects very simple MPI programming errors, such as MPI data type mismatches, invalid argument types, and unmatched/missing MPI calls. Some other detectors need to monitor the execution of the target MPI program to detect MPI programming errors [6,13,25,29,33,34] or synchronization errors [1,2,5,7]. For example, MUST [6] intercepts MPI library calls to examine call arguments for MPI programming error detection. But it has no support for data race detection. Traditional data race detectors, such as ThreadSanitizer [26] and Helgrind [16], are mainly developed for programs written in shared-memory programming models, e.g., OpenMP and Pthreads [31], and therefore, it is hard to apply them directly to distributed programs written in MPI.

To address the above limitations, this paper presents **MPIRace**, which is a *static* data race detector specifically designed for MPI programs. MPIRace augments existing MPI programming error detectors with the key capability of detecting data races. Further, compared to dynamic data race detectors, MPIRace does not need to run target MPI programs with sample inputs. That means it does not have the notorious coverage problem. MPIRace creates novel and effective static *compiler-based* program analysis techniques to analyze the entire code base of the target MPI program for data race detection.

We have implemented a research prototype of MPIRace based on LLVM [15]. Specifically, MPIRace takes as input the LLVM intermediate representation (IR) of the target MPI program and reports data races in the program. To evaluate MPIRace, we apply it to MPI-CorrBench [12], a recent MPI correctness benchmark suite, and a broad range of real-world MPI applications, including Ember [9], miniFE [21], Presta [10], SuperLU_DIST [14], and U.S. Naval MPI Tutorials [11]. MPIRace successfully reports 20 data races in these applications. Among them, 12 are found in real-world applications, and it is the first time these data races are discovered by a data race detector. This demonstrates the effectiveness and practicability of MPIRace. We believe MPIRace will provide strong support for developing correct, reliable, and sustainable MPI programs. The source code of MPIRace is available at https://github.com/mpirace/mpirace.

In summary, this paper makes the following contributions:

- We present MPIRace, which is, to the best of our knowledge, the first-ever static data race detector for MPI programs. MPIRace vastly strengthens the capability of existing MPI programming error detection tools.
- We propose novel and effective static program analysis techniques to overcome the technical challenges of MPIRace. We anticipate other MPI-related programming/debugging tools can also benefit from these techniques.
- We implement a research prototype based on LLVM, a popular compiler infrastructure, to demonstrate the feasibility of MPIRace. We also properly address several practical problems during the implementation process.
- We evaluate MPIRace using both micro benchmarks in MPI-CorrBench and real-world MPI applications. The results show that MPIRace can successfully discover previously unknown data races in these applications.

2   Background and Motivation

Data Races. In general, a data race is triggered by three conditions. First, a shared memory location is accessed *concurrently*. Second, the two accesses are *not ordered* by any synchronization. Finally, at least one access is a *write* operation. Since the *happens-before* order of the two shared memory accesses in a data race is *nondeterministic* [35], data races often lead to unexpected execution results [32]. In this paper, we use op(start_address, size) to represent a shared memory access. op denotes the *type* of the access, i.e., R or W. start_address and size are the two *operands* of the access, indicating the start address of the accessed memory location and the size of the access (in bytes), respectively.

Message Passing Interface (MPI). MPI [18] is a standardized and portable interface for programming parallel and distributed computers. It defines the syntax and semantics of a set of library routines that can be used to build highly efficient and scalable distributed parallel programs. Though MPI is not shipped with an official implementation, there are several popular MPI implementations maintained by independent organizations, such as MPICH [20], Open MPI [19], Microsoft MPI [17], and IBM Spectrum MPI [8].

In MPI, a group of processes that can communicate with one another is called a *communicator*. Each process in a communicator is assigned with a unique *rank*, which can be used to communicate with other processes in the same communicator. The communications are implemented by passing *messages*. For example, a rank can send/receive a message to/from another rank by invoking the MPI_Send()/MPI_Recv() routine and passing the receiver/sender rank to the routine. An MPI routine is usually *blocked* until the corresponding communication is completed. Nevertheless, in practice, communications between different nodes are very expensive. Therefore, in addition to blocking routines, MPI also supports *nonblocking* routines, e.g., MPI_Isend()/MPI_Irecv(), which can return immediately without waiting for the completion of the communications. Through nonblocking routines, an MPI program can hide the long latency of communications by overlapping them with local computations.

Motivation. Although MPI dramatically simplifies distributed parallel programming, it is still quite challenging for developers to write highly efficient yet correct MPI programs. One major obstacle is data races. Although MPI programs are implemented using processes and, in general, it is unlikely to form data races between different processes, there are still many scenarios in an MPI program in which *concurrent* shared memory accesses can be issued. For instance, the program code and the MPI library may be executed in parallel because nonblocking MPI library routines. This can generate numerous concurrent shared memory accesses and therefore, potentially introduce data races.

Figure 1 shows an example of MPI data race. In this example, there are two ranks, and rank 0 needs to send the variable data to rank 1. To achieve this, rank invokes the MPI library routine MPI_Isend() at line 9. This routine will read

```
1  MPI_Comm comm;
2  MPI_Request req;
3  int rank, data = 0;
4  comm = MPI_COMM_WORLD;
5  MPI_Comm_rank(comm, &rank);
6  if (rank == 0) {
7    data = 1;
8    // Send data to rank 1
9    MPI_Isend(&data, 1, MPI_INT, 1, ..., &req);
10   data = 2; // Conduct computations on data
11   MPI_Wait(&req, ...);
12 } else if (rank == 1) {
13   // Receive data from rank 0
14   MPI_Recv(&data, 1, MPI_INT, 0, ...);
15   if (data != 1)
16     printf("ERROR: data is wrong!\n");
17 }
```

Fig. 1. An MPI data race, caused by the accesses to data at line 9 and line 10.

the value of data and send it to rank 1. Here, the first, second, third, fourth, and last arguments of MPI_Isend() mean the start address of the data to be sent, the number of the data elements to be sent, the type of each data element, the receiver rank, and the handle of the send request, respectively. We omit other arguments to facilitate the discussion. However, MPI_Isend() is a nonblocking routine. That means, when the routine returns, the send operation may have not been completed. In other words, it is very likely that the MPI library reads data and sends it out after the routine returns. As a result, this read operation can form a data race with the following write operation to data at line 10, due to their nondeterministic happens-before order. If the write operation happens before the read operation, the value 2 will be sent to rank 1. This will eventually lead to an error in rank 1. As we can see in this example, data races in MPI programs can produce unexpected results and disrupt program execution. Therefore, it is of paramount importance to detect and fix them.

3   Technical Challenges

In this section, we explain the technical challenges and briefly describe our proposed solutions in MPIRace. It is worth pointing out that these challenges are *unique* to MPI programs, and therefore, not addressed by previous research work.

Process-based Parallel Execution Model. The first challenge is caused by the parallel execution model of MPI. Different from thread-based shared memory programs, such as those written in OpenMP and Pthreads, MPI programs are often implemented using *processes*. This renders it challenging to determine whether two memory accesses in an MPI program are from the same address space. In particular, if they are issued by different ranks, they are less likely to form a data race. The reason is that such memory accesses actually access different memory locations in different address spaces, even if the name of the accessed variable is the same. Recall the example in Fig. 1. The variable data is accessed by both rank 0 and rank 1. But such accesses actually access different memory locations in different address spaces. For instance, the write to data at line 10, issued by rank 0, and the read from data at line 15, issued by rank 1, are from different address spaces and thus not shared memory accesses.

A straightforward solution for this challenge is to analyze all memory accesses and classify them based on the ranks by which they are issued. However, this will slow down the entire detection process and make it unscalable for large-scale MPI programs. Instead, to overcome this challenge, our key observation is that it is actually unnecessary to analyze all memory accesses in an MPI program for data race detection. This is because data races in MPI programs usually only happen in specific parallel regions. In this paper, we call such regions *may-have-races* (MHR) parallel regions. By identifying MHR regions, we can detect all potential data races in an MPI program. More importantly, it allows us to narrow down the analysis scope and boost the analysis efficiency. We will describe more details about how to identify MHR parallel regions in the next section.

Shared Memory Accesses from MPI Library. In general, to statically detect data races in a program, we need to collect memory accesses in the program and analyze those accessing the same memory location. However, the fact that most data races in MPI programs involve shared memory accesses coming from the MPI library makes this static analysis process quite challenging. Again, take the data race in Fig. 1 as an example. One of the two shared memory accesses of the data race resides in the MPI routine MPI_Isend(). That means, if we only analyze memory accesses in the target MPI program, we will not be able to detect this data race, as line 9 is a function call not a memory access.

An intuitive solution for this problem is to also analyze memory accesses in the MPI library. However, this solution is impractical because of two reasons. First, the MPI library may contain massive memory accesses and most of them are irrelevant to our data race detection problem. Note that detecting data races in the MPI library is out of the scope of this paper. Second, even though the source code of many MPI implementations is available, it is still possible that the target MPI program uses a closed-source MPI implementation. In that case, only the executable code of the MPI library is available, which makes it extremely hard to analyze memory accesses in the library.

To address this problem, we propose a novel *memory access modeling* technique in MPIRace. This is inspired by the observation that the semantics of MPI library routines are well defined in the MPI standard [4]. Therefore, we can model the relevant memory access behavior of an MPI routine based on its semantics specified in the standard. For example, MPI_Isend() in Fig. 1 can be modeled as a read operation from the variable data. This way, we can exclude irrelevant memory accesses in the MPI library without loss of the capability to detect data races in MPI programs.

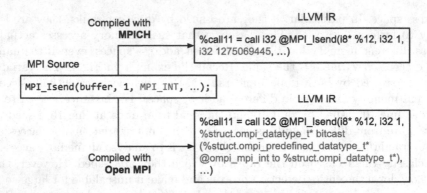

Fig. 2. The implementation divergence of MPI_INT leads to different LLVM IRs.

Implementation Divergences of MPI Library. The last but certainly not the least technical challenge is the divergences between different MPI implementations. In particular, the same MPI data type can be implemented in completely different ways, which makes it challenging to accurately identify MPI data types. Figure 2 shows an example. Here, we use LLVM [15] to compile the *same* MPI program with two representative MPI implementations: MPICH [20] and Open MPI [19]. As we can see, the compiled LLVM intermediate representations (IRs) are *not* the same due to different implementations of MPI_INT. Specifically, MPICH implements MPI_INT as a 32-bit integer, while Open MPI implements it as a sophisticated type. As a result, we cannot simply use the same approach to identify MPI data types compiled with different implementations.

To address this issue, our observation is that for the same MPI implementation, different MPI data types are generally implemented in the same way. For example, MPICH implements different MPI data types as different integers. This allows MPIRace to identify MPI data types in the same implementation using the same approach, e.g., checking the values of the integers. To support different MPI implementations, MPIRace further creates a *type identification table*, each entry of which describes what identification approach should be used for a specific MPI implementation. Note that this table can be created even without the source code of the MPI implementation. Also, MPIRace only needs to look up this table at the beginning of the analysis process, as an MPI program is typically compiled with only one MPI implementation.

4   MPIRace

In this section, we first present a high-level overview of MPIRace, and then div[e] into the technical details.

Figure 3 shows the workflow of MPIRace. As shown in the figure, MPIRac[e] takes as input the LLVM IR of the target MPI program. The first step [of] MPIRace is to identify may-have-races (MHR) parallel regions. Typically, the[y]

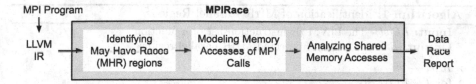

Fig. 3. The high-level workflow of MPIRace.

are two types of MHR parallel regions: *intra-rank* and *inter-rank*. In an intra-rank MHR parallel region, the MPI program code of a rank can be executed in parallel with the MPI library code, or two MPI library routines are executed concurrently. The parallel execution may produce shared memory accesses to a variable defined in the rank. Differently, an inter-rank MHR parallel region involves two ranks and its execution may generate shared memory accesses to a variable defined in one of the ranks, because another rank may remotely access the variable through MPI library routines. To detect both types of MHR parallel regions, MPIRace first analyzes every MPI library call in the target MPI program to figure out whether it is a start point of an MHR parallel region, based on the semantic of the called MPI library routine. If yes, MPIRace further analyzes the following code to find the end point(s) of the region. We will describe more details in the following subsection.

After MHR parallel regions are identified, MPIRace next collects shared memory accesses in each region and analyze them for data race detection. There are two major sources of shared memory accesses: the target MPI program and the MPI library. For shared memory accesses in the target program, MPIRace can collect them by analyzing the input LLVM IR. However, for shared memory accesses from the MPI library, it will incur heavy analysis overhead if we simply analyze the MPI library code. To avoid this problem, MPIRace models shared memory access behaviors of MPI library calls based on their semantics. More specifically, MPIRace creates *artificial* shared memory accesses to emulate the shared memory access behavior of each MPI library call. By analyzing these artificial accesses, MPIRace is able to decouple the analysis from the implementation details of the MPI library and scale up the detection process.

The final step of MPIRace is to analyze shared memory accesses in each MHR parallel region to detect data races. To this end, MPIRace checks whether two shared memory accesses may *concurrently* access the *same* memory location. If yes, they may form a data race. It is quite common in MPI programs that a memory access only touches specific elements in a memory buffer, e.g., odd- or even-indexed elements: `buf[i]`/`buf[i+1]`. That means, two shared memory accesses may not access the same memory location even if they access the same memory buffer. Besides, the memory location that is accessed by a memory access can also be influenced by the control flow, e.g., different memory addresses are assigned to the same pointer on different program paths. Hence, it is essential to thoroughly analyze shared memory accesses for accurate data race detection.

Algorithm 1: Identification of MHR Parallel Regions

Input: *LList* - The LLVM IR instruction list of a function
Output: *RSet* - The set of detected MHR parallel regions

1 *RSet* ← ∅
2 **for** *I* ∈ *LList* **do**
3   **if** *I* is not an MPI call **then**
4 | continue
5   **end**
6   **if** *I* does not start an MHR parallel region **then**
7 | continue
8   **end**
9   *ESet* ← ∅
10   **for** *J* ∈ *LList* **do**
11   **if** *J* is not reachable from *I* **or** not an MPI call **then**
12 | continue
13   **end**
14   **if** *J* may end the MHR parallel region of *I* **then**
15 | *ESet* ← *ESet* ∪ {*J*}
16   **end**
17   **end**
18   *RSet* ← *RSet* ∪ {< *I*, *ESet* >}
19 **end**
20 **return** *RSet*

To this end, MPIRace conducts *field-sensitive* and *path-sensitive* shared memory access analysis to limit potential false positives and false negatives.

Once a data race is detected, MPIRace will report detailed information about the data race to facilitate the following manual investigation and debugging activities. This includes the two shared memory accesses that form the data race and the memory location accessed by them.

4.1 Identifying MHR Parallel Regions

To identify MHR parallel regions, MPIRace analyzes every MPI library call in the target MPI program to see whether it may start an MHR region. If yes MPIRace continues to analyze the following code to find the end of the region. Algorithm 1 explains how MPIRace identifies MHR parallel regions. As shown in the algorithm, MPIRace conducts the identification at the function granularity. More specifically, MPIRace scans the LLVM IR instructions of the input function to find all MPI calls in the function. For each MPI call, MPIRace checks whether it starts an MHR parallel region by examining the semanti of the called MPI library routine. For example, an MPI call to a nonblockin library routine, e.g., MPI_Isend(), can start an intra-rank MHR parallel region which allows the following program code to be executed in parallel with th called library routine for enhanced performance and scalability. Note that th

Table 1. Sample MPI routines denoting the start/end of an MHR parallel region.

		Sample MPI Library Routines
intra-rank	Start	MPI_Isend(), MPI_Irecv(), MPI_Ireduce(), MPI_Put(), MPI_Get(),
	End	MPI_Wait(), MPI_Test(), MPI_Waitany(), MPI_Win_fence(),
inter-rank	Start	MPI_Win_fence(), MPI_Win_start(), MPI_Win_lock(),
	End	MPI_Win_fence(), MPI_Win_complete(), MPI_Win_unlock(),

semantics of each MPI library routine is clearly defined in the MPI standard [4]. Table 1 lists some sample MPI library routines that can start an MHR parallel region. By identifying MPI calls to such routines, MPIRace is able to detect the start of an MHR parallel region.

If an MPI call I is recognized as the start of an MHR parallel region, MPIRace next tries to find the MPI call(s) J that can serve as the end of the region. This will delimit the scope of the following shared memory access analysis for data race detection. In general, there are three conditions for J. First, it needs to be reachable from I on the control-flow graph. This is easy to understand because J should be executed after I. Second, it should have the semantic of ending an MHR parallel region. Table 1 shows some sample MPI library routines that have such semantics. Finally, the arguments passed to it can match with those passed to I. This is important, as unmatched arguments often imply different MPI communications. For example, in Fig. 1, the first argument of MPI_Wait() is the same as the last argument of MPI_Isend(), i.e., &req, which denotes the handle of the communication request. Therefore, they correspond to the same MPI communication. Based on these three conditions, MPIRace is able to find MPI call(s) that end an identified MHR parallel region.

4.2 Modeling Memory Accesses of MPI Library Calls

MPIRace models the shared memory access behavior of an MPI library call mainly based on the semantics of the called MPI routine. In particular, if an MPI routine reads from (or writes to) a memory buffer passed to it, MPIRace will create an artificial read (or write) operation to model the access. In other words, the artificial read (or write) operation is *semantically equivalent* to the MPI call from the perspective of data race detection.

Similarly, we use op(start_address, size) to represent an artificial memory access operation, where op is the access type, i.e., R_B, R_N, W_B, or W_N, and B and N are used to denote the type of the corresponding MPI call, i.e., blocking or nonblocking. To determine the two operands of an artificial memory access, MPIRace further analyzes the arguments of the MPI call. Typically, if an MPI library routine needs to access a memory buffer, it provides three arguments, denoted as $\mathscr{S}$, $\mathscr{C}$, and $\mathscr{T}$, to receive the information of the buffer: the start address of the buffer ($\mathscr{S}$), the number of elements to be accessed ($\mathscr{C}$), and the data type of each element ($\mathscr{T}$). For instance, the first three arguments of

MPI_Send() are used for this purpose. Therefore, the operands of the artificial memory access operation can be derived from the arguments as follows:

$$\begin{aligned} \texttt{start\_address} &= \mathscr{S} \\ \texttt{size} &= \mathscr{C} \times \text{sizeof}(\mathscr{T}) \end{aligned} \tag{1}$$

For the first two arguments, $\mathscr{S}$ and $\mathscr{C}$, we can simply extract them from the MPI call. But, for the argument $\mathscr{T}$, we need to know which identification approach should be used, due to the differences between different MPI implementations (see Sect. 3). This can be solved by looking up the type identification table. Once the type is identified, MPIRace can quickly figure out the size. For example, MPI_CHAR represents one byte, while MPI_INT indicates four bytes.

4.3   Analyzing Shared Memory Accesses

The last step of MPIRace is to analyze shared memory accesses for data race detection. Given two shared memory accesses, A and B, in an MHR parallel region $\mathcal{R}$, MPIRace classifies them as a data race if they satisfy the following conditions. First, at least one of A and B is a memory write operation. Second, A and B may access the same memory location. Third, A and B can be executed concurrently in a nondeterministic happens-before order. For instance, if $\mathcal{R}$ is an intra-rank MHR region, A and B may be executed by the MPI program and the MPI library within the rank, respectively. Or, they should be executed by different ranks if $\mathcal{R}$ is an inter-rank MHR region. Note that these conditions align with the conditions of a data race we discussed in Sect. 2. Next, we explain how MPIRace checks these conditions.

Analyzing Access Types and Locations. It is quite intuitive to check whether a memory access is a write operation or not, as both the memory accesses in the MPI program and the artificial memory accesses created by MPIRace have the access type information. To determine whether two memory accesses may access the same memory location, MPIRace checks whether there is any *overlap* between the two accessed memory locations. Suppose b_1 and b_2 are the start addresses, and s_1 and s_2 are the sizes of the two accesses, respectively. An overlap means the following logical expression is true: $b_1 \leq b_2 < b_1 + s_1 \vee b_2 \leq b_1 < b_2 + s_2$. To evaluate this expression, MPIRace conducts a path-sensitive backward data-flow analysis to find all potential definitions of b_1 and b_2. For example, an address may be derived from a pointer that points to a stack or heap buffer. In case s_1 or s_2 is not a constant, MPIRace also finds their definitions. Due to the inherent limitation of static program analysis techniques [27,28], it is possible that MPIRace cannot accurately find the definitions. Therefore, MPIRace conducts the analysis conservatively to avoid potential false negatives. Though this may pose a risk of more false positives, our experimental results on real-world MPI applications show that the detection results are satisfactory.

Analyzing Access Concurrency. To determine whether two shared memory accesses in an intra-rank MHR region can be executed concurrently, MPIRace checks that at least one of the memory accesses is an artificial memory access and their happens-before order is not determined by the program order. This allows the two accesses to be executed concurrently by the MPI program and the MPI library within the rank. Take the following code as an example:

```
1 || int buf = 0;
2 || MPI_Isend(buf, 1, MPI_INT, ...); // R_N(buf, 4)
3 || buf = 1; // W(buf, 4)
4 || MPI_Irecv(buf, 1, MPI_INT, ...); // W_N(buf, 4)
```

In this code, $W(buf, 4)$ forms a data race with $R_N(buf, 4)$, because they can be executed concurrently in a nondeterministic happens-before order. However, there is no data race between $W(buf, 4)$ and $W_N(buf, 4)$. The reason is that their happens-before order is determined by the program order. That is, $W(buf, 4)$ always happens before $W_N(buf, 4)$. Note that $R_N(buf, 4)$ and $W_N(buf, 4)$ also form a data race in this example, as they may be executed concurrently by the MPI library in a nondeterministic happens-before order.

In case the two shared memory accesses are in an inter-rank MIIR region, MPIRace checks that they can be executed by two different ranks. This can be done by tracking the MPI routine MPI_Comm_rank() because most MPI programs use this routine to get the rank information. This allows MPIRace to figure out the rank(s) that will execute a code region.

5   Implementation

We have implemented a research prototype of MPIRace based on LLVM (version 13.0.0). In this section, we report the issues we encountered during the implementation process and our solutions.

Compiling MPI Programs to LLVM IR. To compile an MPI program to LLVM IR, we pass the LLVM compiler to MPI wrapper compilers with the flags "-S -emit-llvm." We also skip the linking stage at the end of the compilation process without combining all LLVM IR files to generate a single file. This allows us to apply MPIRace to an MPI program even if its source code can only be compiled partially with LLVM.

Identifying MPI Calls. In LLVM IR, MPI library calls are treated in the same way as normal library function calls. In most cases, an MPI call is compiled to 'call' instruction. However, in some cases, especially for C++ programs, it possible that an MPI call is compiled to an 'invoke' instruction. Hence, we ed to check both of them to identify MPI calls.

Collecting Memory Accesses. In general, memory accesses are compiled 'load' and 'store' instructions in LLVM IR. Both of them have a *pointer* operand, which specifies the address of the accessed memory location. To determine the size of a memory access, we can check the type of the pointer operand, as LLVM IR requires that the type must be a first-class type with a *known* size. Apart from these instructions, our implementation also supports C standard library routines, e.g., `memcpy()` and `strcpy()`, and C++ STL containers, e.g., `std::vector` and `std::list`. This is realized by recognizing corresponding function calls in LLVM IR and replacing them with normal 'load' and 'store' instructions, similar to modeling shared memory access behaviors of MPI calls.

6   Experimental Results

In this section, we evaluate MPIRace. The goal of the evaluation is to answer the following two questions: 1) Can MPIRace detect data races in MPI programs? 2) How is the detection efficiency of MPIRace? To this end, we apply MPIRace to MPI-CorrBench [12], a benchmark suite for evaluating MPI programming error detection tools, and a wide range of real-world MPI applications, including Ember [9], miniFE [21], Presta [10], SuperLU_DIST [14], and U.S. Naval MPI Tutorials [11]. Our experimental platform is powered by an Intel Xeon E5-2697 14-core CPU with hyper-threading enabled and 194GB main memory. The operating system is Ubuntu 20.04 with the Linux kernel (version 5.11.0).

6.1   Detection Effectiveness

Table 2 shows the data races detected by MPIRace. For some data races, e.g., #3, #13, and #16, the two shared memory accesses come from the same source line. This is because the source line is in a loop and thus forms a data race with itself. To summarize, MPIRace successfully finds 20 data races. This shows the effectiveness of MPIRace on detecting data races in MPI programs.

MPI-CorrBench. For MPI-CorrBench, 8 data races are reported by MPIRace. Here, an interesting observation is that MPIRace successfully uncovers 4 data races in the presumably correct version of the microbenchmark programs, i.e., data races #3, #4, #5, and #6. The paths of the source files of these data races imply that the corresponding micro benchmarks are located in the "correct" directory. This demonstrates the natural stealthiness of data races and the inherent difficulty to recognize them during the development process.

Comparing with Existing Tools. We compare MPIRace with existing representative tools, including MPI-Checker [3], MUST [6], ThreadSanitizer [26], and Helgrind [16]. Table 3 shows the comparison results for the data races in MPI-CorrBench. As shown in the table, MPI-Checker fails to detect any data races. This is expected because MPI-Checker is designed to catch simple MPI programming errors rather than data races. Surprisingly, MUST detects six out of eight data races. Our further study shows that this is not because MUST is ab

Table 2. The details of the data races detected by MPIRace.

Application	ID	Source File	Source Lines
MPI-CorrBench	1	micro-benches/0-level/conflo/pt2pt/ ArgMismatch-MPIIrecv-buffer-overlap.c	36 MPI_Irecv(buffer, N, ... 37 MPI_Irecv(tar_2, N/2, ...
	2	micro-benches/0-level/conflo/pt2pt/ MisplacedCall-MPIWait.c	35 MPI_Isend(buffer, 100000, ... 37 buffer[0] = 10;
	3	micro-benches/0-level/correct/pt2pt/ dtype_send.c	84 MPI_Irecv(rcv_buf, 1, ... 84 MPI_Irecv(rcv_buf, 1, ...
	4	micro-benches/0-level/correct/pt2pt/ inactivereq.c	92 MPI_Irecv(rbuf, 10, ... 92 MPI_Irecv(rbuf, 10, ...
	5	micro-benches/0-level/correct/pt2pt/ patterns.c	87 MPI_Irecv(buffer, buf_size, ... 88 MPI_Irecv(buffer, buf_size, ...
	6	micro-benches/0-level/correct/pt2pt/ patterns.c	116 MPI_Irecv(buffer, buf_size, ... 117 MPI_Irecv(buffer, buf_size, ...
	7	micro-benches/0-level/pt2pt/ ArgMismatch-MPIIrecv-buffer-overlap.c	28 MPI_Irecv(buffer, N, ... 29 MPI_Irecv(&buffer[N/2], N/2, ...
	8	micro-benches/0-level/pt2pt/ MisplacedCall-MPIWait.c	35 MPI_Isend(buffer, 100000, ... 36 buffer[0] = 10;
Ember	9	mpi/halo3d-26/halo3d-26.c	446 MPI_Irecv(edge, nz*vars, ... 488 MPI_Irecv(edge, ny*vars, ...
	10	mpi/halo3d-26/halo3d-26.c	446 MPI_Irecv(edge, nz*vars, ... 495 MPI_Irecv(edge, ny*vars, ...
	11	mpi/halo3d-26/halo3d-26.c	488 MPI_Irecv(edge, ny*vars, ... 495 MPI_Irecv(edge, ny*vars, ...
miniFE	12	ref/src/make_local_matrix.hpp	259 MPI_Irecv(&tmp_buf[i], 1, ... 266 MPI_Send(&tmp_buf[i], 1, ...
Presta	13	com.c	582 MPI_Irecv(comBuf, bufsize, ... 582 MPI_Irecv(comBuf, bufsize, ...
	14	com.c	764 MPI_Irecv(rBuf, bufsize, ... 764 MPI_Irecv(rBuf, bufsize, ...
SuperLU_DIST	15	SRC/psymbfact.c	4776 MPI_Irecv (&sz_msg, 1, ... 4782 if (sz_msg > INT_MAX)
U.S. Naval MPI Tutorials	16	src/MPI_Recv_init.c	150 MPI_Irecv(rbuf, 10, ... 150 MPI_Irecv(rbuf, 10, ...
	17	src/MPI_Request_free.c	135 MPI_Irecv(rbuf, 10, ... 135 MPI_Irecv(rbuf, 10, ...
	18	src/MPI_Send_init.c	159 MPI_Irecv(rbuf, 10, ... 159 MPI_Irecv(rbuf, 10, ...
	19	src/MPI_Ssend_init.c	152 MPI_Irecv(rbuf, 10, ... 152 MPI_Irecv(rbuf, 10, ...
	20	src/MPI_Start.c	106 MPI_Irecv(rbuf, 10, ... 106 MPI_Irecv(rbuf, 10, ...

detect data races. Instead, it considers the programs have misuses of MPI library routines. Since MUST only monitors MPI calls, it cannot detect data races that involve both the MPI library and the target MPI program. Also, it is a dynamic detector and thus suffers from the well-known coverage issue. Both ThreadSanitizer and Helgrind cannot find the data races detected by MPIRace. Overall, we can conclude that MPIRace outperforms existing tools in detecting data races in MPI programs.

Table 3. The comparison between existing tools and MPIRace.

	1	2	3	4	5	6	7	8
MPI-Checker	✗	✗	✗	✗	✗	✗	✗	✗
MUST	✓	✗	✓	✓	✓	✓	✓	✗
ThreadSanitizer	✗	✗	✗	✗	✗	✗	✗	✗
Helgrind	✗	✗	✗	✗	✗	✗	✗	✗
MPIRace	✓	✓	✓	✓	✓	✓	✓	✓

Real-World MPI Applications. As shown in Table 2, MPIRace successfully reports 12 data races in the evaluated real-world MPI applications. To our surprise, every evaluated MPI application has at least one data race. This shows the importance of conducting data race detection for MPI programs. Among the 12 data races, #15 is caused by concurrent shared memory accesses between the MPI application and a nonblocking MPI library routine, while #12 is caused by a nonblocking MPI routine and a blocking MPI routine. Also, the shared variable of data race #12 is a C++ STL container. This shows that MPIRace is capable of detecting MPI data races in various types.

False Positives and False Negatives. Although MPIRace is a static detector, it does not report any false positives in the detection results. A potential reason is that most MPI programs have regular shared memory accesses, which makes static analyses more accurate, compared to general multithreaded programs. Regarding false negatives, we manually created a group of micro benchmarks with artificially injected data races to evaluate MPIRace. The evaluation results show that MPIRace can detect all injected data races. We believe the probability that MPIRace may miss a data race is rather low because of its general design.

6.2 Detection Efficiency

Figure 4 shows the detection time (in seconds) required by MPIRace. For all evaluated MPI applications, the detection time is less than one minute. The longest detection time is spent on MPI-CorrBench, because it contains more than 500 micro benchmarks. As a result, it takes a relatively long time for MPIRace to load the LLVM IR files. In fact, the actual detection time is quite short, i.e. less than 15% of the total time. Overall, we are confident that MPIRace can be applied to large-scale MPI applications for data race detection.

7   Related Work

Many MPI programming tools have been proposed to help developers to fin programming errors in MPI programs [1–3, 5–7, 13, 24, 25, 29, 33, 34]. For exam ple, MPI-Checker [3] analyzes the AST of the target MPI program to dete

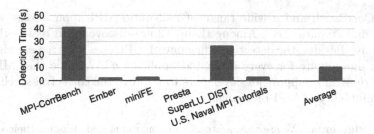

Fig. 4. Detection time of MPIRace.

MPI programming errors. MUST [6] dynamically verifies the correctness of each MPI library call. Besides, it can also detect deadlock errors [5,7]. MC-Checker [1] and SyncChecker [2] are two dynamic checkers that aim to detect memory consistency and synchronization errors in MPI programs. However, they are limited to specific types of MPI programs. Similarly, PARCOACH [24] aims to validate MPI collective communications. ParaStack [13] is dedicated to MPI hang detection. NINJA [25] explores noise injection techniques to expose MPI message races. In addition, some other tools [29,33,34] leverage symbolic execution and formal verification techniques to check the correctness of MPI programs.

Though data race detection has been researched for decades, traditional detectors, such as ThreadSanitizer [26] and Helgrind [16], can only detect data races in thread-based shared-memory programs [30]. Some previous research work attempts to detect data races in distributed programs [22,23]. Unfortunately, they only support the UPC programming model, rather than MPI.

MPIRace is clearly distinguished from existing tools in two aspects. First, it focuses on MPI data race detection, which is generally much harder than detecting simple MPI programming errors. Therefore, MPIRace augments existing tools, as most of them lack support for data race detection. Second, it is a static data race detector. That means, it can analyze the entire code base of the target MPI program without the need to run the program with sample inputs. In other words, it does not suffer from the notorious coverage issue that confronts existing dynamic tools, such as MUST. Also, since it does not need to run the MPI program, the analysis process can be completely decoupled from the execution environment of the program. This further enhances the practicability of MPIRace, as many MPI programs need to run on dedicated supercomputers, which are typically not available for a tool like MPIRace.

Conclusion

In this paper, we present MPIRace, a static data race detector designed specifically for MPI programs. It creates several novel and effective static analysis techniques to overcome the technical challenges of conducting static data race detection for MPI programs. We also implement a research prototype of MPIRace based on the popular LLVM compiler infrastructure. After applying MPIRace to MPI-CorrBench and a wide range of real-world MPI applications, we successfully find 20 data races. Among them, 12 are discovered in real-world MPI applications. Besides, the detection efficiency of MPIRace is extremely high, i.e., less than one minute for every evaluated application. We hope that MPIRace will provide strong support for developers to improve the correctness, reliability, and sustainability of MPI programs.

Acknowledgments. We are very grateful to anonymous reviewers for their valuable feedback and comments. This work was supported in part by the M. G. Michael Award funded by the Franklin College of Arts and Sciences at the University of Georgia and a faculty startup funding offered by the University of Georgia.

References

1. Chen, Z., et al.: MC-Checker: detecting memory consistency errors in MPI one-sided applications. In: Proceedings of the International Conference for High Performance Computing, Networking, Storage and Analysis, pp. 499–510. SC '14, IEEE Press (2014). https://doi.org/10.1109/SC.2014.46
2. Chen, Z., Li, X., Chen, J.Y., Zhong, H., Qin, F.: Syncchecker: detecting synchronization errors between MPI applications and libraries. In: 2012 IEEE 26th International Parallel and Distributed Processing Symposium, pp. 342–353 (2012). https://doi.org/10.1109/IPDPS.2012.40
3. Droste, A., Kuhn, M., Ludwig, T.: MPI-checker: static analysis for MPI. LLVM '15, Association for Computing Machinery, New York, NY, USA (2015). https://doi.org/10.1145/2833157.2833159
4. Forum, M.P.I.: MPI: a message-passing interface standard, version 4.0 (Accessed: January 2022). https://www.mpi-forum.org/docs/mpi-4.0/mpi40-report.pdf
5. Hilbrich, T., Protze, J., Schulz, M., de Supinski, B.R., Müller, M.S.: MPI runtime error detection with must: advances in deadlock detection. In: Proceedings of the International Conference on High Performance Computing, Networking, Storage and Analysis. SC '12, IEEE Computer Society Press, Washington, DC, USA (2012)
6. Hilbrich, T., Schulz, M., de Supinski, B.R., Müller, M.S.: Must: a scalable approach to runtime error detection in MPI programs. In: Müller, M.S., Resch, M.M., Schulz, A., Nagel, W.E. (eds.) Tools for High Performance Computing 2009, pp. 53–66. Springer, Berlin Heidelberg, Berlin, Heidelberg (2010)
7. Hilbrich, T., de Supinski, B.R., Nagel, W.E., Protze, J., Baier, C., Müller, M.S.: Distributed wait state tracking for runtime MPI deadlock detection. In: Proceedings of the International Conference on High Performance Computing, Networking, Storage and Analysis. SC '13, Association for Computing Machinery, New York, NY, USA (2013). https://doi.org/10.1145/2503210.2503237
8. IBM: IBM spectrum MPI: Accelerating high-performance application parallelization (Accessed: January 2022). https://www.ibm.com/products/spectrum-mpi
9. Laboratories, S.N.: Ember communication pattern library (Accessed: January, 2022). https://proxyapps.exascaleproject.org/app/ember-communication patterns
10. Laboratory, L.L.N.: Presta MPI benchmark 1.3.0 (Accessed: January, 2022). https://github.com/LLNL/phloem/tree/master/presta-1.3.0
11. Laboratory, U.N.R.: Message passing interface (MPI) tutorials (Accessed: January 2022), https://github.com/USNavalResearchLaboratory/mpi_tutorials

12. Lehr, J.P., Jammer, T., Bischof, C.: MPI-Corrbench: towards an MPI correctness benchmark suite. In: Proceedings of the 30th International Symposium on High-Performance Parallel and Distributed Computing. p. 69–80. HPDC '21, Association for Computing Machinery, New York, NY, USA (2021). https://doi.org/10.1145/3431379.3460652

13. Li, H., Chen, Z., Gupta, R.: Parastack: efficient hang detection for MPI programs at large scale. In: Proceedings of the International Conference for High Performance Computing, Networking, Storage and Analysis. SC '17, Association for Computing Machinery, New York, NY, USA (2017). https://doi.org/10.1145/3126908.3126938

14. Li, X.S., Demmel, J.W.: Superlu_dist: a scalable distributed-memory sparse direct solver for unsymmetric linear systems. ACM Trans. Math. Softw. **29**(2), 110–140 (2003). https://doi.org/10.1145/779359.779361

15. LLVM: the LLVM compiler infrastructure (Accessed: January, 2022). https://llvm.org

16. Manual, V.U.: Helgrind: a thread error detector (Accessed: January, 2022). https://www.valgrind.org/docs/manual/hg-manual.html

17. Microsoft: Microsoft MPI (Accessed: January 2022). https://docs.microsoft.com/en-us/message-passing-interface/microsoft-mpi

18. MPI: MPI forum (Accessed: January 2022). https://www.mpi-forum.org

19. MPI, O.: Open source high performance computing (Accessed: January 2022). https://www.open-mpi.org

20. MPICH: High-performance portable MPI (Accessed: January 2022). https://www.mpich.org

21. Organization, M.: minife finite element mini-application (Accessed: January, 2022). https://proxyapps.exascaleproject.org/app/minife

22. Park, C.S., Sen, K., Hargrove, P., Iancu, C.: Efficient data race detection for distributed memory parallel programs. In: Proceedings of 2011 International Conference for High Performance Computing, Networking, Storage and Analysis. SC '11, Association for Computing Machinery, New York, NY, USA (2011). https://doi.org/10.1145/2063384.2063452

23. Park, C.S., Sen, K., Iancu, C.: Scaling data race detection for partitioned global address space programs. In: Proceedings of the 27th International ACM Conference on International Conference on Supercomputing, pp. 47–58. ICS '13, Association for Computing Machinery, New York, NY, USA (2013). https://doi.org/10.1145/2464996.2465000

24. Saillard, E., Carribault, P., Barthou, D.: Parcoach: combining static and dynamic validation of MPI collective communications. Int. J. High Perform. Comput. Appl. **28**(4), 425–434 (2014). https://doi.org/10.1177/1094342014552204

25. Sato, K., Ahn, D.H., Laguna, I., Lee, G.L., Schulz, M., Chambreau, C.M.: Noise injection techniques to expose subtle and unintended message races. In: Proceedings of the 22nd ACM SIGPLAN Symposium on Principles and Practice of Parallel Programming, pp. 89–101. PPoPP '17, Association for Computing Machinery, New York, NY, USA (2017). https://doi.org/10.1145/3018743.3018767

26. Serebryany, K., Iskhodzhanov, T.: Threadsanitizer: data race detection in practice. In: Proceedings of the Workshop on Binary Instrumentation and Applications, pp. 62–71. WBIA '09, Association for Computing Machinery, New York, NY, USA (2009). https://doi.org/10.1145/1791194.1791203

27. Tan, T., Li, Y., Ma, X., Xu, C., Smaragdakis, Y.: Making pointer analysis more precise by unleashing the power of selective context sensitivity. Proc. ACM Program. Lang. 5(OOPSLA) (Oct 2021). https://doi.org/10.1145/3485524

28. Thiessen, R., Lhoták, O.: Context transformations for pointer analysis. In: Proceedings of the 38th ACM SIGPLAN Conference on Programming Language Design and Implementation, pp. 263–277. PLDI 2017, Association for Computing Machinery, New York, NY, USA (2017). https://doi.org/10.1145/3062341.3062359

29. Vo, A., Aananthakrishnan, S., Gopalakrishnan, G., Supinski, B.R.D., Schulz, M., Bronevetsky, G.: A scalable and distributed dynamic formal verifier for MPI programs. In: Proceedings of the 2010 ACM/IEEE International Conference for High Performance Computing, Networking, Storage and Analysis, pp. 1–10. SC '10, IEEE Computer Society, USA (2010). https://doi.org/10.1109/SC.2010.7

30. Wang, W., Lin, P.H.: Does it matter? ompsanitizer: an impact analyzer of reported data races in openmp programs. In: Proceedings of the ACM International Conference on Supercomputing, pp. 40–51. ICS '21, Association for Computing Machinery, New York, NY, USA (2021). https://doi.org/10.1145/3447818.3460379

31. Wang, W., et al.: Localization of concurrency bugs using shared memory access pairs. In: Proceedings of the 29th ACM/IEEE International Conference on Automated Software Engineering, pp. 611–622. ASE '14, Association for Computing Machinery, New York, NY, USA (2014). https://doi.org/10.1145/2642937.2642972

32. Wang, W., et al.: Dynamically tolerating and detecting asymmetric races. J. Comput. Res. Dev. **51**(8), 1748–1763 (2014). https://doi.org/10.7544/issn1000-1239.2014.20130123

33. Ye, F., Zhao, J., Sarkar, V.: Detecting MPI usage anomalies via partial program symbolic execution. In: Proceedings of the International Conference for High Performance Computing, Networking, Storage, and Analysis. SC '18, IEEE Press (2018). https://doi.org/10.1109/SC.2018.00066

34. Yu, H., et al.: Symbolic verification of message passing interface programs. In: Proceedings of the ACM/IEEE 42nd International Conference on Software Engineering, pp. 1248–1260. ICSE '20, Association for Computing Machinery, New York, NY, USA (2020). https://doi.org/10.1145/3377811.3380419

35. Yuan, X., et al.: Synchronization identification through on-the-fly test. In: Wolf, F., Mohr, B., an Mey, D. (eds.) Euro-Par 2013. LNCS, vol. 8097, pp. 4–15. Springer, Heidelberg (2013). https://doi.org/10.1007/978-3-642-40047-6_3

Wordless Integer and Floating-Point Computing

Henry Dietz(✉) iD

University of Kentucky, Lexington, KY 40506, USA
hankd@engr.uky.edu

Abstract. In most programming languages, data is organized in structures that
are explicitly mapped to machine words each containing a fixed number of bits.
For example, a C variable declared as an int might be specified to be represented
by a 32-bit word. Given computer hardware in which data are organized as fixed-
size words, this seems intuitive and efficient. However, if the integer is known
to always have a value between 0 and 100, at most only seven of those 32 bits
are needed; the other 25 bits are always 0. Programming languages like C allow
integer variables to be declared as having any of several bit precisions, so declaring
the variable as uint8_t could reduce waste to just one bit. The catch is the index is
only seven bits long when it holds a value greater than 63. Operating on more bits
than necessary dramatically increases both the storage space and the number of
gate operations needed to perform operations like addition or multiplication. The
solution proposed here is to implement a programming model in which integer and
floating-point variables are represented by just enough bits to represent the values
they contain at that moment in execution. The overhead involved in dynamically
adjusting precision is significant, thus it is only used for SIMD-parallel variables
implemented using the PBP execution model.

Keywords: Parallel Bit Pattern computing · SIMD · bit slice · bit-serial
arithmetic · variable precision arithmetic · integer arithmetic · floating point

1 Introduction

Through decades of exponential growth in the number of gates that can be cost-effectively
put on a chip, the best way to make programs execute faster was to use increasing amounts
of parallelism. Unfortunately, the happy prophecy of Moore's Law is no longer being
met; as the rate of increase is decaying, it has become prudent to seek ways to increase
computation speed without using more hardware parallelism. This concern is amplified
by the fact that power consumed per gate action has not been dropping even as fast as
the number of gates that can be placed on a chip has grown. There are many ways that
the power consumed per computation might be reduced, ranging from adiabatic logic
to quantum computing, but one of the most immediately practical methods is to simply
avoid performing gate-level operations that do not produce a useful result.

One of the most fundamental concepts in optimizing compilers is the elimination of
unnecessary operations. Optimizations like common subexpression elimination, which
removes repeated computations of the same value, were well known by 1970 [1] and are

© The Author(s), under exclusive license to Springer Nature Switzerland AG 2023
C. Mendis and L. Rauchwerger (Eds.): LCPC 2022, LNCS 13829, pp. 91–105, 2023.
https://doi.org/10.1007/978-3-031-31445-2_7

implemented in nearly all modern compilers. These optimizations are quite effective in reducing the amount of work that must be performed to execute a program, but they are performed at the level of operations on values sized as machine words. In a 2017 paper [2], it was suggested that the key to dramatically reducing power consumed per computation is to instead focus on performing similar optimizations at the level of individual gate operations on bits. The methods recommended for minimizing the number of active gates in performing a word-level computation can be broadly divided into two categories: minimizing the number of bits that must be processed and minimizing the number of gate-level operations that must be executed for a given bit-level computation.

1.1 Minimizing the Number of Bits

Several techniques have been suggested toward minimizing the number of bits that must be stored and processed for each value. The most obvious is that choices between data types should be made more carefully; although C/C++ programs commonly declare most integer variables as int, variables that do not need that large a value range, or that are never negative, should be declared using types that instantiate fewer bits, such as uint8_t. This type of transformation also can be automated by the compiler performing integer range analysis. In fact, the concept of using compile-time range analysis to infer variable types dates from the mid-1960s [3]. The 2017 work also suggested that precision of floating-point values should be a function of the accuracy required for the result, and that accuracy requirements for operations should be specified rather than precision of variables. It was noted that such accuracy requirements would even allow dynamic choices between float and double representations, or even the use of alternative approximate real-number formats such as LNS (log number systems). Finally, it was noted that smaller representations can be packed to hold more values in a fixed number of memory locations or registers, thus reducing the power associated with storing or transmitting each useful bit.

In the current work, the approach taken is to be able to treat any integer or floating-point variable as inherently variable precision, with the number of bits dynamically varying as the value is changed. Excess bits are dynamically trimmed as new values are generated. Even the signedness of an integer is treated as a dynamic property of the current value. For example, a variable with the value 4 would be represented as an unsigned 3-bit integer, and decrementing it to 3 would change the type to an unsigned 2-bit integer. If that value of 3 was then negated, the type of that variable would change to a signed 3-bit integer. Operations on integer values thus effectively eliminate redundant bit positions from the most significant bit (MSB) position downward. In effect, the normalization of ordinary floating-point values similarly removes redundant bit values from the MSB downward. It is possible to extend this notion further so that, using different normalization rule, redundant bits are also removed from the least significant bit (LSB) upward. For example, while the fractional part of the representation of the floating-point value 3.0 would require two bits, the fractional part of 256.0 can be just single bit long. The exponent also can dynamically change in size. These methods are discussed in Sect. 2.

1.2 Minimizing the Number of Gate-Level Operations

Minimizing the number of gate-level operations that must be executed for a given bit-level computation seems impossible for computers that inherently operate on a machine word at a time. However, it was noted that bit-slice hardware, in which word-level operations were performed one bit at a time, was once extremely common – and it might be time to revive that model. Bit-serial processing of values was particularly common in SIMD supercomputers and was used in the ICL Distributed Array Processor (DAP) [4], STARAN [5], Goodyear Massively Parallel Processor (MPP) [6], Thinking Machines CM and CM2 [7], and NCR GAPP [8]. The key benefit in using SIMD-parallel execution of bit-serial operations is that it allows simpler hardware to execute with a faster clock. For example, a throughput of one 32-bit addition per clock cycle can either be obtained by having a fast 32-bit addition circuit perform one addition in one clock cycle or by executing one-bit ripple-carry addition steps in a sequence of 32 clock cycles, but with a parallelism width of 32. Bit serial addition of 32 32-bit values in 32 clock cycles requires only 32 one-bit full adders, for a total of approximately 5×32 gates, yielding 32 results after a total of roughly $5 \times 32 \times 32 = 5120$ gate actions. In contrast, a single fast 32-bit adder built using carry lookahead will require at least twice as many gates, doubling the number of gate actions and hence power consumed for computing the same 32 results; each clock cycle also will be at least an order of magnitude longer, because the longest path through the 32-bit carry lookahead is more than ten times the delay of a one-bit full adder. The bit-serial SIMD machines leveraged this benefit, but used a fixed, microcoded, sequence of bit-level operations for each word-level operation; by optimizing at the bit level across multiple word-level operations, as well as performing constant folding where bit values are known, the number of bit-level gate operations can be reduced even more dramatically. It also was suggested that such analysis could target implementation using a quantum computer, potentially leveraging the ability of such systems to have a individual gate-level operation applied to exponentially many superposed bit values with unit cost.

The approach discussed in the current work is best described as a layered application of symbolic execution. In the top layer, each operation on a dynamic-precision variable can be translated into the simplest possible equivalent set of bit-level operations, and the bookkeeping necessary to adjust precision is performed. This symbolic manipulation is expensive, so it is rarely used for scalar variables. Variables that are massively parallel SIMD data structures multiply the operation cost without incurring additional bookkeeping, so the benefit in performing the symbolic manipulation can far outweigh the overhead. The layers below are logically performing SIMD-parallel operations on large bit vectors distributed across single-bit processing elements. However, the implementation recognizes and removes redundancies in four lower layers leveraging the new, quantum-inspired, parallel bit pattern (PBP) [9] model of computation. In PBP, the value of an E-way entangled superposition is represented as a SIMD-parallel 2^E-bit value, and the current work treats it as precisely that: a collective reference to corresponding bits of 2^E SIMD processing elements (PEs). The dynamically optimized execution of the bit-level SIMD operations is detailed in Sect. 3.

Section 4 summarizes a few preliminary performance results obtained by executing a prototype C++ implementation on a conventional processor using only SIMD hardware parallelism within a 32-bit or 64-bit word. Although use of a conventional processor prevents the power savings from being realized, the system does allow precise counting of gate-level operations needed for conventional word-level SIMD execution, bit-level optimized SIMD execution, and the execution of bit-level SIMD operations using PBP entangled superpositions.

The contributions of this work are summarized in Sect. 5, along with directions for future work.

2   Wordless Integer and Floating-Point Variables

The primary contribution of the current work is the concept and implementation of an efficient mechanism for wordless variables: variables for which the number of bits used to represent a value dynamically is adjusted at runtime to minimally cover the specific values being represented.

Although there are languages in which arbitrary numbers of bits may be used to represent a variable, such as Verilog [10] and VHDL [11], bit precision is fixed at compile time. This is not surprising in that most such languages are intended to be used to specify hardware designs, and bit precision thus corresponds to the physical number of wires in a datapath. In allowing runtime adjustable precision for a variable, the most similar prior work is not minimizing the number of bits in a representation but facilitating computations upon multi-word "Big Numbers." There are many libraries providing variable-length multi-word value manipulation, including The GNU Multiple Precision Arithmetic Library (GMP) [12], BigDigits [13], and ArPALib [14]. Such libraries often use clever implementations of operations to improve speed when operating on high-precision values; for example, multiply is often implemented by algorithms other than the usual shift-and-add sequence. In contrast, most values used in programs fit within an individual machine word with space to spare, and none of the above libraries attempts to avoid storing or operating on those unnecessary bits within a word.

2.1   Wordless Integers

In most computers, an unsigned integer is represented as an ordered set of k bits, b_{k-1}, $b_{k-2}, \ldots, b_1, b_0$, such that the value of bit b_i is $b_i \times 2^i$. That is essentially the representation proposed here. The main difference is that the value of a bit position b_i is not a single bit, but an entire vector of bits distributed one per PE across the $nproc$ PEs of a SIMD machine. Thus, rather than representing an integer as an ordered set of bits, it would be more accurate to say an integer is an ordered set of bit-index values, x_i, such that the corresponding bit value in each PE $iproc$ is $PE[iproc].mem[x_i]$. The value of k, the number of bits in the representation, is variable and therefore must be recorded as part of the integer data structure.

Removal of Redundant Leading Bits. An unsigned integer's value is not affected by any bit position holding zero. Thus, it would be possible to record only the position of potentially non-zero bit values: that is, only values of x_i such that there exists least one PE $iproc$ where $PE[iproc].mem[x_i] \neq 0$. In practice, unsigned integer value close to zero are used much more frequently than larger values, thus the probability of a potentially non-zero bit value in position i dramatically decreases as i increases. This suggests that general-purpose methods for encoding sparse data are not needed; it is typically sufficient to truncate any leading bit positions that are zero and keep a count of the number of bit positions retained.

Signed integers, represented as 2's-complement values, present a significantly different encoding problem. Leading zero bits still have no effect on the value because, in effect, a positive value represented in 2's-complement uses the exact same encoding as that value would have as an unsigned quantity. However, negative values treat leading bits in the inverted sense: leading one bits have no effect on the value of a negative number. In other words, the usual gate-level description of sign extension, converting a signed integer value to a larger number of bits, involves filling the additional leading bits with copies of the originally most significant bit. Thus, to reduce the number of bits in a signed integer while maintaining the value, one repeatedly removes the most significant bit, bk_{-1}, until either $b_{k-1} \neq b_{k-2}$ or $k = 1$. However, if the value is positive, this bit-removal process will stop with one more bit in the representation than the same value would have if considered unsigned. For example, the value 3 as an 8-bit signed integer is 00000011, and as an unsigned integer it can be reduced to 11, but as a signed integer the simplest representation would be 011 because 11 would be interpreted as the value -1.

At this point it is useful to recall that a bit position does not hold just one bit in our system, but a vector of bit values spread across the SIMD PEs. Thus, the leading bits do not need to be all zero across the machine, nor all one, for precision to be reduced. Consider a 2 PE system representing the 8-bit value 00000011 (3) in PE 0 and the value 11111011 (-5) in PE 1. Across the machine, the bit-level representation could be summarized as $\{0,1\}, \{0,1\}, \{0,1\}, \{0,1\}, \{0,1\}, \{0,0\}, \{1,1\}, \{1,1\}\}$. The rule is that if the same ordered set of bit values occurring in the most significant position is repeated below it, the leading bit position may be removed. Thus, the bit-level representation here reduces to $\{0,1\}, \{0,0\}, \{1,1\}, \{1,1\}\}$. In classical SIMD terminology, the most significant bit, b_{k-1}, can be removed iff PE[$iproc$].mem[x_{k-1}] = PE[$iproc$].mem[x_{k-2}] for all PEs, which would seem to require a comparison operation within each PE followed by an ALL reduction.

The apparent complexity of this precision minimization is, however, misleading. Using the PBP model for our SIMD execution, each of the bit vectors stored across the SIMD PEs is implemented by a pbit (pattern bit) [9]. Each pbit value is identified by a pattern register number, the x_i value described above. However, these pbit values are assigned register numbers based on uniqueness: whenever a pbit value is created, is hashed to determine if that same pbit value has appeared before. If it has, the system ensures that the same register number is used to identify the result; otherwise, it allocates a new register number for the result. Thus, the comparison PE[$iproc$].mem[x_{k-1}] PE[$iproc$].mem[x_{k-2}] for ALL PEs is implementable as simply $x_{k-1} = x_{k-2}$, and the actual bit vectors are never accessed. Once completing that minimization, if the most significant remaining bit of a signed integer references the register that holds all zeros, then all values are positive, and the value can be treated as unsigned with that leading zero bit removed.

96   H. Dietz

As a result, the data structure used to represent a variable-precision integer, henceforth called a pint (pattern integer), is:

```
bool has_sign; // has a sign bit?
uint8_t prec; // current number of active pbits
pbit bit[PINTBITS]; // pbit register numbers
```

2.2 Manipulation of Integer Values

It would be valid to consider a pint to have a "normal form" that is minimized as described above. However, given that two different pint values may have different precisions, and perhaps even different signedness, there are a few library-internal routines needed to manipulate these properties so word-like operations can deal with arguments consistently.

Minimize. The **pint Minimize() const;** operation simply returns the normal-form version of a pint value. This is done at the end of every library operation that might otherwise result in an unnormalized result.

Extend. The **pint Extend(const int p) const;** operation returns the "denormalized" version of a pint value with exactly **p** pbit precision. This may be used to add extra leading bits or to truncate a value by clipping leading pbits. Note that, in an implementation using lazy evaluation, clipping leading pbits could cause the entire computations that would have created those pbits to be removed.

Promote. The **pint Promote(const pint& b) const;** operation returns the unnormalized version of a pint value promoted to the smallest precision and signedness that can represent both its value and the value **b**. For example, this operation is a necessary precursor to bitwise operations like AND, OR, and XOR.

2.3 Wordless Floating Point

The IEEE standard for floating-point arithmetic defines the internal structure of a word to be used to represent the approximate value of a real number, as well as various accuracy and other constraints on operations.

IEEE 754 [15] specifies that a single-precision floating-point value, a float, is packed into a 32-bit word. The most significant bit is the sign of the fraction, 0 for zero or positive 1 for negative. The 23 least-significant bits are the magnitude of the fractional part of the value, with an implicit 24th bit which is treated as a leading one for normalized value. The remaining eight bits are the exponent, which is a power-of-two multiplier for the fractional part. The exponent is encoded as a 2's-complement integer, but a bias of 12 is added so that the minimum value presents as 0 rather than -128.

Many details are specified by the IEEE standard. For example, zero is not representable as a normalized number because normalization specifies that the (not stored most significant bit of the fractional part is a 1. Values with the minimum allowed exponent are treated specially – as *denormals*, in which the implicit most significant bit of the fraction is essentially ignored, and normalization is not performed. For example, this allows representing zero as a fractional part that is 0 and an exponent that is the minimum value; conveniently making float zero have the same bit-level representation as the 32-bit integer value zero. Similarly, the fact that the exponent bits reside above the fraction bits means that floating-point comparisons for less than and greater than can use the same logic employed for integer comparisons to compare the absolute values of floats. The IEEE standard also provides for direct representation of $\pm$ infinity and NaN (not-a-number) values, and further specifies rounding modes and accuracy requirements for operations.

The wordless floating-point representation for a pfloat is based loosely on the IEEE specification but differs in many important ways. A single pfloat value represents not just one float value, but one float value per virtual SIMD processing element. The component fields within a pfloat are functionally much like the sign, exponent, and mantissa components of an IEEE float but, as is described below, they are represented and manipulated differently. Similarly, the normal form for a pfloat, and the normalization algorithm, is quite different from that of an IEEE float.

Sign. The pfloat representation of the value sign uses a pint that contains a single pbit. That pbit normally has the exact same meaning as the sign bit in the IEEE standard format: 1 is negative and 0 is non-negative (positive or zero). However, because a pfloat value of 0 is always given a 0 sign bit, the encoding that would represent -0 is instead available for other use, such as representation of NaN.

Exponent. The exponent is stored as a pint specifying a power-of-two multiplier. This differs from the standard in that IEEE 754 uses the minimum possible exponent value to indicate that the value is a denormal, and further requires adding a bias factor to make the minimum exponent value be stored as a field full of 0s.

There would be no significant benefit in adding a bias to the pfloat exponent pint value. There also is no well-defined minimum possible exponent value for a pfloat because the int exponent field has runtime-variable precision; thus, picking a bias value would artificially impose a minimum bound on the exponent value. It is important to remember that a single pfloat can represent an exponential number of float values, so the overhead of maintaining a scalar variable holding the current precision of the exponent is negligible comparison to the amount of float data being represented.

There are two motivations for denormals in the IEEE standard. The first is the need be able to represent the value zero, which is impossible to represent as a normal value – and a pfloat cannot circumvent this issue. The second motivation is to allow values between the smallest representable normal number and zero. Without denormals, the difference between the second smallest and smallest normal values would be much less than the difference between the smallest normal value and zero. However, non-zero normal values could be represented as normals if the exponent field had a larger range. The variable precision of the pint exponent field of a pfloat means that expanding the exponent range naturally occurs as needed – and the number of pbits used to represent the exponent is not artificially increased to cover representation of a fixed minimum value. Thus, the only ordinary pfloat value that is denormal is zero.

Mantissa. In the IEEE standard, the exponent value distinguishes between normal and denormal values, and the mantissa of a normal number has an implicit leading 1 bit, whereas a denormal has an implicit leading 0. In effect, the implicit leading bit is the value of (exponent ! = *minimum*), a test that is nonsensical for a pfloat because there is no fixed *minimum* exponent value. Instead, the single denormal value, zero, is represented by the mantissa pint having the value 0. This implies that the exponent field is meaningless when the mantissa is 0. The smallest pint representation occurs for the values 0, 1, or -1 all of which are representable using a single pbit. Giving the value zero an exponent of 0 seems the obvious choice. We further suggest that a mantissa of zero with an exponent of 1 represents infinity. Thus, NaN, zero, infinity, and negative infinity – all values distinguished by having the mantissa field be zero – are not subject to normalization. These pfloat values not subject to normalization are given in Table 1; each is represented using only 3 pbits because the normal pint handling removes leading 0 pbits.

Table 1. The pfloat value representations not subject to normalization.

Decimal Value	Sign	Exponent	Mantissa (8 bit precision)
0.0	0	0	0
NaN	1	0	0
Infinity	0	1	0
Negative Infinity	1	1	0

Normalization. A normal form for floating-point numbers provides a unique representation for each possible value. Without normalization, each number would have many different representations thus wasting multiple bit patterns on encoding a single value, just as the decimal float value 42.0×10^0 is equivalent to 4.2×10^1 and also 420.0×10^{-1}. For an IEEE float, the normal form places the most-significant non-zero bit in the mantissa one bit to the left of the mantissa bits stored. That bit value does not need physical storage because 1 is the only non-zero bit value. However, for a pfloat, the mantissa can be variable size, so which pbit position would correspond to the most-significant bit position? There are two choices; one obvious, the other not.

The obvious normal form is derived by modeling the normal form used by traditional float values. Rather than letting the mantissa of a pfloat vary in size completely dynamically, suppose that a particular mantissa precision is selected. Normalization can be performed by simply adjusting the pfloat so that the most significant bit of the mantissa is 1 for all the values within that pfloat. Table 2 gives some examples of the number of pbits used to encode various decimal values.

This type of floating-point normalization was often implemented by an expensive process in bitwise SIMD computers: one-bit-position-at-a-time disabling of processor

Table 2. Some pfloat value representations, MSB normalized.

Decimal Value	Sign	Exponent	Mantissa (8 bit precision)
1.0	0	0	10000000
2.0	0	1	10000000
5.0	0	10	10100000
0.5	0	−1	10000000
−42.0	1	101	10101000

with values already in normal form, shifting the selected mantissas one bit position, and decrementing their exponents. However, bitwise normalization can be performed in log(precision) steps. For example, with 8-bit mantissa precision, the checks would be for top 4 bits all 0, then top 2 bits, and finally top bit, completing in just three steps rather than eight. The problem with this conventional MSB normalization is that the pint mantissa fields naturally trim leading zeros, but not trailing zeros. Thus, the number of apparently active bits can be inflated.

The less obvious option would be to normalize values not based on the position of their most significant 1 bit but based on the position of their least significant 1 bit. Normalizing so that the least-significant 1 bit is in the least significant bit position is stripping trailing 0 bits and combining that with the stripping of leading 0 bits inherently done by pint processing should result in the shortest possible mantissas. This can be seen in Table 3, which shows that the same values given in Table 2 with MSB normalization become significantly shorter with LSB normalization. However, LSB normalization increases overhead in operations like addition and tends to increase entropy, so the current system defaults to MSB normalization.

Table 3. Some pfloat value representations, LSB normalized.

Decimal Value	Sign	Exponent	Mantissa (8 bit maximum precision)
1.0	0	0	1
2.0	0	1	1
1.0	0	0	1011
.5	0	−1	1
42.0	1	1	10101

Runtime Optimizations

e key concept being leveraged in the current work is that the new Parallel Bit Pattern P) computing model, which was inspired by quantum computing, also can be treated as an extremely efficient model for massively parallel bit-serial SIMD computation. Instead of viewing the PBP implementation of an E-way entangled superposition as a quantum-like phenomenon, the current work treats it as 2^E virtual bit-serial SIMD processing elements (PEs): i.e., *nproc* is 2^E and *iproc* values range from 0 to 2^E-1. This enables two classes of work-reducing optimizations: compiler-like optimizations performed at the bit level at runtime and optimizations based on recognizing value patterns across groups of PEs.

3.1 Compiler-Like Optimization at Runtime

Compiler optimizations such as constant folding, recognition of algebraic simplifications, and common subexpression elimination are normally applied to word-level expressions at compile time. However, by applying these transformations to symbolic descriptions of massively parallel bit-level operations, the number of actual massively parallel bit-level operations that must be performed can be dramatically reduced.

In a traditional bit-serial SIMD computer, each gate-level operation would cause each processing element to produce a single-bit result in its own local memory or register file, and fixed gate-level sequences would be used to implement each word-level operation. For example, adding 4 to a 32-bit variable in each PE would typically invoke the standard 32-bit ripple-carry add sequence rather than taking advantage of the fact that adding 4 can be accomplished by a ripple-carry 30-bit increment sequence applied to the top 30 bits of the variable. In contrast, if the current value of that potentially 32-bit variable in each PE fit in just 12 bits, the methods used here would recognize both that fact and the fact that adding 4 is equivalent to incrementing starting at bit position 2. Thus, the gate-level operation sequence used would be equivalent to a 10-bit ripple-carry incrementer – a much cheaper sequence in both execution time and total energy expended for the computation.

The recognition of such redundancies lies primarily in the concept of a pbit. A pbit logically represents a vector of *nproc* bits but is actually a descriptor with the interesting property that any two equivalent bit vectors will always have the same descriptor value. This allows the system to dramatically reduce storage space by keeping only a single copy of each unique bit pattern, but also implies that comparing for equality is accomplished by simply comparing descriptors, and never requires examining the actual bits. As each pfloat or pint operation is lowered to pbit operations, the lowering is done by calling a function that not only is parameterized by the current precisions of the operands, but also applies standard compiler optimizations rather than simply generating a fixed sequence of operations.

Constant Folding. At the bit level, there are only two constants: 0 and 1. In the current PBP implementation, these are represented by pbit descriptors with the corresponding values, 0 for a vector of all 0s and 1 for a vector of all 1s. When any gate-level operation on a pbit value is requested, the descriptors are first checked, and where all operands are constants the gate result is computed by performing the operation on the descriptor. For example, OR of descriptor 0 and descriptor 1 produces a result which is simply OR 1 $\Rightarrow$ descriptor 1, without accessing any actual bit vector.

Algebraic Simplifications. Because the mapping between bit vector values and descriptors is 1:1 and *onto*, a wide range of algebraic optimizations can be applied without accessing any actual bit vector. For example, pbit 601 AND pbit 601 yields pbit 601. Similarly, pbit 601 AND pbit 1 yields pbit 601 and pbit 601 AND pbit 0 yields pbit 0.

Common Subexpression Elimination. The key bookkeeping problem in recognizing common subexpressions is mapping to a "single assignment" form, but the pbit descriptors already have that property. Thus, if pbit 42 XOR pbit 601 was found to produce pbit 22, pbit 42 XOR pbit 601 will always produce pbit 22, and the operation does not need to be repeated.

Applying these symbolic compiler optimizations at runtime implies significant overhead, but that overhead is independent of the value of *nproc*. Thus, as *nproc* is increased, the overhead quickly becomes negligible.

3.2 Optimizations Using Pattern Recognition Across PEs

Although classical SIMD models have the concept of values being spread across PEs, most do not provide a means for describing patterns across PEs. In contrast, using the new PBP model to implement bit-serial SIMD computations provides several layers of mechanisms for describing value patterns across PEs, and these can be used to dramatically increase the number of gate-level operations that can be recognized as redundant and avoided.

If the number of SIMD PEs is virtualized so that it may be different from the number of physical PEs, larger numbers of virtual PEs are classically simulated by multiple passes and excess physical PEs are disabled. For example, if there are 1024 physical PEs and 10000 virtual PEs are requested, each gate-level operation would be repeated 10 times and, in the last round, the last 240 physical PEs would be disabled. The hierarchical SIMD-like execution model employed by GPUs improves upon the classical virtualized SIMD model by fragmenting the PEs into SIMT warps [16], typically of 32 PEs each, which allows skipping execution of an entire warp if all the virtual PEs it contains are disabled. Continuing the example, those last 240 virtual PEs occupy the last 7.5 warps; thus, a GPU would skip the last 7 warps entirely and apply enable masking only for the half-enabled warp. The PBP model also fragments each 2^E-bit entangled superposition into smaller chunks but allows use of far more sophisticated logic to determine when chunk computations can be skipped.

In the PBP model, the layer below pbit is RE, a layer in which each vector of bits represented by a regular expression that would generate the bit vector. The regular expressions are not patterns of bits per se, but patterns of "chunks" that roughly correspond to the concept of warps in GPUs. Like pbits, both REs and chunks implement 1:1 and *onto* mappings between bit vectors and descriptors, and only a single copy of each unique chunk bit vector is stored. Thus, the same compiler optimizations that were discussed for pbit operations also can be applied for chunks. For example, in the current PBP system, there is an AC layer between REs and chunks that performs applicative caching – implementing common subexpression elimination on chunks.

To appreciate the value of this chunk handling, it is useful to consider a simple example. For example, suppose that the chunk size is (the ridiculously tiny) 8 bits and *nproc* is 32. As bit vectors with the PE0 bit in the rightmost position, in order of LSB to MSB, the value of *iproc* would look like this:

```
10101010 10101010 10101010 10101010
11001100 11001100 11001100 11001100
11110000 11110000 11110000 11110000
11111111 00000000 11111111 00000000
11111111 11111111 00000000 00000000
```

However, the actual chunk pattern is:

```
chunk(2) chunk(2) chunk(2) chunk(2)
chunk(3) chunk(3) chunk(3) chunk(3)
chunk(4) chunk(4) chunk(4) chunk(4)
chunk(1) chunk(0) chunk(1) chunk(0)
chunk(1) chunk(1) chunk(0) chunk(0)
```

Thus, the total storage used for the above vectors is just 5 chunks, or $5 \times 8 = 40$ bits, not $5 \times 32 = 160$ bits. Low entropy of values across SIMD PEs is common. Consider adding 1 to each value (incrementing each 5-bit value to produce a 6-bit result). The chunk pattern for 1 is:

```
chunk(1) chunk(1) chunk(1) chunk(1)
```

The LSB of the result should be four copies of chunk(1)^chunk(2), which we will call chunk(5), and the computation is performed once to produce the new bit vector chunk. The next three chunk operations would all be hits in the applicative cache. However, the RE layer does not necessarily need to even check the AC for this factoring, because it could represent the LSB as $chunk(2)^4$ and 1 as $chunk(1)^4$, thus directly recognizing that there are three copies of the result from the first chunk operation.

In summary, whereas GPUs can improve performance over classical SIMD by skipping disabled warps, using the PBP model for bit-serial SIMD execution allows much more generalized skipping of chunk computations – as well as skipping of "disabled" chunks. It also has the significant benefit of potentially dramatically reducing storage space. However, the storage space reduction is compromised in the current system by the fact that once a unique chunk value has been created, the current system never deallocates it. A garbage collection scheme would be needed to prevent continued growth of memory use over long sequences of computations.

4   Implementation and Performance

The current PBP library for bit-serial SIMD computation is implemented as 3,644 lines of portable C++ source code. It supports pfloat and pint classes with a wide varie of primitive operations and currently runs on a single processor core using bitwise parallelism within either 32-bit or 64-bit words. This is much narrower than the desired hardware parallelism width, and also makes power savings unmeasurable, but hardware directly implementing PBP execution [9] is not yet available. The chunk size for the library may be any power of 2 no smaller than the host word size, and the maximum supported *nproc* is 4294967296.

For the pint class, operations include: conversion to/from C++ int, reading from and writing to a variable in a selected PE; scatter and gather; initialization to a range of values; logical NOT, AND, OR, and XOR; bitwise NOT, AND, OR, and XOR; comparisons for EQ, NE, GT, LT, GE, and LE; shift right and left; negation, absolute value, addition, subtraction, multiplication, division, and remainder; SIMD ANY and ALL reductions; reductions and scans (parallel prefix) for AND, OR, XOR, addition, multiplication, minimum, and maximum; and sort to increasing or decreasing order. Where appropriate, the C++ operators have been overloaded so that pint behaves like a built-in type.

The pfloat class implements most of the same operations implemented for pint, but not bitwise logic nor remainder. In addition, it implements reciprocal, exponentiation, logarithm, square root, sine, cosine, tangent, and arctangent. The maximum settable precision for a mantissa is 32 bits, although some operations work correctly only for 16 or fewer mantissa bits. The exponent is dynamically sized and can be as large as 32 bits. C++ operators also have been overloaded for pfloat.

We have not yet run any significant applications at this writing but have benchmarked several simple programs and the pint library validation suite. Given that the PBP code only uses a hardware parallelism width of 32 or 64, one would expect that the book-keeping overhead would make SIMD code run slower than optimized sequential code on the same processor. However, even for simple programs executed with modest *nproc* values, the PBP run times were within a factor of 2–3 × faster or slower than the opti-mized sequential code. For the pint library validation suite, one would expect poorer performance than from most application codes due to the higher entropy associated with testing all the different library routines. To better understand the performance, the PBP library was augmented with various performance counters and the validation suite was run ten times, each with freshly created random data, for each of 8 sets of parameters.

The measured performance of the validation suite is summarized in Table 4. The first column gives the number of virtual PEs (*nproc*) used and the second column specifies how many bits were in each chunk, which is giving the equivalent of the warp size in GPU terminology. The validation suite creates random data scaled in proportion to the number of bits in a chunk, thus entropy of the test data increases with larger chunk sizes, whereas increasing *nproc* multiplies the total amount of work to be done but has no direct effect on entropy of the test data. The two "Gates" columns respectively show the average total number of active gate operations that were needed to perform the validation suite's computations. The "Gates (Words)" column measures the number of gate actions assuming that each pint was treated as typical older bit-serial SIMD systems commonly did, using a fixed gate sequence to handle each value as if it were holding up to 32 bits; it would be noted that this is still a far lower number of gate actions than would be counted using non-bit-serial hardware because, for example, it assumes addition is done by ripple

Table 4. Active gate counts for 32-bit word operations vs. proposed PBP model.

nproc	Chunk bits	Gates (Words)	Gates (PBP)	Ratio
65536	256	12279113318	3209523	3826:1
262144	256	55522282700	3141452	17674:1
262144	512	55520002048	6563379	8459:1
1048576	256	252845228032	3135360	80643:1
1048576	1024	252876370739	13902438	18189:1
4194304	2048	1154496017203	29179904	39565:1
16777216	4096	5277432676352	61104947	86366:1
67108864	8192	24153849174425	128459571	188027:1

carry rather than by a much more complex circuit (e.g., implementing carry lookahe
as is commonly used in word-oriented arithmetic. As can be seen from the "Gates (PB
column numbers, the method proposed in this paper dramatically reduces the num
of gate actions used to perform the exact same computation. The rather surprising rat
are given in the final column, making it obvious that the savings from operating o
on active bits and performing various bit-level optimizations at runtime *can be* far m
than the 32:1 best case that one might have expected.

5 Conclusion

The current work has introduced and explored the concept of wordless integer a
floating-point computation, in which precision varies dynamically and aggressive sy
bolic bit-level optimizations are performed at runtime – all with the goal of minimiz
the total number of gate actions needed to perform each computation. The high ov
head of precision bookkeeping is managed by applying these types only to massiv
parallel data structures being operated upon in a SIMD fashion. The quantum-inspi
PBP model is shown to have the potential to be a dramatically more efficient virtuali:
SIMD execution model by combining this bit-level optimization with the ability to s
chunks of SIMD computation not only if all PEs were disabled for the chunk, but als
equivalent computations had been performed by *any* PEs before. The preliminary res
shown here suggest *4–6 orders of magnitude reduction in gate actions per computat*
is feasible.

This work is still at an early stage, largely because neither PBP hardware nor l
serial SIMD computers is readily available, but the portable C++ library implementat
will soon be released as open source. Beyond that, the highest priority is resolving
issue of how to garbage collect chunks that are no longer needed.

References

1. Cocke, J., Schwartz, J.T.: Programming Languages and Their Compilers, Preliminary Notes, New York University, Second Revised Version. Courant Institute of Mathematical Sciences (1970)

2. Dietz, H.G.: How Low Can You Go? In: Rauchwerger, L. (ed.) Languages and Compilers for Parallel Computing (LCPC) 2017, LNCS, vol. 11403, pp. 101–108. Springer, Cham (2017). https://doi.org/10.1007/978-3-030-35225-7_8

3. Klerer, M., May, J.: A user oriented programming language. Comput. J. **8**(2), 103–109 (1965). https://doi.org/10.1093/comjnl/8.2.103

4. Reddaway, S.F.: DAP - a distributed array processor. In: Proceedings of the 1st Annual Symposium on Computer Architecture, pp. 61–65. ACM Press (1973)

5. Batcher, K.E.: STARAN parallel processor system hardware. In: National Computer Conference, pp. 405–410 (1974)

6. Batcher, K.: Design of a Massively Parallel Processor. IEEE Trans. Comput. **C-29**(9), 836–840 (1980)

7. Tucker, L.W., Robertson, G.G.: Architecture and applications of the connection machine. IEEE Comput. **21**(8), 26–38 (1988)

8. Morely, R.E., Sullivan, T.J.: A massively parallel systolic array processor system. In: Proceedings of the International Conference on Systolic Arrays, pp. 217–225 (1988)

9. Dietz, H., Eberhart, P., Rule, A.: Basic operations and structure of an FPGA accelerator for parallel bit pattern computation. In: 2021 International Conference on Rebooting Computing (ICRC), pp. 129–133 (2021).https://doi.org/10.1109/ICRC53822.2021.00029

10. IEEE 1364-2001. IEEE Standard Verilog Hardware Description Language (2001). https://standards.ieee.org/ieee/1364/2052/

11. IEEE 1076-2019. IEEE Standard for VHDL Language Reference Manual (2019). https://standards.ieee.org/ieee/1076/5179/

12. Granlund, T.: GNU MP 6.0 Multiple Precision Arithmetic Library. Samurai Media Limited, Hong Kong (2015)

13. BigDigits multiple-precision arithmetic source code, https://www.di-mgt.com.au/bigdigits.html, Accessed 15 August 2022

14. Macheta, J., Dąbrowska-Boruch, A., Russek, P., Wiatr, K.: ArPALib: a big number arithmetic library for hardware and software implementations. a case study for the miller-rabin primality test. In: Wong, S., Beck, A., Bertels, K., Carro, L. (eds.) Applied Reconfigurable Computing (ARC) 2017, LNCS, vol. 10216, pp. 323–330. Springer (2017). https://doi.org/10.1007/978-3-319-56258-2_28

15. IEEE 754-2019. IEEE Standard for Floating-Point Arithmetic (2019). https://standards.ieee.org/ieee/754/6210/

16. Lindholm, E., Nickolls, J., Oberman, S., Montrym, J.: NVIDIA tesla: a unified graphics and computing architecture. IEEE Micro **28**(2) (2008). https://doi.org/10.1109/MM.2008.31

Exploiting the New Power ISA™ Matrix Math Instructions Through Compiler Built-ins

José E. Moreira[1]([✉])(iD), Kit Barton[2], Peter Bergner[7], Puneeth Bhat[4], Gordon Fossum[3], Nemanja Ivanovic[2], Satish Sadasivam[4](iD), Baptiste Saleil[5], Bill Schmidt[6](iD), and Rajalakshmi Srinivasaraghavan[3]

[1] IBM Research, New York, USA
jmoreira@us.ibm.com
[2] IBM Systems, Markham, Canada
{kbarton,nemanjai}@ca.ibm.com
[3] IBM Systems, Austin, USA
Rajalakshmi.Srinivasaraghavan@ibm.com
[4] IBM Systems, Bengaluru, India
{puneebha,satsadas}@in.ibm.com
[5] Université de Montréal, Montreal, Canada
baptiste.saleil@umontreal.ca
[6] Intel Corporation, Santa Clara, USA
william.schmidt@intel.com
[7] IBM Systems, Rochester, USA
bergner@us.ibm.com

Abstract. Power ISA™ Version 3.1 has introduced a new family of matrix math assist instructions, collectively known as the Matrix-Multiply Assist (MMA) facility. The instructions in this facility implement numerical linear algebra operations on small matrices and are meant to accelerate computation-intensive kernels. We advocate the use of compiler built-ins as the preferred way of leveraging these instructions. MMA built-ins are currently available in the GNU Compiler Collection and the LLVM-based IBM Open XL compilers. The built-ins are compatible across both compiler suites. We show that programming with these built-ins leads to efficient code that fully exploits the new facility.

Keywords: Power ISA · Compiler built-ins · Numerical linear algebra

1 Introduction

Power ISA™ Version 3.1 has introduced an entirely new facility: the VS[
Matrix-Multiply Assist (MMA) instructions [2,7]. These instructions directl[
implement numerical linear algebra operations on small matrices and vecto[
and can be used to speed up the execution of important computational kerne[
such as matrix multiplication, convolution, and discrete Fourier transform.

B. Saleil and B. Schmidt—They were with IBM Systems in Canada and the Unit[
States of America, respectively, when this work was performed.

© The Author(s), under exclusive license to Springer Nature Switzerland AG 2023
C. Mendis and L. Rauchwerger (Eds.): LCPC 2022, LNCS 13829, pp. 106–122, 2023.
https://doi.org/10.1007/978-3-031-31445-2_8

Although there are ongoing activities to develop compilation techniques that will translate programs written in high-level languages to the new MMA instructions, we expect most MMA code to continue to be manually generated for the near future. To facilitate both the development and maintenance of this handwritten code, we advocate the use of compiler built-ins that encapsulate the new operations provided by the MMA facility.

Compiler built-ins are source-language functions with an interface and semantics known to the compiler. As a result, the compiler can directly emit code for those built-in functions. Compiler built-ins have been a standard feature of the GNU Compiler Collection for many years and are also available in LLVM-based compilers. Most built-ins, including those for the MMA facility, translate one-to-one to machine instructions in the target architecture.

Section 2 of this paper presents the new MMA facility architecture, including the new registers and instructions added to Power ISA 3.1. Section 3 introduces the new compiler built-ins that support programming the new facility. In particular, we discuss two ancillary built-ins that implement transfers between the traditional vector-scalar registers of the Power ISA and the new *accumulator* registers in the MMA facility. Section 4 illustrates programming the MMA facility with compiler built-ins through an example of a DGEMM (double-precision matrix multiply) kernel. We show the source code in C, with the various built-in calls, and the compiler generated object code, which makes efficient use of the new instructions. Section 5 presents an evaluation of the performance of code developed with the built-ins, including a comparison with hand-optimized assembly code. Finally, Sect. 6 presents our conclusions.

2   Instruction Set Architecture of the MMA Facility

The MMA facility is fully integrated in the Power ISA. That is, MMA instructions can appear anywhere in the instruction stream and can interleave with any other Power ISA instruction. They are executed by a dedicated functional unit, with access to both the Power ISA vector-scalar registers (VSRs) and a new set of *accumulator registers*, described below. In a superscalar, out-of-order processor, such as the IBM POWER10 processing core, execution of MMA instructions can completely overlap with the execution of other Power ISA instructions.

1   MMA Registers

The MMA facility defines a set of eight 512-bit accumulator registers. Each accumulator register can hold one of three different kinds of data:

A 4×2 matrix of 64-bit double precision floating-point elements (fp64).
A 4×4 matrix of 32-bit single precision floating-point elements (fp32).
A 4×4 matrix of 32-bit signed integer elements (int32).

Each of the eight accumulator registers (ACC[0 : 7]) is associated with a group of four vector-scalar registers from the set VSR[0 : 63], as shown in Fig. 1. The architecture requires that as long as a particular accumulator register is in use,

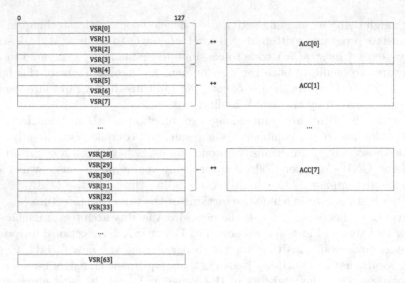

Fig. 1. The MMA facility adds eight 512-bit accumulator registers (ACC[0 : 7]) to the Power ISA register set. That set also includes 64 vector-scalar registers (VSR[0 : 63]) of 128 bits each. Each accumulator is associated with a group of four consecutive 128-bit vector-scalar registers. The VSR[32 : 63] vector-scalar registers are not associated, nor do they conflict, with any accumulator.

the associated four vector-scalar registers must not be used. Vector-scalar registers VSR[32 : 63] are not associated with any accumulator register and therefore can always be used while the MMA facility is active.

2.2   MMA Instructions

MMA instructions fall into one of three categories:

1. *Accumulator Move Instructions*: These instructions move data between the accumulator registers and their associated vector-scalar registers. (See Table 1(a).)
2. *Integer rank-k Update Instruction*: These are integer arithmetic instructions that update the elements of an accumulator with the product of input matrices. (See Table 1(b).)
3. *Floating-point rank-k Update Instructions*: These are floating-point arithmetic instructions that update the elements of an accumulator with the product of input matrices or vectors. (See Table 1(c).)

The arithmetic instructions (integer and floating-point) have both a *prefix form* which always begins with **pm**, and a *conventional form*, without the prefix. We will start our discussion with the conventional forms of the instructions and cover the prefix forms later.

Table 1. MMA instructions. Those instructions with a pm prefix belong to the new class of *prefix instructions* in Power ISA, which are 64 bits in size. The others have the traditional format (32-bit fixed size). The arithmetic instructions have an optional 2-letter suffix that indicates how the product of the input matrices/vectors should be added to the target accumulator: pp – positive product, positive accumulator, np – negative product, positive accumulator, pn – positive product, negative accumulator, nn – negative product, negative accumulator. The optional s suffix indicates the use of saturating arithmetic for the integer instructions.

(a) Accumulator Move Instructions.

Instruction	Description
xxsetaccz	Set all elements of the target accumulator to 0
xxmfacc	Move the contents of the source accumulator to the associated group of vector-scalar registers
xxmtacc	Move the contents of a group of vector-scalar registers to the associated accumulator

(b) Integer rank-k update instructions.

Instruction	Description
[pm]xvi16ger2[s][pp]	Update a 4×4 matrix of int32 elements with the product of two 4 × 2 matrices of int16 elements
[pm]xvi8ger4[pp,spp]	Update a 4×4 matrix of int32 elements with the product of two 4 × 4 matrices of int8/uint8 elements
[pm]xvi4ger8[pp]	Update a 4×4 matrix of int32 elements with the product of two 4 × 8 matrices of int4 elements

(c) Floating-point rank-k update instructions.

Instruction	Description
[pm]xvbf16ger2[pp,np,pn,nn]	Update a 4 × 4 matrix of fp32 elements with the product of two 4 × 2 matrices of bfloat16 elements
[pm]xvf16ger2[pp,np,pn,nn]	Update a 4 × 4 matrix of fp32 elements with the product of two 4 × 2 matrices of fp16 elements
[pm]xvf32ger[pp,np,pn,nn]	Update a 4 × 4 matrix of fp32 elements with the outer product of two 4-element vectors of fp32 elements
[pm]xvf64ger[pp,np,pn,nn]	Update a 4 × 2 matrix of fp64 elements with the outer product of 4/2-element vectors of fp64 elements

Accumulator Move Instructions: The three Accumulator Move Instructions can be used to initialize the elements of an accumulator to 0, to move data from vector-scalar registers into an accumulator register, or to move data from an accumulator register into vector-scalar registers. When data is moved from vector-scalar registers into an accumulator, or when the accumulator elements are initialized to zero, the accumulator is said to be *primed*. From this point on, the associated vector-scalar registers should not be used again, until the accumulator is *deprimed* by moving data from the accumulator into the associated vector-scalar registers. After a depriming event, an accumulator should not be used until primed again.

Integer Rank-k Update Instructions: These instructions have the general form

$$A \leftarrow XY^{\mathrm{T}}[+A] \tag{1}$$

where A is an accumulator register, holding a 4×4 matrix of int32 elements, and X and Y are vector-scalar registers that must not overlap the accumulator, holding matrices of either 16-, 8- or 4-bit integers. (The bracketed term $[+A]$ is optional and Y^{T} denotes the transpose of Y.) The exact shape of the input matrices depends on the type of input data, which also defines the value of k in the rank-k update operation. For 16-, 8-, and 4-bit input types, the XY^{T} matrix multiply is defined as the addition of either 2, 4, or 8 different 4×4 outer products, respectively.

Vector-scalar registers in Power ISA are always 128 bits wide. Therefore, when the input data are 16-bit integers (int16), the X and Y registers are interpreted as 4×2 matrices, so that XY^{T} produces a 4×4 matrix as a result. That product matrix can be optionally added to the current value of the accumulator or directly stored in the accumulator. Instructions that simply write the value of XY^{T} into the target accumulator automatically prime that accumulator. The accumulation form of the instructions, with the pp suffix in case of integer types, require that the target accumulator be previously primed with an initial value.

When using 16-bit integer inputs, there are two choices for the arithmetic model: the more conventional *modulo* arithmetic, where the largest representable integer is followed by the smallest representable integer, and *saturating* arithmetic model, where adding positive values to the largest representable integer or negative values to the smallest representable integer does not change the target value.

For 8-bit integer inputs, the X and Y registers are interpreted as $4 \times$ matrices. While the contents of X are a 4×4 matrix of signed 8-bit intege elements (int8), the contents of Y are a 4×4 matrix of unsigned 8-bit intege elements (uint8). This mixing of signed and unsigned 8-bit integer inputs ha been common practice since early generations of vector instructions, and is als present in modern deep learning libraries. As with the 16-bit inputs case, th product can be optionally added to the current value of the accumulator. Th same requirements, as with 16-bit integer inputs, regarding automatic primir of the target accumulator also hold.

The xvi8ger4 instructions offer the same choice of modulo *vs* saturating arit metic as the xvi16ger2 instructions. Saturating arithmetic is only available in t accumulation-form of the instruction (suffix spp), since a product of 4×4 8-bit matrices cannot overflow a 32-bit integer result.

The final family of integer rank-k update instructions consist of the xvi4ger8 instructions. In this case, the contents of X and Y are interpreted as signed 4-bit integer elements (int4). The product XY^T can be optionally added to the contents of the target accumulator (suffix pp). Only a modulo arithmetic version is provided, since the chance of overflowing a 32-bit result with the sum of products of 4-bit inputs is small.

Floating-point Rank-k Update Instructions: These instructions have the general form

$$A \leftarrow [-]XY^T[\pm A] \tag{2}$$

where A is an accumulator register, holding either a 4×2 matrix of double-precision (fp64) elements or a 4×4 matrix of single-precision (fp32) elements. X and Y are vector-scalar registers that must not overlap the accumulator, holding matrices or vectors of 16-, 32- or 64-bit floating-point values. (In one case discussed below, X is a pair of vector-scalar registers.) The product of the input matrices or vectors can be optionally negated and then added to the current contents of the target accumulator, or its negation. The optional pp, np, pn, and nn suffixes control the accumulation operation.

There are two families of rank-2 update instructions for 16-bit input elements. The xvbf16ger2 instructions treat the inputs in *brain float 16* format (bf16) [10], whereas the xvf16ger2 instructions treat the inputs in IEEE half-precision format (fp16) [1]. In both cases, X and Y are 4×2 matrices of 16-bit elements, producing a 4×4 matrix product (optionally negated) that can then be added to the (optionally negated) target accumulator. Just as with the integer rank-k update instructions, the nonaccumulation-form of the floating-point instructions automatically prime the target accumulator.

For 32-bit inputs, the xvf32ger instructions use X and Y as 4-element vectors of single-precision (fp32) values, computing a 4×4 outer product that can then be optionally negated and added to the (optionally negated) target accumulator.

The double-precision instructions (xvf64ger family) break the usual conventions for the rank-k update instructions. First, the accumulator is treated as a 4×2 matrix of double-precision elements (fp64). The X input is a 4-element vector of fp64 values (consisting of an even-odd pair of adjacent vector-scalar registers) and the Y input is a 2-element vector of fp64 values. None of the input vector-scalar registers can overlap the accumulator. The XY^T outer product is computed, producing a 4×2 result. That result is optionally negated and added to the (also optionally negated) accumulator.

3   Prefixed Instructions

One of the main innovations of Power ISA™ Version 3.1 is the introduction of *prefixed instructions*. While all Power ISA instructions pre-dating Version 3.1

consist of a single 32-bit word encoding, prefixed instructions are 64 bits long, consisting of a 32-bit prefix word followed by a 32-bit suffix word.

Each of the integer and floating-point rank-k update instructions in the MMA facility has a prefix version that extends the previously discussed functionality of the base instruction. That extended functionality consists of immediate *mask* fields that specify the exact rows of X and columns of Y^T to be used in the computation. When the MMA instruction is of rank 2 or higher ($k \geq 2$), a third *product mask* field can specify the exact outer products to use when computing the XY^T multiplication result.

The masking feature of the prefixed variants is better illustrated with an example. Consider the multiplication of two 4×2 matrices X and Y of half-precision floating-point elements (`fp16`) through the instruction

   `pmxvf16ger2pp` A, X, Y, x, y, p

where A is the accumulator, x and y are the 4-bit immediate fields specifying the masks for input matrices X and Y respectively, and p is the 2-bit immediate field specifying the product mask. Let $x = x_0x_1x_2x_3$, $y = y_0y_1y_2y_3$ and $p = p_0p_1$, where the x_i, y_j and p_k are single bit values (0 or 1). The resulting value of each element A_{ij} of accumulator A is computed by

$$A_{ij} \leftarrow \sum_{k=0,1} [(p_k(x_i X_{ik} \times y_j Y_{jk})] + A_{ij}. \tag{3}$$

In other words, the x mask enables/disables rows of X, the y mask enables/disables columns of Y^T and the p mask enables/disables the specific partial products along the inner dimension (the k from rank-k) of the matrix multiply. Computations on disabled rows and columns are not performed, and, therefore, exceptions are not generated for those computations.

The prefix variant of the rank-k update instructions can be used to compute operations on matrices of shape different than the shape directly supported by the conventional instructions. This can be useful when computing residual loop iterations after a matrix is blocked into multiples of the default size. For the `xvf32ger` and `xvf64ger` families of instructions, only the x and y masks can be specified, since the rank of those operations is always one ($k = 1$).

3   Programming the MMA Facility with Compiler built-ins

Generation of MMA facility code from high-level language constructs is an active area of research [3,4]. Currently, most code that uses those new instructions is manually generated, with explicit invocation of the new operations. While directly programming in assembly instructions is always an option for MMA exploitation, we advocate the use of compiler built-ins as a preferred alternative.

Built-ins are functions with pre-defined semantics, known to the compiler. The compiler can directly emit code for these built-in functions, and quite often they translate one-to-one to native machine instructions. They represent a compromise in abstraction. The programmer has detailed control of the operations performed by the machine while implementation of the built-ins in the compiler can choose to include additional semantics about the instructions. This additional information can then be used throughout the compilation to enable optimizations. Furthermore, low-level optimizations such as instruction scheduling and register allocation are left to the compiler.

The open source GNU Compiler Collection (GCC), starting with version 10.2, and the new generation of IBM Open XL compilers [8,9] have already been augmented with built-ins for the MMA facility. This is in addition to the various built-ins that were already implemented, including architecture agnostic and Power ISA-specific built-ins. This provides performance and functional portability across the different compilers. For this reason, and the simplicity compared with direct assembly programming, we believe programming with built-ins is the preferred approach for broader exploitation of the MMA facility.

MMA built-ins make use of three data types to specify data manipulated by those built-ins:

__vector unsigned char – a 16-byte vector, used for most rank-k update operations;

__vector_pair – a 32-byte vector, used for the fp64 rank-1 update operations;

__vector_quad – a 64-byte accumulator.

The new MMA built-ins are summarized in Table 2. Most built-ins correspond one-to-one to machine instructions, as shown in the table. Two of the built-ins provide an ancillary role to the compiler, by constructing accumulators from vectors and extracting vectors from accumulators.

The __builtin_mma_build_acc performs a *gather* operation, collecting four 16-byte vectors x, y, z, and t into an accumulator A. At first glance, this built-in may seem identical to the xxmtacc instruction but that instruction and the corresponding __builtin_mma_xxmtacc built-in) only transfers data between an accumulator and its corresponding vector-scalar registers, whereas the __builtin_mma_build_acc built-in can initialize an accumulator from any set of four vectors.

Similarly, the __builtin_mma_disassemble_acc built-in performs a *scatter* operation, extracting the contents of an accumulator into an array of vectors that can then be used individually in the code. This is different than the transfer accomplished by the xxmfacc instruction (and respective __builtin_mma_xxmfacc built-in). We give an illustration of using the __builtin_mma_disassemble_acc built-in in Fig. 3.

When programming with built-ins, there are some general guidelines to follow in order to help the compiler generate good quality code. First, instead of explicitly using the __builtin_mma_xxmfacc and __builtin_mma_xxmtacc built-ins, it is better to provide the compiler with the list of vectors for initializing the accumulator, using the __builtin_mma_build_acc built-in. Correspondingly, is better to have the compiler decompose an accumulator into a group of vectors, using the __builtin_mma_disassemble_acc built-in. Second, although

Table 2. MMA built-ins. Each MMA instruction has a corresponding built-in function with pre-defined semantics known to the compiler. By programming with built-ins, the programmer can specify the exact operations to be performed by the hardware, while leaving register allocation and instruction scheduling to the compiler. In the table below, A represents an accumulator (and $\&A$ its address), while x, y, z and t are vectors. Q is a vector pair, used to hold a 4-element vector of fp64 values. Finally, u2, u4 and u8 are 2-, 4- and 8-bit unsigned integer literals used to define the masks in the prefixed form of the instructions.

Instruction	built-in
	$\_\_$builtin$\_$mma$\_$build$\_$acc($\&A$,x,y,z,t)
	$\_\_$builtin$\_$mma$\_$disassemble$\_$acc($\&x$,$\&A$)
xxsetaccz	$\_\_$builtin$\_$mma$\_$xxsetaccz($\&A$)
xxmfacc	$\_\_$builtin$\_$mma$\_$xxmfacc($\&A$)
xxmtacc	$\_\_$builtin$\_$mma$\_$xxmtacc($\&A$)
xvi16ger2[s][pp]	$\_\_$builtin$\_$mma$\_$xvi16ger2[s][pp]($\&A$,x,y)
pmxvi16ger2[s][pp]	$\_\_$builtin$\_$mma$\_$pmxvi16ger2[s][pp]($\&A$,x,y,u4,u4,u2)
xvi8ger4[pp,spp]	$\_\_$builtin$\_$mma$\_$xvi8ger4[pp,spp]($\&A$,x,y)
pmxvi8ger4[pp,spp]	$\_\_$builtin$\_$mma$\_$pmxvi8ger4[pp,spp]($\&A$,x,y,u4,u4,u4)
xvi4ger8[pp]	$\_\_$builtin$\_$mma$\_$xvi4ger8[pp]($\&A$,x,y)
pmxvi4ger8[pp]	$\_\_$builtin$\_$mma$\_$pmxvi4ger8[pp]($\&A$,x,y,u4,u4,u8)
xvbf16ger2[pp,np,pn,nn]	$\_\_$builtin$\_$mma$\_$xvbf16ger2[pp,np,pn,nn]($\&A$,x,y)
pmxvbf16ger2[pp,np,pn,nn]	$\_\_$builtin$\_$mma$\_$pmxvbf16ger2[pp,np,pn,nn]($\&A$,x,y,u4,u4,u2)
xvf16ger2[pp,np,pn,nn]	$\_\_$builtin$\_$mma$\_$xvf16ger2[pp,np,pn,nn]($\&A$,x,y)
pmxvf16ger2[pp,np,pn,nn]	$\_\_$builtin$\_$mma$\_$pmxvf16ger2[pp,np,pn,nn]($\&A$,x,y,u4,u4,u2)
xvf32ger[pp,np,pn,nn]	$\_\_$builtin$\_$mma$\_$xvf32ger[pp,np,pn,nn]($\&A$,x,y)
pmxvf32ger[pp,np,pn,nn]	$\_\_$builtin$\_$mma$\_$pmxvf32ger[pp,np,pn,nn]($\&A$,x,y,u4,u4)
xvf64ger[pp,np,pn,nn]	$\_\_$builtin$\_$mma$\_$xvf64ger[pp,np,pn,nn]($\&A$,Q,y)
pmxvf64ger[pp,np,pn,nn]	$\_\_$builtin$\_$mma$\_$pmxvf64ger[pp,np,pn,nn]($\&A$,Q,y,u4,u2)

it is possible to pass accumulators across function calls, the arguments will be copied through memory, which is likely to cause a performance degradation. The exception to this guideline is when one can be certain the compiler will inline the function, and therefore remove superfluous copies. (This is a common practice in C++ template libraries.) For most cases, it is advisable to limit accumulator usage to within a function and avoid having function calls while using accumulators. Third, one must be conscious of the actual number of accumulators supported by the architecture (8) and not create too many live accumulator objects in a function. Otherwise, the compiler may be forced to spill extra accumulators to and from memory, which also causes a performance degradation. Finally, and this is a rule rather than a guideline, it is important not to use an accumulator that has not been primed. Accumulators can be primed either by the $\_\_$builtin$\_$mma$\_$build$\_$acc built-in, by the $\_\_$builtin$\_$mma$\_$xxsetaccz built-in, or any of the nonaccumulating arithmetic rank-k operations.

4   Case Study - DGEMM Kernel

DGEMM is the general matrix-multiply routine from BLAS, computing

$$C \leftarrow \alpha A^{[T]} B^{[T]} + \beta C \qquad (4)$$

where A, B, C are matrices and α, β are scalars, all of type double-precision floating-point. We consider here only the innermost kernel found in the more popular high-performance numerical linear algebra libraries [5].

The inner-most kernel of DGEMM computes a register-contained $m \times n$ block of matrix C as the product of a $m \times k$ block of matrix A and a $k \times n$ block of matrix B. Typically, $k \gg m$ and $k \gg n$, to help amortize the cost of loading and storing the C block into/from registers.

For our example, we will use all eight architected accumulators to create a virtual 8×8 accumulator of double-precision elements, as shown in Fig. 2 (a). The accumulator numbers in the figure are for illustration purpose only. Since we are programming with built-ins, we cannot control the precise allocation of registers. The compiler is free to choose a particular allocation that guarantees correctness and that will not hurt performance.

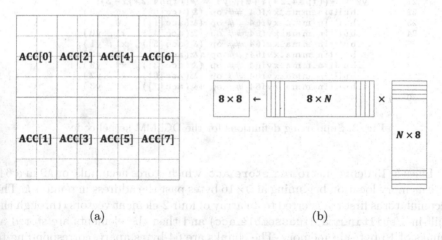

(a)   (b)

ig. 2. The DGEMM kernel uses all architected accumulators to create a virtual 8×8 :cumulator of double-precision elements (a). The accumulator is used to compute the ·oduct of an $8 \times N$ and a $N \times 8$ matrix (b).

1   The Code with Built-ins

pporting definitions to make our code more compact are shown in Fig. 3. Lines 3 redefine the data types directly supported by the compilers to names that ·· more related to our computation: A 16-byte vector data type (__vector signed char) is used to represent a two-element vector of double-precision floating-point numbers (fp64_2), whereas a pair of vectors (__vector_pair) represents a four-element vector of double-precision floating-point numbers (fp64_4) and a group of four vectors (__vector_quad) represents a 4 × 2 matrix of double precision floating-point numbers (fp64_4x2).

```
1   typedef __vector_quad           fp64_4x2;
2   typedef __vector_pair           fp64_4;
3   typedef __vector unsigned char  fp64_2;
4
5   #define mma_store_acc(AS, A, D)                          \
6   {                                                        \
7       fp64_2      a[4];                                    \
8       __builtin_mma_disassemble_acc(a,&(AS));             \
9       *((fp64_2*)A+D+ 0) = a[0];                          \
10      *((fp64_2*)A+D+ 4) = a[1];                          \
11      *((fp64_2*)A+D+ 8) = a[2];                          \
12      *((fp64_2*)A+D+12) = a[3];                          \
13  }
14
15  #define mma_xvf64_8x8(acc, op, X, Y)                     \
16  {                                                        \
17      fp64_4      x0, x1;                                 \
18      fp64_2      y0, y1, y2, y3;                         \
19      x0 = *((fp64_4*)X+0); x1 = *((fp64_4*)X+1);         \
20      y0 = *((fp64_2*)Y+0); y1 = *((fp64_2*)Y+1);         \
21      y2 = *((fp64_2*)Y+2); y3 = *((fp64_2*)Y+3);         \
22      __builtin_mma_xvf64 ## op (&(acc[0]), x0, y0);      \
23      __builtin_mma_xvf64 ## op (&(acc[1]), x0, y1);      \
24      __builtin_mma_xvf64 ## op (&(acc[4]), x1, y0);      \
25      __builtin_mma_xvf64 ## op (&(acc[5]), x1, y1);      \
26      __builtin_mma_xvf64 ## op (&(acc[2]), x0, y2);      \
27      __builtin_mma_xvf64 ## op (&(acc[3]), x0, y3);      \
28      __builtin_mma_xvf64 ## op (&(acc[6]), x1, y2);      \
29      __builtin_mma_xvf64 ## op (&(acc[7]), x1, y3);      \
30  }
```

Fig. 3. Supporting definitions for the DGEMM kernel code.

Lines 5–13 define macro mma_store_acc, which stores accumulator AS in a 64-byte memory location beginning at D×16 bytes past the address in pointer A. The accumulator is first transferred to an array of four 2-element vectors (through the built-in __builtin_mma_disassemble_acc) and then the elements are stored a chunks of 16 bytes in memory. The chunks are 64 bytes apart, corresponding to the size of one row (8 elements) of the virtual 8 × 8 accumulator. (See Fig. 2(a).

Lines 15–30 of Fig. 3 define macro mma_xvf64_8x8 which computes the oute product of two 8-element vectors of double precision floating-point numbers (and Y), accumulating the result into an 8 × 8 accumulator (acc) represented ε an array of eight 4 × 2 accumulators. The exact operation (accumulating or no inverting signs or not) is specified by the op argument, which must be one ε ger, gerpp, gernp, gerpn, or gernn.

The kernel function that computes the product XY^T of two $8 \times N$ double-precision matrices X and Y is shown in Fig. 4. Line 9 tests for an empty multiply. Line 11 declares the array of 4×2 accumulators that implement the virtual 8×8 accumulator. Line 13 is the initial multiply without accumulation, which initializes the 8×8 accumulator. Lines 15-19 are the main loop, which performs the remaining $N-1$ outer products, with accumulation. Finally, lines 21-28 store the components of the 8×8 accumulator into the result matrix A, as 8 rows of 8 elements each.

```
1   void  dgemm_kernel_8xNx8
2   (
3       double                  *A,
4       const  double           *X,
5       const  double           *Y,
6       const  uint64_t         n
7   )
8   {
9       if (n == 0) return;
10
11      fp64_4x2      acc[8];
12
13      mma_xvf64_8x8(acc, ger, X, Y);
14
15      for (uint64_t i=1; i<n; i++)
16      {
17          X += 8; Y += 8;
18          mma_xvf64_8x8(acc, gerpp, X, Y);
19      }
20
21      mma_store_acc(acc[0], A, 0);
22      mma_store_acc(acc[1], A, 1);
23      mma_store_acc(acc[2], A, 2);
24      mma_store_acc(acc[3], A, 3);
25      mma_store_acc(acc[4], A,16);
26      mma_store_acc(acc[5], A,17);
27      mma_store_acc(acc[6], A,18);
28      mma_store_acc(acc[7], A,19);
29  }
```

Fig. 4. DGEMM $8 \times N \times 8$ kernel code.

.2   The Generated Machine Code

'e compile the source code of Fig. 4 using g++ version 11.2.1 in the IBM Advance ɔolchain version 15.0-2 [6], with the compiler flags

```
-mcpu=power10 -O3
```

ɹich explicitly enable MMA support and higher levels of optimization.

The management of the new accumulator registers presented significant chal-ɪges to their enablement in compilers. In particular, the need to transfer data and from accumulators, and their overlap with existing vector-scalar registers, ce the compiler to insert various register spill and copy operations in the inter-diate representation of the code. Those are successfully removed with higher levels of optimization, which therefore are crucial to get good quality code from built-ins.

Figure 5 shows the object code generated for source lines 9–13 in Fig. 4. The various sftd machine instructions (spread out through lines 6–31 of Fig. 5) save the contents of the non-volatile registers that will be modified by the DGEMM kernel. These values are restored at function exit, as discussed below. The 4-element vector variables x0 and x1 in line 17 of Fig. 3 are assigned register pairs VSR[0 : 1] and VSR[32 : 33], respectively, and loaded through 32-byte load instructions in lines 1-2 of Fig. 5. Correspondingly, the 2-element vector variables y0, y1, y2 and y3 in line 18 of Fig. 3 are loaded through 16-byte load instructions in lines 4–5 and 8–9 of Fig. 5. The 8 × 8 initializing outer product in line 13 of Fig. 4 is implemented by 8 xvf64ger instructions, in lines 16, 17, 20, 21, 24, 27, 32, and 33 of Fig. 5.

1	10000dc0:	00	00	04	18	lxvp	vs0,0(r4)
2	10000dc4:	20	00	24	18	lxvp	vs32,32(r4)
3	10000dc8:	01	00	26	28	cmpldi	r6,1
4	10000dcc:	01	00	45	f5	lxv	vs10,0(r5)
5	10000dd0:	11	00	65	f5	lxv	vs11,16(r5)
6	10000dd4:	70	ff	c1	d9	stfd	f14,−144(r1)
7	10000dd8:	78	ff	e1	d9	stfd	f15,−136(r1)
8	10000ddc:	21	00	65	f4	lxv	vs3,32(r5)
9	10000de0:	39	00	a5	f5	lxv	vs45,48(r5)
10	10000de4:	80	ff	01	da	stfd	f16,−128(r1)
11	10000de8:	88	ff	21	da	stfd	f17,−120(r1)
12	10000dec:	90	ff	41	da	stfd	f18,−112(r1)
13	10000df0:	98	ff	61	da	stfd	f19,−104(r1)
14	10000df4:	a0	ff	81	da	stfd	f20,−96(r1)
15	10000df8:	a8	ff	a1	da	stfd	f21,−88(r1)
16	10000dfc:	d8	51	00	ee	xvf64ger	a4,vs0,vs10
17	10000e00:	dc	51	80	ed	xvf64ger	a3,vs32,vs10
18	10000e04:	b0	ff	c1	da	stfd	f22,−80(r1)
19	10000e08:	b8	ff	e1	da	stfd	f23,−72(r1)
20	10000e0c:	dc	59	80	ec	xvf64ger	a1,vs32,vs11
21	10000e10:	d8	59	80	ee	xvf64ger	a5,vs0,vs11
22	10000e14:	c0	ff	01	db	stfd	f24,−64(r1)
23	10000e18:	c8	ff	21	db	stfd	f25,−56(r1)
24	10000e1c:	dc	19	00	ed	xvf64ger	a2,vs32,vs3
25	10000e20:	d0	ff	41	db	stfd	f26,−48(r1)
26	10000e24:	d8	ff	61	db	stfd	f27,−40(r1)
27	10000e28:	d8	19	00	ef	xvf64ger	a6,vs0,vs3
28	10000e2c:	e0	ff	81	db	stfd	f28,−32(r1)
29	10000e30:	e8	ff	a1	db	stfd	f29,−24(r1)
30	10000e34:	f0	ff	c1	db	stfd	f30,−16(r1)
31	10000e38:	f8	ff	e1	db	stfd	f31,−8(r1)
32	10000e3c:	da	69	80	ef	xvf64ger	a7,vs0,vs45
33	10000e40:	de	69	00	ec	xvf64ger	a0,vs32,vs45
34	10000e44:	50	00	81	40	ble	10000e94
35	10000e48:	ff	ff	26	39	addi	r9,r6,−1
36	10000e4c:	a6	03	29	7d	mtctr	r9

Fig. 5. Object code for the initial part of the DGEMM kernel, including saving nonvolatile registers and initialization of the accumulator through an outer product the first columns of X and Y.

Object code for the loop in lines 15–19 of Fig. 4 are shown in Fig. 6. Each column of X is loaded through two 32-byte load instructions (lines 1–2) and each row of Y^T is loaded through four 16-byte load instructions (lines 5–8). The accumulating outer product of the two 8-element vectors is implemented by 8 xvf64gerpp instructions (lines 9–16). Lines 3 and 4 advance the pointers for Y and X, respectively. Line 17 closes the loop.

```
1     10000e50:    40 00 a4 19    lxvp       vs44,64(r4)
2     10000e54:    60 00 24 18    lxvp       vs32,96(r4)
3     10000e58:    40 00 a5 38    addi       r5,r5,64
4     10000e5c:    40 00 84 38    addi       r4,r4,64
5     10000e60:    09 00 05 f5    lxv        vs40,0(r5)
6     10000e64:    19 00 25 f5    lxv        vs41,16(r5)
7     10000e68:    29 00 45 f5    lxv        vs42,32(r5)
8     10000e6c:    39 00 65 f5    lxv        vs43,48(r5)
9     10000e70:    d6 41 0c ee    xvf64gerpp a4,vs44,vs40
10    10000e74:    d6 41 80 ed    xvf64gerpp a3,vs32,vs40
11    10000e78:    d6 49 8c ee    xvf64gerpp a5,vs44,vs41
12    10000e7c:    d6 49 80 ec    xvf64gerpp a1,vs32,vs41
13    10000e80:    d6 51 0c ef    xvf64gerpp a6,vs44,vs42
14    10000e84:    d6 51 00 ed    xvf64gerpp a2,vs32,vs42
15    10000e88:    d6 59 8c ef    xvf64gerpp a7,vs44,vs43
16    10000e8c:    d6 59 00 ec    xvf64gerpp a0,vs32,vs43
17    10000e90:    c0 ff 00 42    bdnz       10000e50
```

Fig. 6. Object code for the computation loop of the DGEMM kernel. The accumulator is updated by a sequence of 8 × 8 outer products of the columns of X and Y.

Object code for the final part of the DGEMM kernel (lines 21–28 of Fig. 4) are shown in Fig. 7. The values of the accumulators are first transferred to the corresponding vector-scalar registers (lines 1–8) and then stored to memory (lines)–40). Finally, the nonvolatile registers are restored (lines 41–58), and the function returns (line 59).

5   Evaluation

We measure the performance of C code with the built-ins discussed in this paper against a hand-optimized version. The operation we choose is a DGEMM computation of the form $C = C - AB$, where A, B, and C are $N \times 512$, $512 \times N$, and $N \times N$ matrices, respectively. We vary N from 512 to 16384, in increments ' 512.

The hand-optimized version was developed for a LINPACK benchmark. The rnel is written in assembly and optimized for specific matrix sizes. The C code from the POWER10 release of OpenBLAS. It is written entirely in C, with lls to the built-ins discussed in this paper and using various optimizations such tiling and loop unrolling. The DGEMM routine in OpenBLAS is fully generic, pporting all variations of DGEMM required by BLAS. No assembly code is d in this component of OpenBLAS for POWER10.

1	10000e94:	62 01 00 7e	xxmfacc	a4
2	10000e98:	62 01 80 7e	xxmfacc	a5
3	10000e9c:	62 01 00 7f	xxmfacc	a6
4	10000ea0:	62 01 80 7f	xxmfacc	a7
5	10000ea4:	62 01 80 7d	xxmfacc	a3
6	10000ea8:	62 01 80 7c	xxmfacc	a1
7	10000eac:	62 01 00 7d	xxmfacc	a2
8	10000eb0:	62 01 00 7c	xxmfacc	a0
9	10000eb4:	05 00 63 f6	stxv	vs19,0(r3)
10	10000eb8:	45 00 43 f6	stxv	vs18,64(r3)
11	10000ebc:	85 00 23 f6	stxv	vs17,128(r3)
12	10000ec0:	c5 00 03 f6	stxv	vs16,192(r3)
13	10000ec4:	15 00 e3 f6	stxv	vs23,16(r3)
14	10000ec8:	55 00 c3 f6	stxv	vs22,80(r3)
15	10000ecc:	95 00 a3 f6	stxv	vs21,144(r3)
16	10000ed0:	d5 00 83 f6	stxv	vs20,208(r3)
17	10000ed4:	25 00 63 f7	stxv	vs27,32(r3)
18	10000ed8:	65 00 43 f7	stxv	vs26,96(r3)
19	10000edc:	a5 00 23 f7	stxv	vs25,160(r3)
20	10000ee0:	e5 00 03 f7	stxv	vs24,224(r3)
21	10000ee4:	35 00 e3 f7	stxv	vs31,48(r3)
22	10000ee8:	75 00 c3 f7	stxv	vs30,112(r3)
23	10000eec:	b5 00 a3 f7	stxv	vs29,176(r3)
24	10000ef0:	f5 00 83 f7	stxv	vs28,240(r3)
25	10000ef4:	05 01 e3 f5	stxv	vs15,256(r3)
26	10000ef8:	45 01 c3 f5	stxv	vs14,320(r3)
27	10000efc:	85 01 a3 f5	stxv	vs13,384(r3)
28	10000f00:	c5 01 83 f5	stxv	vs12,448(r3)
29	10000f04:	15 01 e3 f4	stxv	vs7,272(r3)
30	10000f08:	55 01 c3 f4	stxv	vs6,336(r3)
31	10000f0c:	95 01 a3 f4	stxv	vs5,400(r3)
32	10000f10:	d5 01 83 f4	stxv	vs4,464(r3)
33	10000f14:	25 01 63 f5	stxv	vs11,288(r3)
34	10000f18:	65 01 43 f5	stxv	vs10,352(r3)
35	10000f1c:	a5 01 23 f5	stxv	vs9,416(r3)
36	10000f20:	e5 01 03 f5	stxv	vs8,480(r3)
37	10000f24:	35 01 63 f4	stxv	vs3,304(r3)
38	10000f28:	75 01 43 f4	stxv	vs2,368(r3)
39	10000f2c:	b5 01 23 f4	stxv	vs1,432(r3)
40	10000f30:	f5 01 03 f4	stxv	vs0,496(r3)
41	10000f34:	70 ff c1 c9	lfd	f14,−144(r1)
42	10000f38:	78 ff e1 c9	lfd	f15,−136(r1)
43	10000f3c:	80 ff 01 ca	lfd	f16,−128(r1)
44	10000f40:	88 ff 21 ca	lfd	f17,−120(r1)
45	10000f44:	90 ff 41 ca	lfd	f18,−112(r1)
46	10000f48:	98 ff 61 ca	lfd	f19,−104(r1)
47	10000f4c:	a0 ff 81 ca	lfd	f20,−96(r1)
48	10000f50:	a8 ff a1 ca	lfd	f21,−88(r1)
49	10000f54:	b0 ff c1 ca	lfd	f22,−80(r1)
50	10000f58:	b8 ff e1 ca	lfd	f23,−72(r1)
51	10000f5c:	c0 ff 01 cb	lfd	f24,−64(r1)
52	10000f60:	c8 ff 21 cb	lfd	f25,−56(r1)
53	10000f64:	d0 ff 41 cb	lfd	f26,−48(r1)
54	10000f68:	d8 ff 61 cb	lfd	f27,−40(r1)
55	10000f6c:	e0 ff 81 cb	lfd	f28,−32(r1)
56	10000f70:	e8 ff a1 cb	lfd	f29,−24(r1)
57	10000f74:	f0 ff c1 cb	lfd	f30,−16(r1)
58	10000f78:	f8 ff e1 cb	lfd	f31,−8(r1)
59	10000f7c:	20 00 80 4e	blr	

Fig. 7. Object code for the final part of the DGEMM kernel, including the transf of accumulator values, the store of those values, and the restoring of the nonvolat registers.

The performance comparison is shown in Fig. 8. The hardware limit is 32 double-precision flops per cycle, for a single-thread. We see that the C version with built-ins (OpenBLAS) consistently achieves 23 flops/cycle (72% of peak) across a wide range of problem sizes. The hand-optimized version performs better, achieving up to 29 flops/cycle (90% of peak) for some problem sizes. For additional reference, the flat green line shows the performance of the code in Fig. 4 when computing an 8×8 block using inputs of size 8×512 and 512×8. That computation achieves 24 flops/cycle (75% of peak).

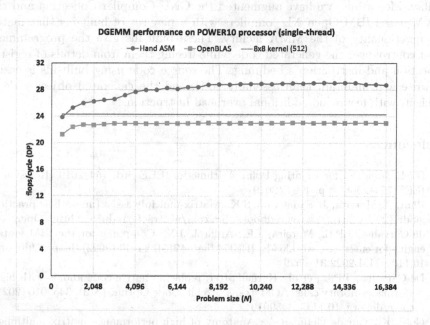

Fig. 8. Performance comparison of a DGEMM computation $(C = C - AB)$ using both hand-optimized assembly (Hand ASM) and C code with compiler built-ins (Open-BLAS). For a given problem size (N), the A, B, and C matrices are of shape $(N \times 512)$, $(512 \times N)$, and $(N \times N)$, respectively. Performance is shown in double-precision flops per cycle, with a hardware limit of 32. The reference flat green line shows the performance of the kernel in Fig. 4 when computing an 8×512 by 512×8 multiplication.

The OpenBLAS C code with built-ins achieves 80% of the performance of the hand-optimized assembly code, while being fully generic, more portable, and more maintainable. These results support our claim that compiler built-ins are the preferred approach to exploiting the new matrix math instructions of Power A.

Conclusions

The MMA facility is a new addition to the Power ISA™ Version 3.1 of the most recent IBM POWER processors. The facility adds a set of instructions tailored for matrix math, directly implementing rank-k update of small matrices of 32-bit signed integers, single-precision floating-point and double-precision floating-point numbers. The new MMA instructions are a significant departure from current vector instruction sets, which typically operate on homogeneous vector registers. The MMA instructions use vector registers as inputs, but update a new set of registers called *accumulators*.

In the face of their nonconventional characteristics, we expect it will take time for compilers to catch up with automatic code generation for the MMA facility. Meanwhile, we have augmented the GNU Compiler Collection and the LLVM-based IBM Open XL compilers with a new set of built-ins that match the functionality of the MMA facility. These built-ins give the programmers great control over the generated code while freeing them from details of register allocation and instruction scheduling. The source code using built-ins is easier to write and maintain than assembly code, and the generated object code is efficient, with few or no additional overhead instructions.

References

1. IEEE Standard for Floating-Point Arithmetic. IEEE Std. 754–2019 (Revision of IEEE 754–2008), pp. 1–84 (2019)
2. Bhat, P., Moreira, J., Sadasivam, S.K.: Matrix-multiply assist (mma) best practices guide (2021). http://www.redbooks.ibm.com/abstracts/redp5612.html?Open
3. de Carvalho, J.P.L., Moreira, J.E., Amaral, J.N.: Compiling for the IBM matrix engine for enterprise workloads. IEEE Micro **42**(5), 34–40 (2022). https://doi.org/10.1109/MM.2022.3176529
4. De Carvalho, J.P.L., et al.: KernelFaRer: replacing native-code idioms with high-performance library calls. ACM Trans. Archit. Code Optim. **18**(3), 3459010 (2021). https://doi.org/10.1145/3459010
5. Goto, K., Van de Geijn, R.A.: Anatomy of high-performance matrix multiplication. ACM Trans. Math. Softw. **34**(3), 1356053 (2008). https://doi.org/10.1145/1356052.1356053
6. IBM Corporation: Advance Toolchain for Linux on Power. https://www.ibm.com/support/pages/advance-toolchain-linux-power
7. Corporation, I.B.M–Power ISA Vers. **3**, 1 (2020)
8. IBM Corporation: IBM Open XL C/C++ for AIX 17.1.1 User's Guide (2022). https://www.ibm.com/docs/en/SSRZSMX_17.1.1/pdf/user.pdf
9. IBM Corporation: IBM Open XL Fortran for AIX 17.1.1 Language Reference (2022). https://www.ibm.com/docs/en/SSWEZ2_17.1.1/pdf/langref.pdf
10. Tagliavini, G., Mach, S., Rossi, D., Marongiu, A., Benin, L.: A transprecision floating-point platform for ultra-low power computing. In: 2018 Design, Automation Test in Europe Conference Exhibition (DATE), pp. 1051–1056 (2018)

Parallelizing Factory Automation Ladder Programs by OSCAR Automatic Parallelizing Compiler

Tohma Kawasumi[1]([✉]), Yuta Tsumura[1], Hiroki Mikami[1], Tomoya Yoshikawa[2], Takero Hosomi[2], Shingo Oidate[2], Keiji Kimura[1], and Hironori Kasahara[1]

[1] Waseda University, 27 Waseda-machi,, Shinjuku-ku Tokyo 1620042, Japan
{tohma,tmtmwaseda,hiroki}@kasahara.cs.waseda.ac.jp,
{keiji,kasahara}@waseda.jp
[2] Mitsubishi Electric Corporation, Tokyo Building, 2-7-3, Marunouchi, Chiyoda-ku, Tokyo 1008310, Japan
Yoshikawa.Tomoya@aj.mitsubishielectric.co.jp,
Hosomi.Takero@ap.mitsubishielectric.co.jp,
Oidate.Shingo@dx.mitsubishielectric.co.jp

Abstract. Programmable Logic Controllers (PLCs) and their programming language, or Ladder language, have been widely used for over 50 years to control plants like Factory Automation or FA. Demands for higher performance of Ladder programs on PLCs are increasing along with increasing functionality and complexity of plants, as well as growing numbers and variety of sensors and actuators. Traditional clock frequency improvement of a CPU in a PLC is inappropriate to satisfy them since high reliability and robustness are essential for plant control because of surrounding electrical noise. Instead, parallel processing on a multicore is a promising approach. However, Ladder programs have poor loop parallelism and basic block level fine task granularity. This paper proposes a parallelization technique of Ladder programs by the OSCAR automatic parallelizing compiler. It first translates a source Ladder program into an OSCAR compiler-friendly C program by a newly developed automatic translation tool. Then, the compiler parallelizes it. At the parallelization, the OSCAR compiler employs parallelism among macro tasks, each composed of a basic block in this application. However, the execution time of a basic block is relatively short compared with data transfer and synchronization overhead. Therefore, macro-task fusion is applied considering data dependency among macro tasks on a macro task graph so that the execution time of the fused macro task can be longer than the overhead and the parallelism among the fused macro tasks can be kept. Before the macro task fusion, the duplication of the basic block having a conditional branch and the graph transformation changing a macro task graph with control-dependence edges into a macro-task graph with just data dependence edges applied. Finally, the macro tasks on the macro task graph having data dependence edges are statically scheduled on processor cores. A performance evaluation on two ARM Cortex A53 cores on a Zynq UltraScale+ MPSoC ZCU102

The Author(s), under exclusive license to Springer Nature Switzerland AG 2023
Mendis and L. Rauchwerger (Eds.): LCPC 2022, LNCS 13829, pp. 123–138, 2023.
https://doi.org/10.1007/978-3-031-31445-2_9

shows the proposed technique can reduce 17% of execution clock cycles, though a parallel program before the proposed task fusion needs twice longer execution time on two cores against a sequential execution.

Keywords: Ladder-program · Parallelizing compiler · Task fusion · Static scheduling

1   Introduction

Instead of classic hardwired relay circuit-based sequence controllers, Programmable Logic Controllers (PLCs) consisting of CPUs have been widely used for plant control because of their flexibility, low maintenance cost, and small footprint. Among several PLC programming languages, Ladder language is a representable one. It can represent relay circuits and offers a low transition cost from classic sequence controllers. A Ladder program consists of two kinds of circuit blocks: condition parts and execution parts. Condition parts process boolean operations and check their results. Execution parts include operations, which are executed according to the results from condition parts.

Along with the advancement of plant control technology, demands for higher execution speed of Ladder programs are also increasing. Lower response time of PLC obtained by reduced Ladder program execution time allows more sensors and actuators resulting in precise target plant control. Further, recent plants' scale tends to become larger and more complicated, and their Ladder programs are also more extensive. This trend also introduces the motivation for faster Ladder program execution time.

A traditional approach of increasing the clock frequency of a CPU in a PLC is inappropriate because it makes keeping high reliability and durability difficult in a high electrical noise plant environment. Parallel processing of a Ladder program seems to be a promising approach to accelerate it. However, it usually has low loop parallelism and fine task granularity, resulting in the difficulty of employing conventional loop-level parallel processing and simple task parallel processing. Since a PLC is usually used in a severe environment, low heat dissipation realized by low power consumption is also expected.

Several parallel acceleration techniques for Ladder programs have been proposed. One focuses on logic operations in a program and reduces execute instructions. Another tries to parallelize Ladder programs. However, they are difficult to deal with indirect access by an index register, which a Ladder program characteristically uses. Program restructuring techniques for program acceleration are also challenging.

In contrast, we have developed OSCAR (Optimally SCheduled Advanced multiprocessoR) automatic parallelizing compiler [3–5]. It employs coarse grain task parallel processing and near-fine grain parallel processing, in addition conventional loop iteration-level parallel processing. Further, we parallelize engine control programs, which have poor loop parallelism. At this time, branch duplication and task-fusion were employed to make task granularity coarse and enable static scheduling to cope with basic block fine granularity avoiding dynamic scheduling overhead. While they can be also efficiently used for Ladder programs, finer task granularity in a target program must be overcome.

This paper proposes an acceleration technique for Ladder programs by OSCAR automatic parallelizing compiler. It first translates a source Ladder program into a C program. Then, the compiler parallelizes it. At the parallelization, the compiler exploits coarse grain task parallelism from a translated C program. The compiler also combines coarse grain tasks considering available parallelism to mitigate synchronization overhead, in addition to previously proposed branch-duplication and task-fusion for hiding if-statements. Finally, the parallelized program is statically scheduled on processor cores.

This paper includes the following contributions:

- We developed a Ladder-to-C translator. It enables the OSCAR compiler to parallelize Ladder programs.
- We propose a task-fusion technique to mitigate synchronization overhead from fine task granularity in a Ladder program.
- We conducted an experimental evaluation using industry-provided programs. It reveals that the proposed technique can reduce 17% of execution clock cycles.

The rest of the paper is organized as follows. Section 2 introduces the related works. Section 3 describes Ladder language. Section 4 introduces the proposed Ladder transformation method in this paper. Section 5 provides an overview of the OSCAR automatically parallelization compiler. Section 6 shows the evaluation results of our proposed methods on the application from the industry. Section 7 concludes the paper.

2   Related Works

Yasu proposed a parallelization technique for Ladder programs called Soft-PLC. [8]. It converts a Ladder program into an intermediate representation, performs dependency analysis on it for each circuit block using a Python program, and achieves speed-up through parallelization by using Python's multi-process execution model.

Regarding parallelization of control programs, several studies on model-based design, such as MATLAB/Simulink have been studied. Zhong achieved parallelization by using parallelism between blocks in a model [10]. Umeda realized speed-up by exploiting parallelism within blocks in addition to the parallelism between blocks in a model [7]. Similar to model-based development, a Ladder program can be represented as a block diagram. However, its program structure is difficult to grasp, resulting in the difficulty of parallelization. To overcome this problem, this paper proposes a Ladder program-to-C translator. OSCAR compiler takes the result C code by the translator, exploits parallelization, and generates a parallelized C code by inserting OpenMP or OSCAR-API directives. In addition, the compiler generates a macro task graph that represents the data and control dependencies of the program, making it possible to easily check the program structure.

3 Ladder Language

A Ladder program is a model of sequence control [9], which was conventionally performed by relays and switches. There are two types of representations of a Ladder program: Ladder diagrams, which directory represents a control circuit as a block diagram and instruction lists (ILs) represent a Ladder diagram in a text format. A developer usually develops a program in a Ladder diagram on a development tool, and it can output ILs from the diagram format.

A Ladder diagram consists of Ladder rungs and Ladder instructions. Ladder instructions are connected with both ends of a Ladder rung. A circuit that starts with an instruction connected to the left Ladder rung and ends with an instruction connected to the right Ladder rung is called a circuit block. A Ladder diagram is composed by connecting these circuit blocks. A circuit block represents an instruction and its execution condition. A Ladder instruction referring to a memory value is called a device. Typical devices include input X and output Y with logic values, internal relay M that holds bit information inside the PLC, device K that holds an immediate value, word device D that handles 16-bit word data, timer device T that measures time, and counter device C that counts numbers. A device is represented by a pair of device symbols and numbers, which indicates the location of the device to be accessed. For example, X3 uses the value of the third element of input device X.

In a conditional part of a circuit block, (1) "Open contact" and (2) "Close contact" in Fig. 1 are used. An open contact in this figure is turned on when X0 is 1, and a close contact is turned on when X0 is 0. An execution part of a circuit block uses (3) "OUT instructions" and so on. An OUT instruction is a special instruction that is always executed and holds 1 in M0 when the condition is satisfied and holds 0 when the condition is not satisfied. Other instructions are executed when a condition is satisfied, and there are various instructions such as data transfer instructions and four arithmetic operations.

Symbols used in Ladder diagrams are expressed in IL language, such as LD, AND, OUT, +, and so on. A conditional part can have LD and LDI, which handle open and close contacts respectively, as contact start instructions, and AND, OR, ANI, and ORI, which combine contacts. An execution section use IL instructions, including an OUT instruction shown in (3) of Fig. 1, a "+" instruction for addition, a "-" instruction for subtraction, and a MOV instruction for data transfer.

A Ladder program is executed from left to right and top to bottom. The when an END instruction is executed, it is executed again from the top to the bottom. Figure 2 shows an example of a Ladder diagram, and Figure 3 show corresponding Ladder ILs, respectively. The execution flow of this program is follows:

1. If X0 is closed, M0 sets as 1 (close), else M0 sets as 0 (open).

2. If X2 and M0 are closed, add 2 to D2.
3. If X2 and M1 are closed, subtract 2 from D2.
4. Go back to step 1 unconditionally.

Execution time from the first instruction to the END instruction is called scan time, and there is a demand for faster scan time.

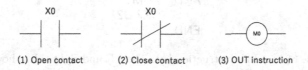

(1) Open contact   (2) Close contact   (3) OUT instruction

Fig. 1. Symbols used in Ladder diagrams

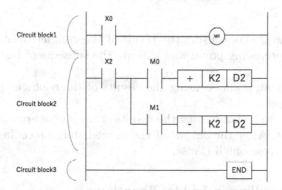

Fig. 2. Example of a Ladder diagram. A Ladder diagram consists of Circuit blocks. They start with a part connected to a power rail on the left side. Circuit block1 includes an open contact X0 and OUT instruction for M0. Circuit block2 includes 3 contacts and 2 instructions. Circuit block3 includes only END instruction.

Ladder Program Transformation

his section explains the proposed Ladder-to-C translator. Because a Ladder ogram consists of conditional parts and execution parts, the translator trans- es a circuit block in a source Ladder program into an if-statement in an output program.

Translation of Instructions Around Contacts

open contact by an LD instruction or a close contact by an LDI instruction ranslated into a single if clause to realize its conditional behaviors explained ect. 3. In addition, a Ladder program has MPS instructions to push contact

```
LD      X0
OUT     M0
LD      X2
MPS
AND     M0
 +      K2 D2
MPP
AND     M1
 -      K2 D2
END
```

Fig. 3. Example of a Ladder instruction list. The left and right sides show instructions and arguments, respectively.

operation results onto the stack, MRD instructions to load from the stack, and MPP instructions to pop from the stack. Our translator handles these three instructions as follows.

- MPS: Start an if clause using the result of the contact operation up to the immediately preceding point, and execute the subsequent instructions inside this if clause.
- MRD: Output an if clause using the results of the contact operations up to the previous point.
- MPP: Output an if clause using the results of the contact operations up to the previous point. After the output of the immediately preceding result section is completed, close one if clause.

4.2 Device Handling in Ladder Translator

The proposed translator translates devices representing data in a source Ladder program into arrays in a generated C program. At this time, each device number explained Sect. 3 corresponds to each array element in the generated array in the C program. By doing so, the compiler can analyze data dependency among Ladder operations accessing the devices, resulting in the exploitation of the parallelism from the Ladder program.

4.3 Translation Example

Figure 4 shows the example of translation by the Ladder-to-C translator. It translates LD instructions into if clauses. As described in Sect. 3, an OUT instruction is executed unconditionally. Thus, as shown in the first five lines on the right side of Fig. 4, the result of "LD X0" is once stored in a temporal variable, then an assign statement corresponding "OUT M0" stores the value in the temporal variable into "M[0]." MPS instruction starts an if clause using the X2 from the previous LD instruction. AND instruction after the MPS instruction also starts an if clause to express the execution condition for the add instruction in Fig. After translating the add instruction, the translator closes the if clause start by the AND instruction placed before the add instruction. MPP instruction and AND instruction start the if clause using the device M1. After translating the subtraction instruction, the translator closes both if clauses opened by the AND and MPS instructions. As mentioned in Sect. 4.2, all devices in the Ladder are translated into arrays. Note that the device K holds an immediate value; therefore, it is translated into an integer value that it holds instead of an array element.

```
                                                       ⎛ tempM0 = 0;
                                                       ⎜ if(X[0x0]){
Circuit block1  ⎧ LD    X0         Circuit block1      ⎜    tempM0 = 1;
                ⎩ OUT   M0                              ⎜ }
                ⎧ LD    X2                              ⎜ M[0] = tempM0;
                ⎪ MPS                           ⇨       ⎨ if(X[0x2]){
                ⎪ AND   M0                              ⎜    if(M[0]){
Circuit block2  ⎨ +     K2 D2                           ⎜        D[2] = D[2] + 2;
                ⎪ MPP                                   ⎜    }
                ⎪ AND   M1         Circuit block2       ⎜    if(M[1]){
                ⎩ -     K2 D2                           ⎜        D[2] = D[2] − 2;
                  END                                   ⎜    }
                                                       ⎝ }
```

Fig. 4. Translation example of a Ladder diagram shown in Fig. 2. One circuit block is translated into one if clause.

5 OSCAR Automatic Parallelizing Compiler

5.1 Macro Task Level Parallelization

One of the main features of the OSCAR automatic parallelizing compiler is the exploitation of Macro Task (MT) level parallelism in addition to conventional loop-iteration level parallelism and statement level near-fine grain parallelism. The compiler defines basic blocks, loops, and function calls in a source program as macro tasks. For Ladder programs, almost all macro tasks are basic blocks.

In macro task level parallel processing, or coarse grain task parallel processing, the compiler divides a source program into macro tasks. Then, the compiler analyses control flow and data dependencies among them. The analysis result is presented as a macro flow graph (MFG). Figure 5 shows an example of MFG. In the figure, a node represents a macro task. A small circle at a bottom of an MT represents a conditional branch. A solid edge represents a data dependence, and a dotted edge represents control dependence, respectively. Next, the compiler performs the earliest executable condition (EEC) analysis from an MFG. For each macro task, an earliest executable condition represents when the macro task can start its execution the earliest considering its data dependence and control dependence. The compiler generates a macro task graph (MTG) as a result of the earliest executable condition analysis, which naturally represents parallelism among macro tasks.

Figure 6 shows an example of MTG. A solid edge represents data dependence and a dotted edge represents a control dependence, respectively. A solid arc in front of a macro task is an AND arc, representing the macro task that can start when all data and control dependencies bound by it are satisfied. Similarly, a dotted arc is an OR arc, which represents the macro task that can start when one of the data and control dependencies bound by it is satisfied.

After generating a macro task graph, macro tasks are assigned to cores in a target multicore for parallel execution. At this time, the compiler chooses dynamic scheduling or static scheduling. Dynamic scheduling determines the allocation at the program execution time, while static scheduling determines it at the compile time. Dynamic scheduling can deal with conditional branches and task execution cost fluctuation appropriately, while it introduces runtime scheduling overhead. On the other hand, static scheduling has no scheduling overhead at runtime because it can schedule in advance when an MTG has no conditional branch [6].

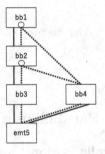

Fig. 5. MFG sample. A small circle at a bottom of an MT represents a conditional branch. A solid edge represents a data dependence, and a dotted edge represents a control dependence, respectively.

5.2   Basic Block Decomposition

If a macro task is a basic block and it can be decomposed into independen groups of statements, the compiler can decompose it into multiple macro task: To do so, the compiler also builds a task graph representing data depender cies among statements in a basic block. According to the built task graph, th compiler can detect the independent groups of statements. Thus, the compil can exploit more parallelism. This basic block decomposition makes finer mac: tasks resulting in relatively larger synchronization and data transfer overhe among macro tasks. To mitigate it, the compiler tries to fuse multiple mac tasks, as explained in the following subsections.

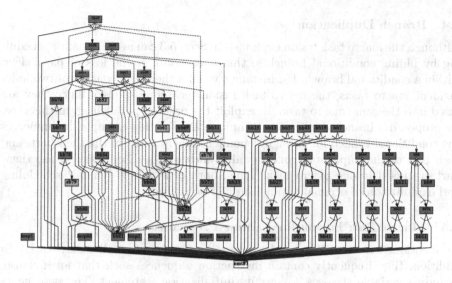

Fig. 6. MTG sample. It is a graph that adds EEC analysis results to an MFG.

5.3 Avoiding Dynamic Scheduling Overhead

A plant control program, like a Ladder program, has many operations which require conditional branches since their behavior is determined by sensor inputs. Thus, dynamic scheduling is required to deal with this dynamic behavior of a program. However, the execution cost of each macro task in a plant control program tends to be small, resulting in the impracticality of dynamic scheduling [7].

To avoid dynamic scheduling, the compiler fuses a macro task containing a conditional branch and macro tasks that have control dependent on the conditional branch macro task so that the fused macro task can hide conditional branches inside it. Therefore, the compiler can employ static scheduling for an MTG after this macro task fusion. It also enlarges the execution cost of a macro task.

Figure 7 shows the result of applying this technique to Fig. 6. All control dependencies are hidden in the macro tasks.

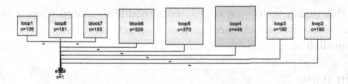

Fig. 7. MTG sample(control flow dependence free). All conditional branches are hidden in the macro tasks. The edges represent the data dependencies.

5.4   Branch Duplication

Although the macro task fusion explained in Sect. 5.3 can avoid dynamic scheduling by hiding conditional branches, this may result in the loss of parallelism within a conditional branch. For instance, when a then-part consists of two independent macro tasks, the macro task fusion technique spoils it since they are fused into the same macro task. To exploit the original parallelism, in this case, we proposed a branch duplication technique [2]. For this example, it duplicates the conditional branch for those independent macro tasks in the then-part, and each pair of the duplicated conditional branch and a macro task in the then-part are fused in one macro task. Thus, both of avoiding dynamic scheduling and exploitation of original parallelism can be realized.

5.5   Macro Task Fusion for Ladder Programs

As mentioned in Sect. 5.3, Ladder programs consist of small macro tasks. In addition, they frequently contain instruction sequences such that an if-clause, including variable accesses, follows its initialization statement. The statements in each of them are data-dependent and worth task fusion. To reduce synchronization overhead and data transfer overhead, we implemented another macro task fusion technique. It fuses macro tasks for the following four cases:

- For two macro tasks MT X and MT Y, if MT X has only a successor MT Y, X and Y are fused.
- For two macro tasks MT X and MT Y, if MT X has only a predecessor MT Y, X and Y are fused.
- If macro tasks have no predecessor macro tasks and they also have common successor macro tasks, they are fused into a single macro task. For instance, in Fig. 8, MT1 and MT2 are fused into MT1-2. Similarly, MT3 and MT4 are fused into MT3-4. This kind of MTs frequently appears in Ladder programs to initialize device values.
- If macro tasks have no successor macro tasks other than the end macro task (EMT), which is the last macro task of an MTG, and they also have common predecessor macro tasks, they are fused into a single macro task. For instance, in Fig. 9, MT3 and MT4 are fused into MT3-4. Similarly, MT5 and MT6 are fused into MT5-6. These kinds of macro tasks correspond to setting the final results to external devices, and they are independent of other macro tasks. They also frequently appear in Ladder programs.

Note that this fusion technique is only employable to macro tasks whose execution costs are less than synchronization and data transfer costs to avoid spoiling available parallelism.

6   Evaluation

6.1   Evaluation Environment

We use a Xilinx ZCU102 board with Cortex-A53 driven at 300MHz (4 core and 4GB memory [1] for the evaluation. Ubuntu 20.04.2 LTS is installed on

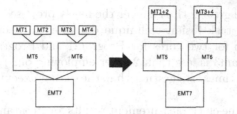

Fig. 8. Macro task fusion for MTs with no predecessors. The upper four MTs are fused, two by two.

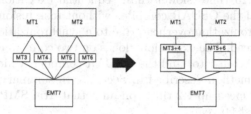

Fig. 9. Macro task fusion for MTs with no successors. The middle four MTs are fused, two by two.

6.2   Evaluation Programs

We evaluated three proprietary factory automation small test programs. Table 1 shows their summary as the numbers of lines and the execution clock cycles. We use them since they appropriately represent real Ladder programs for factory automation usage, and there are no publicly available such Ladder programs. They are labeled from "Program1" to "Program3". Note that they have many basic blocks and a few loop. Thus, ordinary product parallelizing compilers cannot exploit parallelism from the programs composed of a set of basic blocks.

6.3   Evaluation Results

Table 2 shows each evaluated program's average task cost before and after task fusion. Here, "cost" is the estimated clock cycles for a virtual target multicore modeled in the compiler. Figure 11 shows Program2's MTG, and Fig. 13 (a) shows that for Program3, respectively. Similarly, Figs. 10, 12, and 13 (b) show the MTGs for Programs 1, 2, and 3, respectively. The task fusion technique described in Sect. 5.5 is employed for them. As described in Sect. 5.3, a coarse grain parallelization for small macro tasks is ineffective due to the data transfer and synchronization overhead. According to Table 2, our task fusion technique makes task granularity about twice as large for Program1, about 6 times for Program2, and about 10 times for Program3, respectively. Thus, these results indicate a relative reduction in parallelization overhead.

Table 3 shows the summary of the parallelism exploited from the evaluated programs. Here, "parallelism" is calculated as "total task cost" divided by "critical path length" by the compiler [5]. In this table, the parallelism of Program1 and Program2 is still greater than 2 after the newly proposed task fusion. Hence, the newly proposed task fusion technique described in Sect. 5.5 can maintain sufficient parallelism for two cores for Program1 and Program2. Although the parallelism of Program3 is less than 2 after employing our proposal, task granularity increased 10 times, suggesting that the actual execution performance is better.

Figure 14 shows the clock measurement results for Program2 on Xilinx ZCU1-02. According to this figure, the Ladder-to-C translator and GCC's execution clock on one core were 1614. The execution clock on two cores was increased to 3633, namely 2.25 times slower than sequential execution, by the Ladder-to-C translator and the OSCAR compiler without task fusion considering data transfer and synchronization overhead due to a synchronization overhead and a data transfer overhead. The execution clocks on two cores were reduced to 1335 by the Ladder-to-C translator and the OSCAR compiler, which implements the macro task fusion method described in Sect. 5.5. In summary, our current task fusion allows us to speed up 1.2 times on an actual Arm SMP multicore for the first time in the past 50 years.

6.4   Comparison with Soft-PLC

As mentioned in Sect. 2, Soft-PLC also realized Ladder program parallelization [8]. Unlike our parallelization technique, it did not handle indirect device accesses by an index register. Our translator translates a device into an array, and it can naturally, handle indirect accesses. In addition, it was a kind of a simulator that executes Ladder programs though it realized parallel execution. On the other hand, our technique can generate a parallelized native code that can be directly executed on an Arm multicore. Finally, we conducted the experimental evaluation with industry-provided Ladder programs, as shown in this section, while the Soft-PLC was evaluated with randomly generated Ladder programs having around several dozen steps.

Table 1. Summary of the evaluated programs

	Number of steps	Execution clock cycles of translated Ladder programs on ZCU102
Program1	196	269
Program2	1766	1614
Program3	522	383

Table 2. Summary of average task cost estimated in the compiler

	Average task cost without macro task fusion	Average task cost with macro task fusion
Program1	101.95	270.80
Program2	236.30	1,394.92
Program3	36.95	363.71

Table 3. Summary of the parallelism estimated in the compiler

	Parallelism without macro task fusion	Parallelism with macro task fusion
Program1	4.3	4.3
Program2	2.5	2.0
Program3	2.0	1.4

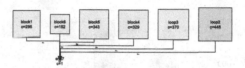

Fig. 10. MTG for Program1 (Newly proposed task fusion described in Sect. 5.5 was employed.)

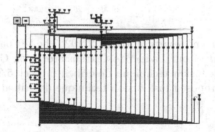

Fig. 11. MTG for Program2 (Task fusion described in Sect. 5.3 was employed.)

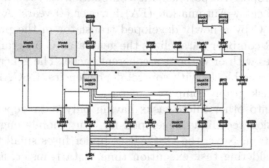

. 12. MTG for Program2 (Newly proposed task fusion described in Sect. 5.5 was loyed.)

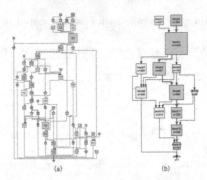

Fig. 13. MTGs for Program3. (a) was employed the task fusion technique described in Sect. 5.3. (b) was employed the newly proposed task fusion technique described in Sect. 5.5.

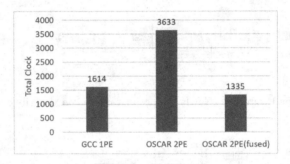

Fig. 14. Clock measurement results on the ZCU102. The left bar is the result obtained by compiling the output of our Ladder-to-C translator with GCC. The center bar is the result with the task fusion technique described in Sect. 5.3. The right bar is the result with the newly proposed task fusion technique described in Sect. 5.5.

7   Conclusion

This paper has proposed a parallelizing compilation method for "Ladder" pro grams used for Factory Automation (FA) for over 50 years. A ladder program is translated into C by a newly developed translator in the proposed method Next, the OSCAR compiler parallelizes the generated C program for any share memory multicores with or without a coherent cache. The generated C program consists of small basic blocks with control dependencies. OSCAR Compiler ge erates a macro task graph composed of basic blocks as macro tasks. It fus the micro-tasks into other micro-tasks having only data dependencies amor them by task fusion technique developed for "automobile engine control pr gram" parallelization. Next, the OSCAR compiler fuses small micro-tasks in coarser ones, considering task execution time, data transfer, and synchroniz tion overhead. By the proposed compilation scheme, this paper succeeded parallelizing the Ladder programs on a real multicore processor. However, th has not existed automatic parallelization of the ladder circuit for over 50 yea

In the evaluation, since the ladder programs directly represent existing control systems that are difficult to use, we used a few small proprietary test programs to evaluate compilation analysis and an executable program with input and output data. This paper conducted an experimental evaluation on an Arm two-core multicore. The execution time on two cores without the proposed task fusion considering data transfer and synchronization overhead was 2.25 times slower than sequential execution. However, the proposed task fusion allows us to speed up 1.2 times on an actual Arm SMP multicore for the first time in the past 50 years. The proposed Ladder-to-C translation and the macro task fusion to reduce data transfer and synchronization overhead has shown for the first time that parallel processing of the real-time sequence control computation on an SMP multicore is possible. Improvement of the macro-task fusion method will allow us more speedups. Also, this method can be easily applied to embedded multicores using distributed shared memory like Renesas and Infineon for automobiles, like in our previous paper [7].

References

1. Zynq UltraScale+ MPSoC ZCU102 evaluation kit. https://www.xilinx.com/products/boards-and-kits/ek-u1-zcu102-g.html
2. Kanehagi, Y., Umeda, D., Hayashi, A., Kimura, K., Kasahara, H.: Parallelization of automotive engine control software on embedded multi-core processor using Oscar compiler. In: 2013 IEEE COOL Chips XVI, pp. 1–3. IEEE (2013)
3. Kasahara, H., Honda, H., Mogi, A., Ogura, A., Fujiwara, K., Narita, S.: A multigrain parallelizing compilation scheme for Oscar (optimzally scheduled advanced multiprocessor). In: Proceedings of the 4th International Workshop on LCPC, pp. 283–297 (1991)
4. Kasahara, H., Obata, M., Ishizaka, K.: Automatic coarse grain task parallel processing on SMP using OpenMP. In: Midkiff, S.P., et al. (eds.) LCPC 2000. LNCS, vol. 2017, pp. 189–207. Springer, Heidelberg (2001). https://doi.org/10.1007/3-540-45574-4_13
5. Obata, M., Shirako, J., Kaminaga, H., Ishizaka, K., Kasahara, H.: Hierarchical parallelism control for multigrain parallel processing. In: Pugh, B., Tseng, C.-W. (eds.) LCPC 2002. LNCS, vol. 2481, pp. 31–44. Springer, Heidelberg (2005). https://doi.org/10.1007/11596110_3
6. Oki, Y., Mikami, H., Nishida, H., Umeda, D., Kimura, K., Kasahara, H.: Performance of static and dynamic task scheduling for real-time engine control system on embedded multicore processor. In: Pande, S., Sarkar, V. (eds.) LCPC 2019. LNCS, vol. 11998, pp. 1–14. Springer, Cham (2021). https://doi.org/10.1007/978-3-030-72789-5_1
7. Umeda, D., Suzuki, T., Mikami, H., Kimura, K., Kasahara, H.: Multigrain parallelization for model-based design applications using the OSCAR compiler. In: Shen, X., Mueller, F., Tuck, J. (eds.) LCPC 2015. LNCS, vol. 9519, pp. 125–139. Springer, Cham (2016). https://doi.org/10.1007/978-3-319-29778-1_8
8. Vasu, P., Chouhan, H., Naik, N.: Design and implementation of optimal soft-programmable logic controller on multicore processor. In: 2017 International conference on Microelectronic Devices, Circuits and Systems (ICMDCS), pp. 1–4. IEEE (2017)

9. Bolton, W.: Programable logic controllers sixth edition. Newnes (2015)
10. Zhong, Z., Edahiro, M.: Model-based parallelizer for embedded control systems on single-isa heterogeneous multicore processors. In: 2018 International SoC Design Conference (ISOCC), pp. 117–118. IEEE (2018)

Invited Papers

Structured Operations: Modular Design of Code Generators for Tensor Compilers

Nicolas Vasilache[1], Oleksandr Zinenko[2], Aart J. C. Bik[3],
Mahesh Ravishankar[4], Thomas Raoux[3], Alexander Belyaev[5],
Matthias Springer[1], Tobias Gysi[1], Diego Caballero[6], Stephan Herhut[5],
Stella Laurenzo[4], and Albert Cohen[2](✉)

[1] Google, Zürich, Switzerland
[2] Google, Paris, France
albertcohen@google.com
[3] Google, Sunnyvale, USA
[4] Google, Seattle, USA
[5] Google, Munich, Germany
[6] Google, San Diego, USA

Abstract. The performance of machine learning systems heavily relies on code generators tailored to tensor computations. We propose an approach to the design and implementation of such code generators leveraging the natural structure of tensor algebra and illustrating the progressive lowering of domain-specific abstractions in the MLIR infrastructure.

1 Introduction

This article tackles the design and implementation of *portable* and *performance-portable* tensor operations in Machine Learning (ML) frameworks. More specifically, we report on code generation efforts in the area of high-performance tensor algebra. We leverage MLIR, a compiler infrastructure that drastically reduces the entry cost to define and introduce new abstraction levels for building domain-specific Intermediate Representations (IRs) [8]. It is part of the LLVM project and follows decades of established practices in production compiler construction. Yet, while MLIR provides much needed infrastructure, the problem remains of defining portable intermediate abstractions and a progressive refinement strategy for tensor compilers. Our strategy involves alternating cycles of top-down and bottom-up thinking: (1) top-down relates to making primitives available to the programmer that *gradually decompose* into smaller building blocks with surprisingly good performance; while (2) bottom-up is concerned with the creation of building blocks that are well-suited to each hardware architecture and their *gradual composition*, connecting to top-down thinking.

As of today, ML frameworks have to make an exclusive choice among domain-specific compilers such as XLA [19], Glow [12], TVM [2], Halide [10], Triton [16], TACO [7], polyhedral compilers [18]. All of these eventually produce some flavor of LLVM IR, but they come with incompatible abstractions and implementations, do not compose, and have complex front-end/back-end compatibility

© The Author(s), under exclusive license to Springer Nature Switzerland AG 2023
C. Mendis and L. Rauchwerger (Eds.): LCPC 2022, LNCS 13829, pp. 141–156, 2023.
https://doi.org/10.1007/978-3-031-31445-2_10

matrices. We propose a portable set of abstractions, composition rules and refinements aiming to break out of this silo-ed world.

The techniques and abstractions described in this paper are used at Google for CPU and GPU code generation, including XLA-based flows [19] and IREE [3] on mobile and edge devices. The extended version of the paper [17] provides additional examples and details the design and implementation.

2   Overview of the Code Generation Flow

MLIR reduces the cost to define, compose and reuse abstractions for the construction of domain-specific compilers. It offers a comprehensive collection of compiler construction solutions by: (1) standardizing Static Single Assignment (SSA) form representations and data structures, (2) unifying compiler analyses and transformations across semantic domains through generic programming concepts such as operation traits and interfaces, (3) providing a declarative system for operations with nested regions and domain-specific type systems, and (4) providing a wide range of services including documentation, parsing/printing logic, location tracking, multithreaded compilation, pass management, etc.

MLIR is designed around the principles of parsimony, progressivity and traceability [8]. The code generation approach presented in this paper has largely contributed to the establishment of these principles and actively leverages them. The Internal Representation (IR) is fully extensible, allowing for user-defined operations (instructions), attributes and types. IR components that are expected to work together are grouped into *dialects*, which can be seen as the IR analog of dynamic libraries. Unlike earlier compilation flows offering a multi-level IR, MLIR affords and encourages the mix of different dialects in a single unit of compilation at any point in the compilation flow. For example, a high-level tensor operation may co-exist with low-level hardware instructions on vector elements in the same function. This provides a great level of modularity, composition and optionality: different abstractions can be assembled into solving a particular problem, instead of having to solve all problems in a unique representation.

2.1   Structured Code Generation

Optimizations for numerical computing have traditionally focused on loop nests. The associated analyses focus on individual array elements, considering memory dependences and aliasing [1]. They are well-suited when starting from an input language like C or Fortran where the problem is already specified in terms of loops over data residing in pre-allocated memory. When focusing on a specific domain such as Machine Learning (ML), we have the luxury of programs defined at a much higher level of abstraction than loops. This opens up the opportunity to revisit classical loop optimizations like fusion, tiling or vectorization without the need for complicated analysis and heuristics. Advantages include reduced complexity and maintenance cost while also enabling extensions like sparse tensors that are even more difficult to analyze at the loop level. It eliminates the need for extracting information from lower level representations by means static analysis, performing optimizations at the highest possible level of abstraction. We refer to this approach as *structured code generation* since the compiler primarily leverages structural information readily available in the source code. And we refer to the tensor operations amenable to structured code generation as *structured operations*.

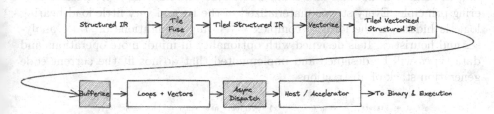

Fig. 1. Bird's eye view of structured and retargetable code generation.

Figure 1 depicts the coarse-grained steps and levels of abstraction involved in a structured code generation flow for a typical tensor compiler. The starting point (Structured IR) is composed of tensor algebra operations, organized as a functional program over dense and sparse tensors. From this level we move to a tiled structured level, which introduces loops by tiling the operations. Multiple, gradual tiling steps are possible, and do not necessarily result in loops around scalars. Instead, tiling produces loops around structured operations similar to the original ones but on smaller tensors. We also perform fusion of tensor operations at this level. The final granularity of operations is chosen to make their hardware mapping efficient. A typical example is to tile a matrix multiplication according to a cache hierarchy and then lower the smaller matrix multiplication directly to a super-optimized microkernel in assembly language. We may do so by mapping computations on sub-tensors to a (retargetable) vector abstraction. This mapping exploits high-level knowledge about the operations that has been carefully preserved. This step might also include enabling transformations like adding and vector masking.

What makes *structured code generation* highly composable and reusable is that tiling and fusion are both fully generic in the operations and data types they operate upon. These transformations only assume a generic, monotonic (regarding set inclusion), structural decomposition pattern associated with computations and composite data. Both dense and sparse tensor algebra exhibit such blockwise decomposition patterns, and the code generation abstractions and infrastructure generically applies to both.

Up until now, computations took place on immutable tensor values. We lower this to a representation on side-effecting buffers in the next step. This results in a representation with nested loops on vectors and side-effects. More optimizations of loops and memory accesses happen at this level.

In the final step, we may translate the representation directly to the `llvm` dialect of MLIR for sequential execution on CPU, or offload a GPU kernel, or split up loops into `async` blocks for a task parallel runtime, etc.

This flow composes with existing affine analyses and loop optimizations as implemented in MLIR, and that have been largely explored in the literature. In fact, the packing and loop peeling transformations in our flow leverage and helped generalize the MLIR affine machinery.

While this flow is but a first stake in the ground, it already demonstrates how to achieve a modular and composable system, following a progressive lowering principle. Every step is materialized in the IR and very little load-bearing logic is hidden in the form of complex C++ implementations of static analyses and heuristics. It is designed with optionality in mind: more operations and data types will be designed and implemented that do not fit the current code generation stack of abstractions.

```
%value_definition = "dialect.operation"(%value_use) {attribute_name = #attr_kind<"value">} ({
// Regions contain blocks.
^block(%block_argument: !argument_type):
  "dialect.further_operation"()[^successor] : () -> ()
^successor: // more operations below
}) : (!operand_type) -> !result_type<"may_be_parameterized">
```

Fig. 2. MLIR concepts in the generic format. MLIR has an open set of attributes, operations and types. Operations may recursively contain regions of blocks holding operations themselves.

2.2   Structured Code Generation in MLIR

The MLIR infrastructure builds on the success of LLVM IR while providing unprecedented extensibility. MLIR has an open, easily extensible set of instructions, called *operations* that typically represent the dynamic semantics of the program. Operations can represent anything from hardware instructions, or even hardware itself, to building blocks for machine learning models such as layers or blocks thereof. They define and use values, which represent units of immutable data in SSA form. The compile-time knowledge about values is captured in *types*, and the knowledge about operations is captured in *attributes*. Attribute and type systems are similarly open and extensible. IR objects can be logically grouped together in libraries, called *dialects*. The MLIR IR has a recursive structure where operations may have additional *regions* containing a graph of (basic) *blocks*, which in turn contain further operations. Figure 2 illustrates key MLIR concepts.

In addition to common components such as the compiler pass infrastructure, MLIR provides tools to manage its extensibility, many of which evolved or were specifically designed to support the code generation flow presented in this document. In particular, MLIR features attribute, operation and type *interfaces*, similar to object-oriented programming languages allowing one to work with abstract properties rather than (fixed) lists of supported concepts. Interfaces can be implemented separately from operations, and mixed in using MLIR's registration mechanism, thus fully separating IR concepts from transformations.

Let us now review the dialects we defined, listed in increasing level of abstraction. Any of these dialects can be mixed with others or simply bypassed if it does not provide a useful abstraction for a particular case.

The vector dialect provides a fixed-rank, static shape, n-D vector type, such as vector<4x3x8xf32>, as wel operations that conceptually extend traditional 1-D vector instructions to arbitrary rank. Such operations decompose progressively into lower-rank variants, and eventually lower to LLVM vector instructions.

The gpu dialect defines a retargetable *GPU programming model*. It features abstractions common to SIMT platforms, such as host/device code separation, a workitem/group (thread/block) execution model, communication and synchronization primitives, etc. This dialect can be produced from the vector dialect and can be lowered to platform-specific dialects such as nvvm, rocdl or spirv .

The memref dialect introduces the memref data type, which is the main representation for n-D memory buffers in MLIR, the entry point to the side-effecting memory-based operations, the way to interoperate with external C code. The dialect also provides the operations to manage buffer allocation, aliasing (memref *views*) and access. Unlike traditional pointers, memref s are multi-dimensional buffers with explicit layout that allows for decoupling the indexing scheme from the underlying storage: memref<10x10xf32, strides: [1,10]> affords column-major access while having row-major storage.

The tensor dialect operates on an abstract n-D tensor type with no specified representation in memory. Later in the compilation flow, sufficiently small tensors of static shape may be placed directly in (vector) registers while larger or dynamically-sized tensors are put into memory storage thanks to the bufferization process. Tensor values are *immutable* and subject to SSA semantics. Operations on tensors are generally free of side-effects. This allows classical compiler transformations such as peephole optimizations, constant sub-expression and dead code elimination, or loop-invariant code motion to apply seamlessly to tensor operations regardless of their underlying complexity. *Since tensor values are immutable, they cannot be written into. Instead, "value insertion" operations create new tensors with a value or a subset thereof replaced.*[1]

The scf or *structured control flow* dialect provides operations that represent looping and conditionals (e.g. regular scf.for and scf.while loops without early exit as well as an scf.if conditional construct) and *embeds them into the SA+regions form* of MLIR. This is structured at a higher-level of abstraction than a control flow graph. Notably, scf loop operations may yield SSA values and compose with other operations and dialects with either side-effecting or value-based semantics.

The linalg dialect provides higher-level compute primitives that operate on both multiple containers, including tensor and memref. These primitives can compose into versions of themselves operating on structured *subsets* of the original input data and producing similarly structured subsets of their results. They also capture program invariants and structural information, such as reduction patterns or the independence of certain parts of the computation.

This is analogous to the design of struct in LLVM IR: %1 = insertvalue {f64, i32, i32} %0, f32 42.0, 1 defines a new value %1 that holds the same elements as %0 except for the element at position 1 that now holds 42.0.

The `sparse_tensor` dialect provides the types and transformations required to make sparse tensor types first-class citizens within the MLIR compiler infrastructure. It bridges high-level `linalg` operations on sparse tensors with lower-level operations on the actual sparse storage schemes that save memory and avoid performing redundant work.

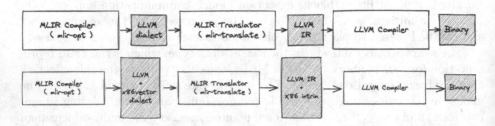

Fig. 3. Simple visual description of the MLIR compiler flow: (top) `llvm` dialect only, (bottom) `llvm` and the `x86vector` dialect of hardware-specific intrinsics.

At the end of the transformation process, MLIR produces low-level dialects common to multiple compilation paths. The `llvm` dialect closely mirrors LLVM IR and is the output we consider in this paper. The MLIR module using this dialect can be *translated* to LLVM IR before being handed off to the LLVM compiler to produce machine code. Figure 3(top) summarizes the tool flow. Similarly to the rest of MLIR, this dialect can be mixed with other ones. In particular, it reuses built-in MLIR types such as integer (`i32`) or floating-point (`f32`) scalars. To support performance-critical scenarios involving specific hardware instructions, MLIR provides low-level platform-specific dialects: `nvvm`, `rocdl`, `x86vector`, `arm_neon`, `arm_sve`, `amx`, etc. These dialects partly mirror the corresponding sets of LLVM IR intrinsic functions, which themselves typically map to hardware instructions. Beyond making these instructions first-class operations, these dialects also provide higher-level abstractions that make use of MLIR's extensible type system and interfaces. For example, the

```
arm_neon.2d.sdot : vector<4x4xi8>, vector<4x4xi8> to vector<4xi32>
```

operation is naturally expressed on a MLIR multidimensional vector type. Before converting to LLVM IR, it is first lowered to

```
arm_neon.intr.sdot : vector<16xi8>, vector<16xi8> to vector<4xi32>
```

that operates on flattened 1-D vectors to match LLVM's convention. The full example is provided in the extended version of the paper [17].

3 Transformations

Let us illustrate the different kinds of transformations available on structured operations, considering a 1-D convolution, named `linalg.conv_1d_nwc_wcf`, a its lowering to a tiled, padded and vectorized form. This is only a sketch of a transformation sequence.

The highest level input is shown in Fig. 4 (left). It operates on SSA values (immutable), with layout information as annotations for a future bufferization step (more on this later).

Fig. 4. Tiling a convolution on tensors introduces loops with secondary induction variables. Parts in italic are simplified for clarity and expanded in callouts. Underscored parts refer to new concepts: (left) operations on immutable tensors, (right) secondary induction variables and tensor slicing.

g. 5. Padding a tiled operation to obtain fixed-size tensors (highlighted). Parts in lic are simplified for brevity. Constants in roman font are attributes, in italic are `ith.constant` operation results.

The operation is fully defined by the following expression, indexed over a 5-D tangular iteration domain, and using/defining 3-D tensors:[2]

$$O[n,w,f] = I[n, w + k_w, c].K[k_w, c, f]$$

'he operation also allows specifying sizes and strides, omitted for simplicity.

The iteration domain is implicit in the operation expression: it is such that iterators span the entire operands' shape. In the example, this yields the inequalities

$$0 \le n < O.0, \quad 0 \le w < O.1, \quad 0 \le f < O.2, \quad 0 \le k_w < K.0, \quad 0 \le c < K.1$$

where $O.d$ denotes the size of the d-th dimension of O. The derivation for these quantities follows the same rules as Tensor Comprehensions [18]. They can be derived with successive applications of Fourier-Motzkin elimination [13].

3.1 Tiling

Among the loop transformations modeled on structured operations, we only describe the simplest form of tiling. Other tiling variants, how to generate parallel SPMD code, various forms of fusion, are described in the extended version of the paper and in the MLIR documentation. In this simple form, tiling introduces scf.for loops as well as subset operations (tensor.extract_slice and tensor.insert_slice) to access tiled subsets, see Fig. 4 (right). The tiled form of the operation is itself a linalg.conv_1d_nwc_wcf operating on the tiled subsets. The derivation of dense subsets is obtained by computing the image of the iteration domain by the indexing function for each tensor. Non-dense iteration domains and subsets involve dialect extensions and inspector-executor [7] code generation that are outside the scope of this paper.

Let us chose tile sizes 1x8x32x1x8 . Some of these do not divide tensor sizes; as a result the boundary tiles are subject to full/partial tile separation. There is no single static tensor type that is valid for every loop iteration; the tiled tensor type !tDyn must be relaxed to a dynamically shaped tensor, whose corresponding dynamic tile sizes are %8, %9 and %11. Later canonicalization steps kick in to refine the types that can be determined to be partially static. The resulting scf.for loops perform iterative yields of the full tensor value that is produced at each iteration of the loop nest. Since tensor values are immutable, new values are produced by each tensor.insert_slice and scf.yield .

This illustrates the structured code generation principle: preserving a high level abstraction on subsets of the original operation, amenable to downstream compositions with further transformations.

3.2 Padding and Packing

Dynamic tile shapes can hamper vectorization which requires static sizes. There are multiple mitigating options: multi-level loop peeling/versioning to isolate statically known constant part, possibly combined with masked vector operatio at domain boundaries; or padding to a larger static size (the padding value mu be neutral for the consuming operation). In Fig. 5, the tensor.pad operati deals with the latter option. Its size is obtained by subtracting the dynamic t size from the static tile size. Elements in the padded region are set to the %c value. A *nofold* attribute enforces additional padding to avoid cache line spli

Note that padding operations can often be hoisted out of tile loops, storing padded tiles in a packed, higher-dimensional tensor. This amortizes copying cost and makes tiles contiguous in memory (reducing TLB misses). The amount of hoisting is configurable per tensor, to trade memory consumption for copy benefits. In the example, input tensor padding is hoisted by 3 loops. This introduces an additional tile loop nest to precompute padded tiles and insert them into a packed tensor of type `tensor<?x?x1x8x8xf32>` containing all padded tiles. This also results in the actual computations accessing the packed tensor `%12= tensor.extract_slice %PI...` .

3.3   Vectorization

After tiling and padding, the convolution operands are statically shaped and amenable to vectorization, see Fig. 6 (left). In the current IR, only 2 types of operations need to be vectorized: `tensor.pad` and `linalg.conv1d_nwc_wcf`.

ig. 6. Operations on tensors of fixed sizes can be directly vectorized. Parts in italic e simplified for brevity.

The vector dialect additionally provides a first-class representation for high-ensity operations. Figure 6 (right) illustrates one of these, `vector.contract`.

4   Bufferization

fferization is the process of materializing `tensor` values into (`memref`) buffers. ypically occurs late in the compilation flow. To achieve good performance, it ssential to allocate and copy as little memory as possible. As a result, buffers uld be reused and updated in-place whenever possible.

Fig. 7. Left-hand side: output tensor arguments, tied with the result of an operation, in destination-passing style. Right-hand side: example of a read-after-write conflict.

Fig. 8. Bufferization assigns tensor values to buffers, taking into account function-level annotations #in, #out from Fig. 4. Data flow is replaced by side effects, unnecessary values are crossed out on the left. "Computational payload" dialects such as **linalg** and **vector** are designed to support both **tensor** and **memref** (buffer) containers.

Allocating a new buffer for every memory write is always safe, but wastes memory and introduces unnecessary copies. On the other hand, reusing a buffer and writing to it in-place can result in invalid bufferization if the original data at the overwritten memory location must be read at a later point of time. When performing transformations, one must be careful to preserve program semantics exposed by dependencies [1]. The right-hand side of Fig. 7 illustrates a potential *Read-after-Write (RaW) conflict* that prevents in-place bufferization. The problem of efficient bufferization is related to register coalescing, the register allocation sub-task associated with the elimination of register-to-register moves.

We propose an "unsurprising" bufferization interface freeing upstream passes of the risk of incurring a large performance penalty when high-level transformations result in unexpected allocation and copying. It is based on the so-called *destination-passing style*: one of the tensor arguments is singled out and tied with the resulting tensor for in-place bufferization. This singled-out tensor argument is called an *output* tensor; see the left-hand side of Fig. 7. After lowering, output tensors are similar to C++ *output parameters* that are passed as non-const references and used for returning the result of a computation. Yet the tie between an output tensor (argument) and the operation's result serve as a bufferization constraint with no observable impact on the functional semantics; in particular, output tensors still appear as immutable. During bufferization, only output tensors are considered when looking for a buffer to write the result of an operation into.

The rationale is two-fold: first of all it provides a non-ambiguous (hence "unsurprising") control mechanism for driving bufferization choices from higher level optimization algorithms; second, notice that the ubiquitous sub-setting operations resulting from tiling and structured control flow naturally consume their tensor argument, making them ideal candidates for in-place bufferization (such as pairs of matching `extract_slice`/`insert_slice` and the `scf.yield` operation). A comprehensive example is shown in Fig. 8. The trade-off is that upstream compilation passes are responsible of rewriting the IR in destination-passing style. In particular, we believe that a global copy elimination problem can be formalized on top of destination-passing style, offering the best of both worlds in terms of allowing passes to optimize memory usage at a global scale, while enabling a robust, in-place bufferization path for the important special case of refining structured operations.

During bufferization, before modifying the, an analysis decides for each tensor OpOperand %t whether *buffer(%t)* (*in-place bufferization*) or a copy thereof (*out-of-place bufferization*), denoted by *copy(buffer(%t))*, should be used with the new memref operation. The analysis simulates *a future in-place bufferization of the OpOperand* and checks if a RaW conflict can be found under this assumption. If not, the analysis greedily commits to this in-place bufferization decision. Furthermore, the analysis stores the fact that the OpOperand and its potentially aliasing OpResult are now *known to alias*, by merging their alias sets. The search for RaW conflicts only involves the traversal of tensor SSA use-def chains. The extended version of the paper [17] details the procedure and covers special cases such as partial updates, cast operations and initialization.

.5   Lowering of Multidimensional Vector Operations to LLVM

At this point, the IR has reached a level of abstraction close to nested loops with vector intrinsics in C, except that we operate on multi-dimensional vectors.

In the simplest case, multi-dimensional `vector.transfer` operations lower multiple 1-D `vector.load` and `vector.store` operations. When supported hardware, they can also lower to n-D operations and DMA transfers. In more complex cases, transfer operations lower to a combination of broadcast, transposition and masked scatter/gather. In the particular case where the `vector.transfer` cannot be determined to be in-bounds, one must resort to an additional separation between full and partial transfer, akin to the full and partial tile separation for non-divisible tile sizes. This is illustrated in Fig. 9 (right) the `else` block around the `linalg.copy(%21, %22)` operation.

The progressive lowering process and resulting code for our example has several dozen operations, as shown in Fig. 10. The detailed discussion of this process is provided in the extended version of the paper [17].

Fig. 9. The `vector` dialect can be lowered progressively to simpler operations on 1-D vectors. Illustrated on lowering contractions to outer products, with parts in italic simplified for brevity and repetitive parts omitted. Lower-level vector operations require constant indices and are produced by unrolling the outer dimensions.

Fig. 10. Progressive lowering of the `vector` operations representing matrix produc (a) vector unrolling to the target shape $2 \times 8 \times 2$ introduces vector slice manipulatio (b) the transfer permutation is materialized as a `transpose` operation; (c) 1-D transfe become loads with shape adaptation; (d) contractions rewrite as outer products (oth options are possible), which in turn lower to (e) fused multiply-add instructions.

3.6   Discussion

The transformations we introduced are legal by design, in the sense that th legality and applicability derive from an operation's properties and structu We refer to this philosophy as *transformations-oriented IR design*.

The traditional compilation for numerical computing [1] revolves around:

- Legality: what transformations can be applied without changing the observed program semantics? Legality conditions are often checked through static analyses. They may be performed upfront or on-demand, and their results may be updated as the IR is transformed.
- Applicability: how complex is the IR matching process for finding where to apply a transformation? Applicability also encompasses considerations related to the loss of high-level semantic information and the ability to apply subsequent transformations.
- Profitability: what are the transformations deemed beneficial for a given metric? For example, polyhedral compilers often focus on finding an objective function to minimize (universal or target-specific) [18], while autotuners may rely on a learned performance model to accelerate search [20].

It is of central importance to control the abstractions on which the transformation legality, applicability and profitability questions relate to. The finer-grained the IR, the more general and canonical the representation, but also the more intractable the analyses and transformations. Indeed, canonicalization to some flavor SSA CFG such as LLVM IR has proven invaluable in enabling the reuse of common infrastructure for middle-end and back-end compilers. But lowering abstractions and domain knowledge too quickly reduces the amount of structure available to derive transformations from. While a loop nest is a net abstraction gain compared to a CFG for the application of loop transformations, important information is still lost. It induces non-trivial phase ordering issues: e.g., loop fusion to enhance temporal locality may alter the ability to recognize an efficient BLAS-2 or BLAS-3 implementation in a numerical library.

The higher-level abstractions we propose facilitate the declarative specification of transformations. It makes it possible to target individual operations in the IR rather than large multi-operation constructs such as loops and control flow graphs. This is the case of tiling, fusion and unrolling.[3] Loops and other constructs may be produced as a result of transformations, but they rarely need to be targeted by further high-level transformations. On the other hand, target specifications can be arbitrarily complex and may use the pattern-matching infrastructure available in MLIR such as the PDL dialect.

Furthermore, transformation orchestration calls for a meta-programming dialect suitable for IR manipulation. Such a dialect makes it possible to capture *transformation schedules* [10] in the IR itself. Transformations schedules can be stored, analyzed, parameterized, and even *shipped separately* from the main compiler. This is paramount to retargeting a tensor compiler to new hardware or to port it to a different ML framework. A declarative approach also facilitates the design of custom passes by selecting specific rewrite rules.

Finally, the multi-level nature of MLIR makes it possible to build higher-level dialects to define IR transformations superimposed on the existing infrastructure and handled by progressive lowering. For example, the transformation

---

[3] Some transformations such as software pipelining remain naturally attached to loops.

sequence and some of the parameters can be reified into a new "strategy" operation that gets lowered into primitive transformation operations with the lowering also specified declaratively. Just as with any other dialect, IR modules using such meta-programming dialects can be created programmatically from any language. The textual or binary IR format enables loosely coupled communication between the front-end language—in which the transformation is written—and the compiler infrastructure. The expressiveness of such transformations is similar to that of RISE/ELEVATE [6] but without restrictions to the specification language.

4   Related Work

The extended version of the paper provides a detailed discussion of design choices and alternatives, illustrated on a survey of related compilers and infrastructure [17]. This survey covers ONNX (https://onnx.ai), XLA [19], Halide [10], TVM [2], Fireiron [4], LIFT [15], Multi-Dimensional Homomorphisms [11], Elevate [5], Glenside [14], Tensor Comprehensions [18], PolyMage [9]. It also discusses the interaction with lower level code generators. The overall conclusion of this survey is that structured operations capture the common abstractions and transformations patterns underlying the different flavors of tensor compilers, from the mathematical specification of tensor algebra down to super-optimized blocks of vector instructions, from polyhedral to more algebraic forms, with or without explicit scheduling languages.

5   Conclusion

We presented the composable multi-level intermediate representation and transformations that underpin tensor code generation in MLIR. This so-called "structured code generation" approach leverages the natural decomposition of tensor algebra operations, doing away with static analyses and applicability checks on low-level IR. The resulting design is modular and built with optionality in mind. Abstractions span data structures and control flow with both functional (SSA form) and imperative (side-effecting) semantics; they serve as generic building blocks for composable, interoperable, retargetable tensor compilers.

References

1. Allen, R., Kennedy, K.: Optimizing Compilers for Modern Architectures: Dependence-Based Approach. Morgan Kaufmann Publishers (2001)
2. Chen, T., et al.: TVM: an automated end-to-end optimizing compiler for deep learning. In: 13th USENIX Symposium on Operating Systems Design and Implementation (OSDI 18), pp. 578–594. USENIX Association (2018). https://www.usenix.org/conference/osdi18/presentation/chen
3. Developers, I.: IREE (intermediate representation execution environment (202 https://google.github.io/iree/

4. Hagedorn, B., Elliott, A.S., Barthels, H., Bodik, R., Grover, V.: Fireiron: a data-movement-aware scheduling language for gpus. In: Proceedings of the ACM International Conference on Parallel Architectures and Compilation Techniques, PACT 2020, pp. 71–82. Association for Computing Machinery, New York (2020). https://doi.org/10.1145/3410463.3414632

5. Hagedorn, B., Lenfers, J., Koehler, T., Gorlatch, S., Steuwer, M.: A language for describing optimization strategies. CoRR abs/2002.02268 (2020). https://arxiv.org/abs/2002.02268

6. Hagedorn, B., Lenfers, J., Kundefinedhler, T., Qin, X., Gorlatch, S., Steuwer, M.: Achieving high-performance the functional way: a functional pearl on expressing high-performance optimizations as rewrite strategies. Proceedings of ACM on Programming Languages 4(ICFP) (Aug 2020). https://doi.org/10.1145/3408974

7. Kjolstad, F., Kamil, S., Chou, S., Lugato, D., Amarasinghe, S.: The tensor algebra compiler. Proc. ACM Program. Lang. 1(OOPSLA) (Oct 2017). https://doi.org/10.1145/3133901

8. Lattner, C., et al.: Mlir: scaling compiler infrastructure for domain specific computation. In: 2021 IEEE/ACM International Symposium on Code Generation and Optimization (CGO), pp. 2–14. IEEE/ACM, IEEE/ACM (2021). https://doi.org/10.1109/CGO51591.2021.9370308

9. Mullapudi, R.T., Vasista, V., Bondhugula, U.: Polymage: automatic optimization for image processing pipelines. In: Özturk, Ö., Ebcioglu, K., Dwarkadas, S. (eds.) Proceedings of the Twentieth International Conference on Architectural Support for Programming Languages and Operating Systems, ASPLOS 2015, Istanbul, Turkey, March 14–18, 2015, pp. 429–443. ACM (2015). https://doi.org/10.1145/2694344.2694364

10. Ragan-Kelley, J., Barnes, C., Adams, A., Paris, S., Durand, F., Amarasinghe, S.: Halide: a language and compiler for optimizing parallelism, locality, and recomputation in image processing pipelines. ACM SIGPLAN Notices 48(6), 519–530 (2013). https://doi.org/10.1145/2499370.2462176

11. Rasch, A., Schulze, R., Gorlatch, S.: Generating portable high-performance code via multi-dimensional homomorphisms. In: 2019 28th International Conference on Parallel Architectures and Compilation Techniques (PACT), pp. 354–369. IEEE, Seattle, WA (2019). https://doi.org/10.1109/PACT.2019.00035

12. Rotem, N., et al.: Glow: graph lowering compiler techniques for neural networks. CoRR abs/1805.00907 (2018). https://arxiv.org/abs/1805.00907

13. Schrijver, A.: Theory of Linear and Integer Programming. John Wiley & Sons (1986)

14. Smith, G.H., et al.: Pure tensor program rewriting via access patterns (representation pearl). CoRR abs/2105.09377 (2021). https://arxiv.org/abs/2105.09377

15. Steuwer, M., Remmelg, T., Dubach, C.: Lift: a functional data-parallel ir for high-performance gpu code generation. In: 2017 IEEE/ACM International Symposium on Code Generation and Optimization (CGO), pp. 74–85. IEEE/ACM (2017). https://doi.org/10.1109/CGO.2017.7863730

16. Tillet, P., Kung, H.T., Cox, D.: Triton: an intermediate language and compiler for tiled neural network computations. In: Proceedings of the 3rd ACM SIGPLAN International Workshop on Machine Learning and Programming Languages, MAPL 2019, pp. 10–19. Association for Computing Machinery, New York (2019). https://doi.org/10.1145/3315508.3329973

17. Vasilache, N., et al.: Composable and modular code generation in MLIR: a structured and retargetable approach to tensor compiler construction. CoRR abs/2202.03293 (2022). https://arxiv.org/abs/2202.03293

18. Vasilache, N., et al.: The next 700 accelerated layers: from mathematical expressions of network computation graphs to accelerated gpu kernels, automatically. ACM Trans. Architecture Code Optim. (TACO) **16**(4), 1–26 (2019). https://doi.org/10.1145/3355606
19. XLA team within Google: XLA: TensorFlow, Compiled. Google Developers Blog (2017). https://developers.googleblog.com/2017/03/xla-tensorflow-compiled.html
20. Zheng, L., et al.: Ansor: generating high-performance tensor programs for deep learning. In: 14th USENIX Symposium on Operating Systems Design and Implementation, OSDI 2020, Virtual Event, 4–6 November, 2020, pp. 863–879. USENIX Association (2020). https://www.usenix.org/conference/osdi20/presentation/zheng

How Can Compilers Help the Additive Manufacturing of Electronics?

Xiaoming Li[✉]

University of Delaware, Newark, DE 19716, USA
xli@udel.edu

Abstract. Additive manufacturing (AM) is becoming a very helpful tool to build electronic systems as well as radio frequency devices. The main driving force behind is the ability of AM to produce complex functional and conforming geometry shapes, manipulate material at extremely high resolution, and process materials such as Zirconium that have desired electronic or RF properties. However, AM is still far away from becoming a scalable and efficient manufacturing scheme. A root cause is the lack of cross-layer design in the AM software stack in the domain. The current software stack don't really convey *why* and *how* for each layer's "thinking", despite the layers do communicate with each other the results of the decisions. This position paper argues for the development of the cross-software-layer optimization capability to enable automated additive manufacturing of electronic and RF systems. We envision the core enabling capabilities include an innovative language and compiler based approach that is capable of representing the constraints, features and goals in designing, material, process and printer involved in the manufacturing, and transmit the internal representation to all layers in a principled way. Extrapolating from the past experience, the cross-layer collaboration will significantly reduce the human intervention necessary to mend between layers, making additive manufacturing the practical, efficient and reliable future manufacturing scheme of electronic and RF systems.

Introduction

Additive manufacturing (AM) is becoming a very helpful tool to build electronic systems as well as radio frequency devices. The main driving force behind is the ability of AM to produce complex functional and conforming geometry shapes, manipulate material at extremely high resolution, and process materials such as Zirconium that have desired electronic or RF properties, in other words, features that are crucial for the fabrication of electronic and RF devices but are challenging for traditional manufacturing technology.

The future of additive manufacturing of electronic and RF systems is bright. Figure 1 shows examples of functional electronic devices fabricated by us. Other investigators in this area are experimenting with or the manufacture of printed sensors [21,23], conformal electronics [4,5,14], stretchable electronics [13,24], custom medical devices [9,11,18] and high frequency RF devices and systems [27]. However, AM is still far away from becoming a scalable and efficient manufacturing scheme. The core missing capability is the inability to automate the manufacturing process. Contrary to many people's expectation, even after a system is designed, the route from the design to the additive manufactured product is still a human driven process. Huge amount of operator intervention is still required to translate a design through layers of software

© The Author(s), under exclusive license to Springer Nature Switzerland AG 2023
P. Pande and L. Rauchwerger (Eds.): LCPC 2022, LNCS 13829, pp. 157–167, 2023.
https://doi.org/10.1007/978-3-031-31445-2_11

such as slicers to G-code, and finally to printer controller. Particularly, much of the human intervention is not rigorously guided by theory or principles. Rather they heavily depend on experience, expertise, or in many cases, "art". This missing capability of automation is what prevents AM from becoming a future manufacturing scheme of electronic and RF systems.

Why do we still need significant human intervention on every step? A root cause is the lack of cross-layer design in the AM software stack in the domain. Every step in the AM workflow is driven by compilers, from the designing, to the slicing that translates design into printable representation, to the g-code that printers understand. To print electronic and RF systems successfully, multiple aspects related to printing need to be right at once, including design requirements, material properties, working processes, and printer characteristics. The layers of compilation make a lot of "local" decisions with regard to one or more of the aspects. However, the compilers involved don't really convey *why* and *how* for each layer's "thinking", despite the layers do communicate with each other the results of the decisions. Without knowing other layer's why and how, the choices made at a layer may very well reverse or compromise other layer's good optimization. This is what we see in today's practices, and is exactly why significant human intervention is needed.

Let's first take a look at four key aspects in AM: design requirements, materials, printing process, and printer characteristics.

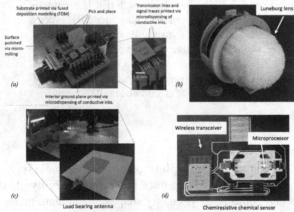

In term of design requirements, the AM of electronics and RF devices need true 3D building capability. The functions of electronics and RF systems are often tied to custom 3D architectures or the direct patterning of complex topographic structures, for example, 3D conforming curves or non-planar resolutions. In contrast, today's 3D model compilation is largely based on 2.5D design, that is 3D shapes are really built in 2D layer-by-layer. The problem

Fig. 1. Examples of printing of electronic and RF systems. (a) Radio frequency communication circuit fabricated via multimaterial AM. (b) Graded index Luneberg lens with integrated electronics for RF beam steering. (c) Structurally integrated antenna printed on a dry fabric and integrated within a fiber reinforced composite. (d) Additively manufactured chemical sensor with integrated microprocessor, energy storage and wireless communication.

that the 2.5D design won't be able to maintain the design requirements along all dimensions. It will be detrimental for the building of products that are sensitive on the properties along those non-planar dimensions.

The materials used in AM of electronic and RF systems also pose challenges for the software stack. First of all, new materials are constantly being introduced. For example, Zirconium has been used in the implementation of RF functions such as Luneburg lens [6,10] that are otherwise very hard to achieve with other materials. In addition, multiple materials are frequently needed for one system, e.g., conductive ink, metal, etc. Significant human efforts are spent to make all material print well in one place and interact in the way that the design desires.

Furthermore, complex electronic and RF systems are usually made with a process involving multiple steps of fabrication. For example, nScrypt [2], Optomec Aerosol Jetting [17,26], and less expensive platforms, such as the System 30M from HYREL 3D [1], resembling a Swiss army knife of DDM, combine a variety of different additive and subtractive manufacturing tools within a single integrated platform. Figure 1a shows a complete RF communication system at 18 GHz that was printed via multi-material AM. This system included passive components (e.g. capacitors and connectors integrated via automated pick & place), active elements (e.g. RF amplifiers and mixers integrated via automated pick & place), ground planes (printed via micro-dispensing), substrates (printed via FDM and polished via micro-milling) and transmission lines (printed via micro-dispensing). Overall, five different tools within a common platform were used to manufacture this one circuit, each with its own compilation workflow.

Moreover, new printers are being equipped with features ahead of the capability of today's software, and the list of unsupported features is getting longer. For example, nScript's Superscrypt machine [2], shown in Fig. 2, supports 6-axis movement, and combines four swappable print heads that include; (1) DW micro-dispensing heads capable of depositing custom and commercial inks and pastes, (2) fused deposition modeling (FDM) print heads capable of extruding a wide range of polymer filaments, (3) aerosol jetting print head capable of printing a range of conductive and non-conductive inks, (4) automated pick-and-place tool capable of integrating passive and active circuit elements, (5) micro-milling tool capable of smoothing surfaces, machining vias and creating other features that require subtractive manufacturing and (6) laser micromachining tools for material removal (i.e. ablation). Maybe ironically, the only way now to use it is manual coding. There misses a principled software strategy to incorporate new features into the workflow and make them visible to all phases of manufacturing.

In summary, the current AM practice is still centered on human operators. Traditional manufacturing of functional systems is based on modular software processing. Multiple layers of software and multiple machines are used with each potentially with own optimization goals and constraints. Current AM practices require extensive operator experience to monitor the print job, and in most cases the processing needs to configured for each different software layers. Current software layers communicate only the outcome of their processing with each other, but they provide no feedback in term of the internal *why* and *how*. The significant need for operator intervention at ever step, and the lack of a coherent compiler stack in AM practices lead to low reliability and very limited scalability.

In this paper, we argue for the creation of cross-software-layer optimization to remove or greatly reduce the need for operator intervention in the loop and at the same time improve the reliability and yield of the printed products. In addition to the potential help on the scale of manufacturing, the new capability will improve the reliability and repeatability for the fabrication of complex structures and devices, another must-have capability for a manufacturing service.

2 How Compiler Can Help?

Next we describe our vision of compiler research that will enable the cross-layer optimization in AM. It includes five areas: (1) semantic metadata encoding in languages used in the AM software stack; (2) dynamic monitoring and feedback loop with sensor fusion; (3) representation of design requirements as static or dynamic optimization constraints; (4) incor-

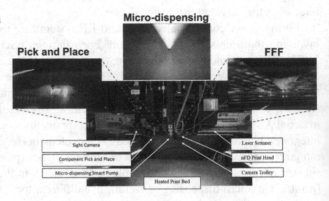

Fig. 2. Testbed: nScrypt multimaterial/multitool platform.

poration of domain expertise as cross-layer optimization heuristics; and (5) adaptable users interfaces for the cross-software-layer optimization capability.

2.1 Semantic Metadata Encoding

The foundation of cross-software-layer optimization is the encoding of semantic information as metadata in languages used between software stack layers. The new semantic metadata capability will make all software stack layers aware of the design intentions and constraints of others, therefore enable the cross-layer optimization from designing through slicing, and till the actual printing.

Currently, the 3D model languages and the G-code are currently the only way to communicate information between the three software stack layers, i.e., CAD, slicer and printer. Essentially, *these language implements, and only implements, the outcome of design, but do not contain any notation of the constraints in design or the reason for design choices.* All those unspoken meta-information is fundamentally important for the success of manufacturing but is lost in translation.

We can see the need for information encoding that contain important hues of the design intention and the constraints that other layers can use to make better decision. The information falls into three categories: parametrical geometry description, material printing properties and printer constraints.

Parametrical Geometry Description. Geometry shapes are important for electronic and RF systems. For example, the RF lens can only function with strict geometric designs. However, the geometric shapes are not really described as they are in the AM process. Rather they are "approximated" with primitive geometry elements. For example, a shape of circle might be the key design element for a RF len. However, some important design requirement is conveyed down the AM process in a very lossy way. The circle may be described or approximated as hundreds of straight lines. In practice a lot of human efforts is spend on tuning this approximation to make it work as the initial circle design intends. If we can encode the parametrical geometry in the model language or G-code, the intention of design can be conveyed along and help the decisions made by all layer of the software stack.

Material Printing Property. In addition to the geometric information, another important aspect in any AM design is the printing material. Here we consider both the material properties that are related to the electronic and AF functions, for example electromagnetic reflection rate, as well as properties that interact with the printing process include the viscosity, adherence with different temperatures, or shrinkage with temperature, etc. The manipulation of material is another area where significant human efforts, or art, are spend to make all moving pieces fall into the right place. It is also the place where a software layer might be able to make better decisions if the information would have been encoded in the languages.

Printing Device Constraints. Software running on printers is the lowest layer in the AM software stack. Usually specifics at this lower level are not made aware at the earlier, higher software stack layers such as CAD. However, designs can be substantially improved if the printing device constraints are known. Furthermore, mending the design requirements and the reality capability of printers is another time-consuming task for human operators. We propose the encoding of printing device constraints in both the model languages and the G-code, so that from the designing stage down-to the printing time monitoring stage, better decisions can be reached with the knowledge from the encoding.

2.2 Dynamic Monitoring and Sensor Fusion

Due to the complex nature of the various AM systems and the lack of feedback control there is currently a large degree of sample-to-sample variability. For the case of printed functional devices, this results in a high percentage of print failures and low yields. For these printing platforms to have widespread use they need to become universally less dependent on human intervention to maintain reliability. The knowledge gap is the ability to automatically monitor and control the printing process. An intelligent software stack, aware of the dynamic monitoring capability at all layers, can compensate for errors or imperfections layer to layer and will make use of robust modeling to track the predicted evolution of the product. Finally, feedback control on the process itself will allow for continuous performance.

Printing Platform: There are several things that commonly cause build failures. The print time has a direct impact of the probability of failure, as these causes are all time dependent. As the build complexity goes up, as is the case with printing the multiple materials needed to realize functional systems, the build time increases, and correspondingly so does the risk of failure. Many printing systems already have integrated cameras. However, these cameras are currently not used along with any kind of image processing to intelligently evaluate the status of the build. The visual feed will be used for feedback control. Additionally, side-channel feedback from printing platforms such as the consumption of the system and the amount of material being used, can model the health of the build platform.

Geometry: It is crucial that the printed geometry meets design expectations. The geometry sensing will utilize vision-based monitoring systems that exist in many of the current printing platforms. For example, nScrypt printers can have multiple optical sensing mechanisms, such as cameras and lasers. The nVision package has a built-in feature for doing topography mapping. This is accomplished using a laser to determine the distance to the targeted print area. Embedding this feature into the printing process will allow for examination of the print layers in-situ. The main challenge is that the topography mapping is very time consuming for high scanning resolutions. If a discrepancy is detected, several corrective actions can be taken. For example, if the feature is too large then the geometry can be trimmed using a laser. Similarly, if the feature is too small, then additional material can be added. To avoid the issue occurring again, the design and manufacturing parameters, such as the pressure, the standoff distance, and the translation speed can be adjusted to prevent reoccurrence of the problem.

Material: The correct functioning of printed electronic and RF systems relies on that the microstructure meets the desired properties. For this monitoring and feedback, DC and low frequency (LF) measurements will be conducted to extract capacitance, inductance, and resistance, using an LCR meter. This will allow the extraction of the permittivity, permeability, and/or resistivity of the deposited materials. These values will then be compared to the desired quantities and if discrepancies are detected, then corrective actions such as laser trimming or local heat up can be applied to change the material properties. The sensing of material can also be helped at the much earlier designing software layer. Custom structures and probes can be incorporated to the design to facilitate the extraction of the data.

Product: The radio frequency (RF) performance of the fabricated parts testing can also be monitored. It will consist of measuring the scattering parameters (S-parameters) of the fabricated device. RF probes and a network analyzer are needed and just like the material monitoring, design software can help by building in specific test structures to extract the high-frequency properties of the devices. Two stages of testing are envisioned, first, calibration test structures will be created. These structures can be included along with every build, which means that an extensive history of process monitoring can be recorded. The second stage will be direct testing of the fabricated parts. This data can be compared to simulated data to evaluate the progression of the device fabrication. Extracting this data will require incorporating probe pads into the device designs that have minimal effect on the overall device performance. Ultimately, the goal will be to probe functional devices as they are being built and adjust build settings to correct for any issues.

2.3 Design Requirements as Optimization Constraints

In AM working flows, a design requirement might not be able to be fully guaranteed at the layer that initializes it. If other layers are aware of it and purposefully guide their optimization and design choices to help, the software stack, as a whole, can d much better job realizing it. For example, the CAD software might want to maintain the density of material in a particular region within a tight range for a particular RF function. With this semantic information, slicers can choose support structures to help maintain the density, and at printing time, the dynamic monitoring can be guided to measure and feedback this particular property.

Encoding of Constraints: Fundamentally what the software stack really do is to change and optimize the internal representation (IR) of the product for each layer's own purpose. Therefore, the constraints are really tests of whether a particular transformation is valid or not. This is very similar to the validity test of transformations in compiler [20,25]. We will borrow the definition of correctness testing from the compiler domain to help the encoding of design constraints for AM. That is, when transforming a representation of an object into other equivalent representations at a software layer, if all design requirements are satisfied, products can be manufactured with the designed property and function.

Testing and Classification of Constraint Violation: Encoding design constraints in the internal representation of AM just solve half of the problem, that is the design intentions of one software layer is conveyed to other layers and maintained there. However, we need to be able to tell if some constraint is violated by a layer's transformation, what causes the violation. In other words, we need to be able to identify the error source. The forward problem of mapping the print to the sensor data series can be solved accurately using simulations; however, the inverse problem is difficult. The main task is to identify what caused the error between real observations (e.g., measured S-parameters as a function of position and frequency or images from cameras that are in turn used to calculate geometry, i.e. transmission line widths, antenna shapes, ...) and intended observations. The AM production platform is a complex system in which it is difficult to predict the response of any single factor (e.g. the humidity in the room varying a bit, which may violate the encoded material constraints).

4 Domain Expertise as Heuristics

Domain knowledge serves as the guidance of optimization in the three stages of designing, slicing and printing. Specifically, the form of the expertise is heuristics at the decision points in the software to optimize function, quality, reliability and efficiency. When e can formally express design requirements and goals, much of the domain expertise n also be formally incorporated as *optimization heuristics*. This provides a methodical capability of using expertise.

Heuristics for Functional Assurance and Improvement: The real-world scenarios printing challenges and how human experts solve the problem can be recorded in abases. Initially at training time, we utilize a database guided by a human expert as supervisor. We rely on the human expert to then suggest corrections for the error. se suggestions are verified on a simulator before implementation as well as stored database corresponding to the fault library. At manufacturing time, the next time milar fault is identified, the mitigation strategy can be identified from the database ctly. The human expert can also provide feedback that can be used to add the observ ons and the parameter choices that resulted in those observations to the database.

As the platform is utilized, the database thus grows in predictive power in terms of the mitigation to be performed.

Heuristics for Printing Quality and Reliability: An AM product might function correctly but with very bad quality, or the product quality can't be reliably repeated in scale manufacturing. Human expert intervention is the only solution today. Our insight is that the key of an automated solution is the modeling of quality and reliability metrics from sensing/imaging inputs. More specifically for the AM of electronic and RF systems, integrating thermal imaging into the process will allow for defect determination in conductive traces. This can be accomplished by running current through the structure and optically observing the formation of hot spots. The captured thermal profile will provide information on the quality of the trace curing/sintering.

Combining these different electrical and thermal sensing methods with visual-based sensing/imaging will result in detailed information on the build status and the quality of the printed parts. This is the basis for us to use sensor fusion to replicate the role of human expert in the current process. Implementing the proposed corrective actions will allow for unprecedented build yields with reliable and repeatable system performances.

Heuristics for Printing Efficiency: Printing efficiency is another aspect that current AM practices heavily rely on human expert to intervene and maintain. Here the printing efficiency means that under the condition that function and quality can be guaranteed, different techniques may spend very different amount time to print and/or use different amount of material. Different printing efficiency leads to different cost, which might not be the first-degree constraint in a research environment, but is crucial for a true manufacturing service.

To optimizing print speed, the goal function is usually to cover all parts exactly once, and minimize the overall time. The goal is very much related many path optimization problems, i.e., finding a path in a finite graph that visits every edge exactly once [15, 16, 19]. Human expertise usually helps on the strategies of planning of visit and minimizing non-functional overhead. Our solution is to include heuristics at several places in software to optimize the total tour. The places include the construction of accessory geometry structures, the choice of next structure to visit. More specifically assisting structures frequently need to be introduced in a product for correct printing. We need to minimize the total amount of the introduced accessory structure to optimiz the total time. Furthermore, the order of visiting carries a significant weight in deter mining the total cost for reasons might not associate with the product itself, but lie i the characteristics of material, printers, or even simple physics.

Adaptable True 3D Tool Path Support: Industry standard computer aided desig (CAD) and computer aided manufacturing (CAM) products were designed and create with traditional subtractive manufacturing in mind. This results in a lack of commerci design software suited for multi-material additive manufacturing. Moreover, comme cially available electronic simulation programs (e.g. Spice) and their associated PC layout tools were designed with conventional electronics manufacturing in mind. A result, these programs are only effective at the design and manufacture of flat mu layered circuit boards. However, new AM tools such as [2] are not constrained by layer-by-layer 2.5D convention, and work in true 3D manner, for example, able to m and add material on 6 axes. In order to design and fabricate complex multi-material structures, it will be necessary to create interfaces in the internal representation that users can customize and support these new tool path capability. In particular, slicer is the most benefited of this adaptable interface. The enhanced slider can take current CAD outputs and translate them to the machine code necessary for multi-material and 3D systems.

Language Pragmas: Users should also be able to specify their own unique design requirements, material properties and printing device constraints, and make such tailored semantic information visible to all software layers. To accommodate such needs into our software stack, we will introduce pragmas into the modeling language and the enhanced G-code. A language pragma directs the compiler and software optimizer to enable an extension or modification of the language. Pragmas are widely supported in almost all computer languages such Java [7], C [8, 12] or Haskell [22]. In practice, users can "program" pragmas to specify new design constraints, new materials or printing devices. Pragmas essentially enhance the existing language. To support the pragmas into existing software, language preprocessors similar to thoses used for other compilers will be developed to translate them into the internal representation, and therefore can be conveyed to all layers of the software stack.

3 Conclusion

This position paper argues for the development of the cross-software-layer optimization capability to enable automated additive manufacturing of electronic and RF systems. If successfully built, the new compilers will significantly reduce human intervention that is needed now to mend between layers, which will make additive manufacturing the practical, efficient and reliable future manufacturing scheme of electronic and RF systems.

References

1. Hyrel 3d system 30m. https://www.hyrel3d.com/portfolio/system-30m/
2. nscrypt superscrypt. https://www.nscrypt.com/
3. Behrmann, G., Hidler, J., Mirotznik, M.: Fiber optic micro sensor for the measurement of tendon forces. Biomed. Eng. Online **11**(77) (2012). https://doi.org/10.1186/1475-925X-11-77
4. Biswas, S., et al.: Realization of modified luneburg lens antenna using quasi-conformal transformation optics and additive manufacturing. Microwave Opt. Technol. Lett. **61**(4), 1022–1029 (2019) https://doi.org/10.1002/mop.31696, https://onlinelibrary.wiley.com/doi/abs/10.1002/mop.31696
5. Biswas, S., Mirotznik, M.: Additively manufactured conformal load-bearing antenna structure (clas). IEEE Trans. Components Packaging Manufacturing Technol., 1 (2020). https://doi.org/10.1109/TCPMT.2020.3019220
6. Biswas, S., Mirotznik, M.: High gain, wide-angle qcto-enabled modified luneburg lens antenna with broadband anti-reflective layer. Nature Sci. Rep., **10** (07 2020). https://doi.org/10.1038/s41598-020-69631-6

7. Cavé, V., Zhao, J., Shirako, J., Sarkar, V.: Habanero-java: the new adventures of old x10. In: Proceedings of the 9th International Conference on Principles and Practice of Programming in Java, pp. 51–61 (2011)
8. Chapman, B., Jost, G., Van Der Pas, R.: Using openmp (2007)
9. Culmone, C., Smit, G., Breedveld, P.: Additive manufacturing of medical instruments: A state-of-the-art review. Additive Manufacturing **27**, 461–473 (2019) https://doi.org/10.1016/j.addma.2019.03.015. https://www.sciencedirect.com/science/article/pii/S2214860418308911
10. Deroba, J.C., Sobczak, K.D., Good, A., Larimore, Z., Mirotznik, M.: Additively manufactured luneburg retroreflector. IEEE Aerosp. Electron. Syst. Mag. **34**(11), 20–24 (2019). https://doi.org/10.1109/MAES.2019.2944050
11. Gibson, I., Srinath, A.: Simplifying medical additive manufacturing: Making the surgeon the designer. Procedia Technol. **20**, 237–242 (2015)
12. Gokhale, M.B., Stone, J.M.: Napa c: Compiling for a hybrid risc/fpga architecture. In: Proceedings of the IEEE Symposium on FPGAs for Custom Computing Machines (Cat. No. 98TB100251), pp. 126–135. IEEE (1998)
13. Greenwood, T.E., Hatch, S.E., Colton, M.B., Thomson, S.L.: 3d printing low-stiffness silicone within a curable support matrix. Additive Manufacturing **37**, 101681 (2021). https://doi.org/10.1016/j.addma.2020.101681, https://www.sciencedirect.com/science/article/pii/S2214860420310538
14. Gulati, G., Liang, M., Xin, H.: A conformal dual-polarized all-metal vivaldi array for feeding broadband luneburg lens. In: 2017 IEEE International Symposium on Antennas and Propagation USNC/URSI National Radio Science Meeting, pp. 2243–2244 (2017). https://doi.org/10.1109/APUSNCURSINRSM.2017.8073164
15. Harris, J.M., Hirst, J.L., Mossinghoff, M.J.: Combinatorics and graph theory, vol. 2. Springer (2008)
16. Hierholzer, C., Wiener, C.: Ueber die Möglichkeit, einen Linienzug ohne Wiederholung und ohne Unterbrechung zu umfahren (March 1873)
17. Hörber, J., Goth, C., Franke, J.: Aerosol-jet printing for functionalization of prototyping materials for electronic applications. In: International Symposium on Microelectronics, vol. 2012, pp. 000741–000748. International Microelectronics Assembly and Packaging Society (2012)
18. Javaid, M., Haleem, A.: Additive manufacturing applications in medical cases: a literature based review. Alexandria J. Med. **54**(4), 411–422 (2018)
19. Jungnickel, D., Jungnickel, D.: Graphs, networks and algorithms. Springer (2005)
20. Kennedy, K., Allen, J.R.: Optimizing compilers for modern architectures: a dependence based approach. Morgan Kaufmann Publishers Inc. (2001)
21. Leal Junior, A., Diaz, C., Avellar, L., Pontes, M., Marques, C., Frizera, A.: Polymer optic fiber sensors in healthcare applications: a comprehensive review. Sensors **19**, 3156 (2019 https://doi.org/10.3390/s19143156
22. Magalhaes, J.P., Dijkstra, A., Jeuring, J., Löh, A.: A generic deriving mechanism for haske ACM Sigplan Notices **45**(11), 37–48 (2010)
23. Martelli, C., Cardozo da Silva, J., Kalinowski, A., Galvão, J., Paes, T.: Biomechanical Se sors, pp. 193–238 (10 2020). https://doi.org/10.1002/9781119534730.ch7
24. Mohammed, M.G., Kramer, R.: All-printed flexible and stretchable electronics. Adv. Ma **29**(19), 1604965 (2017). https://doi.org/10.1002/adma.201604965. https://onlinelibra wiley.com/doi/abs/10.1002/adma.201604965
25. Norrish, M., Strout, M.M.: An approach for proving the correctness of inspector/execu transformations. In: Brodman, J., Tu, P. (eds.) LCPC 2014. LNCS, vol. 8967, pp. 131–1 Springer, Cham (2015). https://doi.org/10.1007/978-3-319-17473-0_9

26. Overmeyer, L., Hohnholz, A., Suttmann, O., Kaierle, S.: Multi-material laser direct writing of aerosol jet layered polymers. CIRP Ann. **68**(1), 217–220 (2019)
27. Pa, P., McCauley, R., Larimore, Z., Mills, M., Yarlagadda, S., Mirotznik, M.: High frequency characterization of conductive inks embedded within a structural composite. Smart Mater. Struct. **24** (2015). https://doi.org/10.1088/0964-1726/24/6/065010

Author Index

© The Editor(s) (if applicable) and The Author(s), under exclusive license
to Springer Nature Switzerland AG 2023
C. Mendis and L. Rauchwerger (Eds.): LCPC 2022, LNCS 13829, pp. 169–170, 2023.
https://doi.org/10.1007/978-3-031-31445-2

Printed in the United States
by Baker & Taylor Publisher Services